ROGER SMITH

TRIAL BY MEDICINE

INSANITY AND RESPONSIBILITY
IN VICTORIAN TRIALS

Edinburgh University Press

© Roger Smith 1981
Edinburgh University Press
22 George Square, Edinburgh
ISBN 0 85224 407 X
Set in Monotype Plantin
by Speedspools, Edinburgh
and printed in Great Britain by
Clark Constable Ltd
Edinburgh

CONTENTS

Responsibility is a highly confused concept. The state and the individual claim – or are assigned – powers and responsibilities which are fundamentally at odds. Even in relation to individuals, we swing between attributing and denying responsibility. Crimes by people whose sanity is questioned force specific answers to the general problem. How to respond to violence which is 'without reason' challenges the limits of comprehension.

The idea of the criminal lunatic developed in the nineteenth century. This book studies the social and intellectual conditions which structured the ascription of responsibility to such people. It deals with individual tragedy, the general framework of thought, and the social administration which the Victorians used to create order.

Notions of crime, insanity and responsibility are formidably complex. I approach these topics primarily as a historian, drawing on other disciplines as the need arises. There is little point in deferring to labels such as medical history, social history, the history of ideas, psychiatry, or jurisprudence. But there are problems in writing for a readership possibly ranging from psychiatrists and lawyers to social historians and historians of science. It is sometimes questioned whether this should be attempted: no group listens to any other. Yet the alternative is to treat certain topics – and I think responsibility is one – from a superficial and one-sided point of view. Different specialists will find sections with which they are familiar and sections where I have not understood meanings from the specialist's viewpoint. But each part contributes to a unified interpretation of how Victorians regarded the line between insanity and responsibility; the result must be judged by its coherence.

I do, of course, concentrate on certain themes. The first is the difficulty of distinguishing different kinds of conduct. How is it that one example of conduct can be described as the product of disease and another as the product of volition ? In debates on criminal lunatics the *same* conduct is described in alternative – even mutually exclusive – ways. What were the institutions and frameworks of thought which made this possible ? These issues are modern as well as historical and it would be perversely academic not to recognise it. Nevertheless, the relationship of the medico-legal past and present will be clarified only with proper attention to the historical sources.

A second theme is the nature of knowledge in the human and medical sciences. The last twenty years has seen considerable shifts in opinion, to a position where scientific knowledge is often claimed to have a social content or meaning. This again is an extremely complex topic. I think there is value in a book-length, though tangential, approach via historical practice. This seeks to reconstruct the history of ideas in response to the new demands being made on it. History of science (and medicine and law) is too important to leave to scientists (and doctors and lawyers). Conversely, historians are over-reluctant to describe scientific knowledge, even when such knowledge is fundamental to lived experience.

Certain issues are raised but not fully discussed. There is scope for establishing with more precision what did happen during crimes and trials; statements of material fact about Victorian cases should be treated with scepticism. Further, this is not a comprehensive study of all Victorian criminal lunacy trials, though I think no significant trials between 1840 and 1870 are missing. The time span is narrow; yet this concentration encourages description of many variables which are hardly contained by the nineteenth century. More historical research is needed – and much is in progress – on the social background of doctors, different medical factions, and the complex relations between economy, the poor laws, administration, medicine, criminal and civil law. Little research has been done on topics such as the evolution of forensic evidence and the content of diagnostic practice. In this book, however, my primary interest is in what people, notably insanity specialists, *thought*.

I came to write medico-legal history through a circuitous route. On the way, I acquired many intellectual debts and received help from many different individuals and institutions; to them I express my gratitude.

To Bob Young's friendship, enthusiasm and integrity, I owe insights and values. He created intellectual excitement and made ideas important.

The present work has a chequered history. At crucial times, John Forrester and Michael Ignatieff separately provided invaluable help and encouragement with the structure and expression of the argument. Lydia Gerend tried to instil some respect for the economy of words and the proper use of language. Her patient and exacting criticism is deeply valued. I owe a debt to Adrian Smith for bringing home to me a sense of what medico-legal issues might mean at the human level.

Many people have helped with ideas, information and mechanics. I am particularly grateful to Patricia Allderidge, Herman Berrios, John Brooke, David Edge, Karl Figlio, Nicholas Fisher, Ludmilla Jordanova, Gordon Phillips, Jacques Quen, Charles Rosenberg, Steven Shapin, Roderick Stirrat, Nigel Walker, Sue Walters, and Brian Wynne.

I am indebted to The Board of Governors of the Bethlem Royal Hospital and The Maudsley Hospital for permission to use and cite material (especially the 'Criminal case books') in the archives of their hospitals. I owe The Wellcome Trust grateful acknowledgement for its financial support, without which it would not have been possible to research historical sources. I would like to thank librarians at the following institutions: University of Lancaster Library (particularly inter-library loans); Cambridge University Library; The British Library; The Institute of Criminology Library, University of Cambridge; The Well-come Institute for the History of Medicine Library. It is also a pleasure to acknowledge the speed and efficiency of Edinburgh University Press.

Finally, I would like to take responsibility – however it may be defined – for the strengths and weaknesses of the final result.

ROGER SMITH

Referencing. This study uses a wide range of sources, both primary and secondary, normally known only to separate groups of specialists. But I do not wish to overburden the text with academic considerations. Refer-ences are therefore noted at the end, and the text may be read without consulting them. The references are not comprehensive but provide support or amplification for the text where this is needed.

Individual trials and medico-legal cases are not given a note each time they are referred to in the text. Instead, I include a list of cases, where material facts and details of sources used (again, not comprehensive) are gathered under the name of the accused person. For convenience, the most cited sources for these cases are listed separately. When citing legal reports, I always refer to volume and *page* number.

CHAPTER ONE

INTRODUCTION

When passing the death sentence on a youth at Maidstone Assizes in 1863, Mr Justice Wightman said that the prisoner had committed a 'barbarous and inhuman murder' so cruel that he 'could not trust himself to dwell upon its shocking details'.[1] Two medical men later wrote: 'What the lawyers and the public should try to realize is that . . . such phenomena as Burton exhibited are explicable on pathological principles . . . his act was exactly that kind of desperate, self-centred, motiveless, impulsive deed which those who have knowledge of insanity know to occur.'[2]

This describes a familiar conflict about an extremely complex issue: legal ritual, the ethics of responsibility, and scientific knowledge of human nature. Lawyers and psychiatrists since the early nineteenth century have disagreed about the proper response. The number of serious crimes where insanity is considered has never been very large; not so the controversy generated. In spite of a strong pressure for giving a medical viewpoint of individual lives, controversy has not died away. Rather, controversy seems to feed upon itself.

The business of history is understanding. History cannot be expected to solve problems of current practice; nor should current practice control what is understood historically. Existing histories of the insanity defence have been written by those professionally involved. Further, since Anglo-American common law is by nature the practice of precedence, a *version* of historical understanding necessarily influences it. This may simply mean juridical acknowledgement of precedent and rules. Or, for psychiatrists and medical psychologists, it may mean that there has been a slow but inevitable progress towards the legal recognition of medical descriptions.

Most writers on the insanity defence try to establish a historical basis for rational practice acceptable to lawyers and doctors alike.[3] By contrast, this book explains why there is no agreement. Further, its purposes are primarily historical, meaning that its explanatory structure is a response to the insanity defence in nineteenth-century British trials. The results may or may not be found useful in a modern debate, but this is not a criterion for their value. Nevertheless, in the conclusion I suggest that they have some modern relevance. Medico-legal controversy is often explained by contingent factors, such as poor communication, narrow professional interests, unfortunate legal rules, or wild medical claims.

This book argues that the conflict is also deeper and unavoidable, given the social and philosophical history which will be described. I support this by analysing theories of human nature and their practical consequences.

History derived from medical and legal reports, and from the debate surrounding many trials, is extremely unreliable about material facts: 'What the judge says is constantly misunderstood, and the facts in relation to which he speaks are constantly left out of the report.'[4] Medical reports, too, were written up with specific purposes in mind and with a special slant. Highly structured accounts of outstanding trials therefore tend to be passed down without attention to the initial reality or to the wider context of the trial.[5] This is appropriate for the establishment of common law, but it does not help medico-legal understanding.[6] By returning to the meanings which such statements originally had, medico-legal reporting – however 'erroneous' – is shown to have great value. It reveals the sources of practice and the constraints operating in thought.

These ends are best served by focusing in depth on individual cases and by demonstrating the ability of different groups to describe differently the same event. Two studies exist which are models for this approach. The first, by Charles Rosenberg, covers the trial of President Garfield's assassin. Guiteau pleaded insanity, a defence supported by evidence of habitual moral insanity owing to inherited degeneration in the nervous system. The trial in 1881–2 revealed a sharp difference between medical factions, which enabled the prosecution to gain medical support for its own depravity theory. Competition between different accounts is also central to Michel Foucault's dossier on the trial in 1835 of Pierre Rivière. In this rare case of a Norman peasant the accused gave a powerful and detailed account of why he murdered his mother, brother and sister. The variety of documents published recaptures the relations between social groups, knowledge and power, in the struggle to reduce Rivière to a problem of social management. My cases are all English or Scottish (while recognising differences in Scottish law), but similar issues are evident. As with Guiteau and Rivière, the trials of Edward Oxford, Martha Brixey, Captain Johnston, and many others, show in a fascinating way how individual tragedy acquires meaning and is reduced to order in our systems of thought.

A different but complementary administrative history exists. Nigel Walker describes the development and use of the insanity defence preparatory to his study of the workings of the English 1959 Mental Health Act (the recent framework for mental health administration).[7] His viewpoint is invaluable, because it is based on a wide reading of the available records rather than on a few conventional cases, and because it shows that the trial must be placed in a wider administrative context before it can be understood.

Several reasons make it worthwhile to investigate medico-legal debate in the mid-nineteenth century. First, the insanity defence did not arouse much medical attention before about 1800. Criminal courts sometimes solicited medical opinion on this and on other matters, but the insanity defence did not exist as a distinct medico-legal problem. Between 1790 and 1830, English coroners' courts and civil and criminal courts made much greater use of medical evidence in general. This created new legal and medical expectations about medical evidence for insanity. Second, the reconstruction of society's attitude towards insanity through legislation culminated in two 1845 Acts, which compelled the building of county lunatic asylums and established a central Commission of Lunacy with wide powers. Along with this came career prospects and professional aspirations for a new medical specialism, alienism or psychological medicine, later known as psychiatry. Third, from about 1830 to 1880, modern scientific physiology expanded to include theories of brain function. Many people, and especially medical men, argued that mental science (or psychology) would make radical progress by studying the brain. It was during this period that the authority of science came to underpin medical statements on insanity. Fourth, the formulation of the M'Naghten Rules (referred to as the 'Rules') in 1843 is considered *the* point of reference for the insanity plea's history. It is essential to describe the context and immediate effect of these Rules. I conclude that it is wrong to accuse the Rules *per se* of causing medical and legal antagonism, and that this perpetuates an over-simple view of the contingency of such antagonism. Rather, the Rules symbolised and exacerbated an endemic conflict.

The final and most important reason concerns the insanity defence's novel visibility, which reached a qualitatively new level of prominence in medical, legal and lay discussion in the mid-nineteenth century. There are difficulties in measuring the incidence of the defence, but for present purposes this is subsidiary to the question, why was this defence so *visible*?[8] Why could the statistical medical expert Professor Guy refer to 'notorious cases that gave rise ... to an amount of controversy which must have carried the fact of their acquittal or condemnation into every household in which public affairs are heard or talked of'?[9] It is, of course, not possible to define 'public opinion', but the extensive book and journal literature certainly assumed the question aroused wide concern. All such literature primarily represents the interests of the writer, and it is necessarily hazardous generalising about his representativeness. However, one can cite parliamentary reports and newspaper comment in further support of what I call the defence's visibility.

Deciding between guilt and insanity has a symbolism transcending an individual's fate. Symbolism exists by virtue of social relations, and as these change, so does the expressiveness of different symbolic elements. Early nineteenth-century Britain experienced dramatic social and industrial change; new forms of power and knowledge reflected this. The statutory criminal law, law enforcement, penology and the legal profession, were all reconstructed. Political economy and the Tudor and Stuart framework for regulating poverty were completely revised. The government of the 1830s and 1840s self-consciously acquired administrative machinery for things like industrial safety and public health, which many historians regard as the foundations of the welfare state. The Reform Bill of 1832 marked a slow shift of political power, while Chartism and other working-class movements maintained a possibility of more radical political change. Against this background, any alteration in public ritual (such as a murder trial) could become a resource for controversy. But there were also changes in the collective attitude towards insanity without which the insanity plea could not have reached prominence.

The question why insanity itself became visible between 1750 and 1850 is stimulating important historical research. Without engaging in debate about what insanity 'is', it can be said that eighteenth-century European and American society decided that there was a social problem caused by the existence of lunatics. The discovery of the response – the asylum – accompanied the discovery of the problem. The asylum movement exemplified a new pattern of social control. A new group with professional expectations, under a central administration, directed specialist institutions for inmates whose lived experience was of routine, discipline and work. These changes were driven through on a wave of reformist sentiment in which humanitarian and medical ideals sometimes became one and the same. Such 'reform', and particularly the special place it seemed to provide for medicine, was the backdrop for controversy about the insanity plea.

Somewhat against the inclinations of psychiatrists, a new historical sociology of medicine has transformed the basis for discussing the history of lunacy. The first part of Foucault's history of the human sciences, *Madness and Civilization* was a powerful catalyst. He poses the problem that insanity, as now constituted, came into being co-incidentally with economic, industrial and urban transformations. Other work, such as Robert Castel's *L'ordre psychiatrique*, Daniel Rothman's *The Discovery of the Asylum*, and Andrew Scull's *Museums of Madness*, reflects the enormous expansion of social history and sociology of medicine. This work contributes to three related areas: medical professionalisation, the prominence (or even dominance) of medicine as social control, and the medicalisation of both social problems and individual deviance.[10] Sociology has become historical in order to demonstrate the social contingency of medicine. By contrast, doctors have expected medical history to demonstrate the progressive objectivity of knowledge and the humanitarian contribution of practice.

Insanity has a history of great complexity. Historians nevertheless agree that philanthropy is not in itself an explanation for the late eighteenth-century changes. There is no incompatibility between revulsion with existing conditions and an ideal of producing citizens for a new economic age. Insanity became an acknowledged social problem at a time when reconciling individualism and the social order seemed to require a new discipline.[11] New institutions separated out madness from poverty, orphanage, vagrancy, and criminality, and each strove for a community to create the good citizen. Treatment of the insane, perhaps the most abject embodiments of suffering, became a potent symbol for society's ability to regulate its affairs. Prior to 1800, lunatics in Britain lived in all manner of circumstances, from custody with private attendants to the freedom of rural villages, from local prisons to charity hospitals. Frequently idiots, petty thieves, tramps, epileptics, the senile, the indigent, and the poverty-stricken were not separated. At the same time, however, some special provisions were being made for the insane (in addition to the medieval foundation of Bethlem), such as the special ward at the Manchester Infirmary (1766) and the new private asylums (the 'trade in lunacy').

The Quaker Retreat (1792) became a model. Its small size, care for physical conditions, and paternalistic moral structure, represented ideals. The reformers' campaigns led through the 1807 Select Committee, the 1808 County Asylums Act, and a series of investigative bodies and *ad hoc* legislative measures, to culminate in the 1845 Lunatics Care and Treatment Act and Lunatics Asylum Act. With these statutory innovations came care at the local level and an interest in non-restraint and 'moral treatment' (or psychological reconstruction) of insane inmates. It was decided that the administration of insanity required medical expertise and that the asylums were medical institutions. Scull, in particular, focuses attention on this development, which was not inherent in the work of the first reformers. Nevertheless, other social interests, particularly a legal one in certification, continued to structure the social response to insanity.[12]

Emphases changed after 1845. Kathleen Jones refers to 'the triumph of legalism', as the Commissioners in Lunacy consolidated the bureaucracy which, rather than medical treatment, ordered insane lives.[13] Alienists became administrators, attending to the running of asylums, problems of staffing, relations with Poor Law Officers, finance, and record-keeping. A flurry of interest in the 1860s about possible alternatives to the asylum system came to nothing. The phenomenon of numbers became the most prominent public issue; however much construction was undertaken, the number of insane people outstripped the available space. The late Victorians pondered the question, which Scull re-opens, why the proportion of insane people grew at such a rate. It was widely feared that this was the grim cost of social progress. The Commissioners in Lunacy (and many alienists, though their views changed

for different audiences) disagreed, explaining the rise in terms of trans-
ferrals from the workhouses, longevity in improved institutional conditions, and fuller registration of the insane. By contrast, Scull concludes
that there was a growing willingness (especially among working-class
people, who supplied the increasing numbers) to have family members
institutionalised; this led to a greater number of people being labelled
insane.[14]

The history of alienism needs to be related to its setting within legal
medicine, the latter having a long but scarcely explored history. The
modern concept of legal medicine originated in late seventeenth-century
Germany and France, in the context of new forms of local and central
administration.[15] Legal medicine was a means for ordering citizens' lives,
and precedents then established under a mercantilist economy were
passed down to the nineteenth century. After 1800, the forensic and
public health branches of legal medicine separated from each other. The
courts increasingly utilised forensic evidence of all kinds, thus establishing precedents for the use of psychiatric evidence. Many medical men
were prepared to give such evidence, but very few (notably Alfred
Swaine Taylor, Professor of Medical Jurisprudence, Guy's Hospital,
1831–77) became known as experts. Two forms of expertise were required: in science, especially in chemistry, and in the legal procedure
which enabled counsel to use medical evidence successfully.

Walker shows that medical considerations were sometimes taken into
account in the insanity plea before 1800.[16] Nevertheless, it was in the
nineteenth century that lawyers, medical men and the public increasingly
expected medicine to be represented in the criminal law. This is partly
explained by social changes, the interest in lunacy, and the establishment
of legal medicine.

But there were also the activities of criminal lunatics themselves. They
were few in number, but bloody in deed. Not responsible, according to
some, they were yet likely to be hanged. To bring discipline to such people,
rather than to duplicate their violence, was the embodiment of reform.
Criminal lunatics had a special position within the legal and penal
systems. Certain prominent trials (Hadfield 1800, Oxford 1840,
M'Naghten 1843) established models which medical humanitarians
hoped would become general. A specialist asylum, Broadmoor, opened
in 1863. The public, however, feared that its interest was not being
served; more specifically, that the use and success of the plea correlated
with a spread of unpunished violence. The insanity plea could attract
anxieties about what rapid social change was doing to the national fabric.

Recent nineteenth-century medical history describes a rise of medical
hegemony. For example, by 1850 medical superintendents were in
charge of day to day asylum administration, and the 1858 Medical Act
defined exclusive rights and obligations for practitioners. Indeed, socio-

logists use doctors to illustrate the developing prominence of the professional middle class. Against this picture, however, must be set both the specific medical failure to dominate medico-legal matters and the general question of novelty in rising professional interests. Sometimes with relation to certification, but most strikingly in relation to the insanity plea, medical men experienced condescension, and even contempt, from lawyers and journalists. Hence the insanity plea became an emotive issue for some medical men; it signalled their struggle for professional autonomy. Matters were made much worse by conflicting interests between medical groups. Some alienists were embittered by the low status of the public health system, by the stigma of associating with insane paupers, and by their unpopularity when defending the repellently aggressive. Criticism from their peers sharpened this bitterness, and it shows through strongly in their tone of writing. However, the question of power and its distribution – between doctors, and between doctors and government – is not the subject of the present book. There is need for a detailed study of the social position, background, careers, and professional affiliations of alienists. Only when this is done will it be possible to explain the position of the insanity defence as a tactic in middle-class politics.[17] This is not attempted here.

The protracted struggle to introduce medical assessments of responsibility was not well received. It was a particularly colourful example of the vexed question, the relationship between human science and human affairs. Over and over again, different groups have claimed that the knowledge of people and societies, as natural objects, is the sure foundation for social progress. I describe medical knowledge which, it was claimed, founded a new basis for assessing non-responsibility. The strengths and weaknesses of these claims are considered. Existing explanations of medico-psychological knowledge usually assume that it derives either inductively from natural facts or professionally from group interest in esoteric expertise. I reject this dichotomy. Cognitive claims do derive content from experience, but no experience can avoid being socially constituted in some way.

Criminal trials display very public choices about the value society attributes to individual actions. Such choices are sustained by a system of legal institutions and rules, which may or may not permit the insertion of other (e.g. medical) institutions or rules. This legal framework is outlined, particularly to emphasise the law's view of human action and its incompatibility with the medical view.

The second half of the book draws on the social, medical and legal background in the first half to explain the drama of the trials themselves. The trials illustrate a unified period (1830s to 1870s), when there was no marked change in the use or success of the plea. This enables one to concentrate on elucidating specific networks of variables (including those which do vary with time). Such an approach is more profitable than moving rapidly from one famous trial to the next in understanding the sources of medico-legal controversy. There was no consensus about the use of the insanity defence. To understand why any particular verdict was reached requires an examination of the special circumstances of the trial. Trials were occasions for expressing theories of human nature and associated value systems; this is the major preoccupation of this study. But it would be wrong to suppose that these theories produced particular verdicts. It is necessary to separate reasons for a specific verdict from reasons for controversy over verdicts in general.

The first group of trials concentrates on the different types of medical evidence – delusions, idiocy, impulsive, or moral insanity. The second group examines the controversy surrounding such evidence in a few highly emotive trials. The distinctive social, medical and legal position of women is discussed in the final group. It was not uncommon for mothers to kill their children (the Victorians loosely referred to infanticide); the insanity plea had a special place in such circumstances.

Medico-legal history raises issues of central importance to the linked development of the human sciences and the modern bureaucratic state. I stress the content and meaning of Victorian statements about human conduct for two reasons. First, there is still much interest at the level of ideas, though the shortcomings of history of ideas divorced from the social context are well known. If history includes understanding the meanings in lived experience, then we need to make intelligible the manner in which people formulated their views.

We are necessarily concerned with the meaning in statements that people make. For present purposes, it does not matter whether meanings inform the motives that cause actions or are the irreducible point of actions.[18] In either case, meanings do not exist in isolation; rather, they derive content from a person's social relationships – in the broadest sense. It follows that meanings are not subjective but exist objectively in practice.

> It is not just that people in our society all or mostly have a given set of ideas in their heads and subscribe to a given set of goals. The meanings and norms implicit in these practices are not just in the minds of the actors but are out there in the practices themselves, practices which cannot be conceived as a set of individual actions, but as essentially modes of social relation, of mutual action.[19]

Ultimately, pseudo-boundaries between the history of ideas and social history may be disregarded. To discuss the content and meaning of medico-legal theories is also to discuss the practical ordering of society.

The second reason for stressing the history of ideas is to counterbalance a weakness in the historical sociology of medicine, namely its indifference to the content of medical knowledge. Nineteenth-century

medical men in general, and alienists in particular, made many rash statements about the 'scientific' standing of their knowledge. It is all too easy
to argue both that their knowledge was 'false' and that the method by
which they derived it did not justify the claim. Some sociologists have
therefore been tempted into supposing that, since medical statements
were not 'science', they were nothing but the rationalisation of group
interest. Other sociologists realise it is not the lack of 'truth' or 'scientific
method' which reveals the group interest; rather, the *type* of any knowledge or method reflects that interest.[20] This argument cannot be ignored,
particularly as the alienists made their social interests very clear. It
would be quite wrong, however, to isolate group self-interest as the
exclusive meaning of the alienists' claims to scientific standing.

Two arguments, the first historical and the second philosophical,
support this contention. Medical claims about lunacy were a small part
of a much wider campaign by social reformers to base policy on facts. In
the 1830s and 1840s, 'social science' became a programme which accompanied major legislative innovations. This new science used a utilitarian
language and devoted a great deal of effort to the collection of facts or
'statistics'.[21] The programme evolved and expanded during the course of
the century, in the 1860s acquiring a stronger biological element
influenced by evolutionary and hereditarian thought. The social science
movement and related legislation partly explains the alienists' choice of
words. It is possible, of course, that everyone advocating a scientific basis
for policy belonged to the same social group, that is the rising professional
middle class.[22] Even so, this says little distinctive about the alienists as a
separate entity, though specialisation of function would add to the professional class's overall authority. Whether such a class had a coherent
identity, and whether its rise was a novel event, may be questioned. This
does not, however, detract from the point that alienists, like every other
group, used knowledge as a resource to propagate a group interest.

On a broader historical scale, the alienists were part of the process
leading towards modern secular society. The nineteenth-century
scientific movement associated with it is sometimes called 'scientific
naturalism': 'Naturalism asserted the universal scope of scientific method
and procedure, the adequacy of science as a universal deterministic
cosmology beyond which no further knowledge or way of knowing exists,
and the universality of natural law.'[23] This claim reached something of a
high point in Britain in the 1860s and 1870s, when clerics were goaded by
scientists into relinquishing their authoritative statements about nature.
Some medical men made a substantial contribution to scientific naturalism; in particular, they elaborated concepts for discussing mind as a part
of physical nature. Naturalism was also an important feature of the
alienists' polemics. As Thomas Laycock, a professor of medicine at
Edinburgh, said about the opponents of the insanity defence: 'In vain

they express their alarm that if these doctrines be admitted as true the foundations of the social fabric will be shaken; the truth is not less the truth.'[24] The alienist Henry Maudsley was not reluctant to become a secular prophet. 'When will man learn that he is at the head of nature only by virtue of the operation of natural laws ? When will he learn that by the study of these laws and by deliberate conformity to them he may become the conscious framer of his own destiny ?'[25] The confidence, hope, even arrogance, of alienists belonged to this tradition.

There are also philosophical reasons why historians should not ignore the detailed content of past knowledge. Sociologists themselves disagree on the value – and even the possibility – of uncovering the meaning of statements for the people who make them. Nevertheless, I consider it necessary to describe medico-psychological knowledge in terms which would be comprehensible to the people for whom this knowledge was meaningful. This implies the need for an account of clinical experience and neurophysiology as science; providing this account is itself a valid historical task.

My analysis is presented in terms of medical and legal discourses. While it is a commonplace (embodied in the very term 'medico-legal') to acknowledge that doctors and lawyers conceptualise humans in different ways, the significance of this for understanding responsibility has not been followed through. To achieve this it is necessary to analyse accepted knowledge in order to uncover the reasons for actions taken. The term 'discourse' has value in this connection.[26] As I use the word, a discourse is the abstract form of first, the language and belief which constitutes a version of reality, and second, the corresponding disciplines, institutions and political choices. There is a danger of treating the discourse itself as an object, which it is not; rather, it is a group of relations between possible objects. The word refers to the set of meanings which exists by virtue of those relations. The discourse is therefore the framework within which particular statements or judgements have validity. Such frameworks are usually unexamined and taken for granted.

Many historians have shifted their interest away from the uniqueness of science to its standing as a social practice. Empirical studies of science (not just 'bad' science) demonstrate aspects of knowledge not reducible to statements about 'objective' nature. This is the case with clinical and neurophysiological knowledge which alienists claimed validated their courtroom evidence. The meaning of medical statements lay not with specific facts but with the medical discourse as a whole, and it is at this level that they must be examined.

The simplest way to distinguish medical and legal discourse is to say that the former is determinist and that the latter is voluntarist. While there are philosophical difficulties in giving a satisfactory account of either a determining cause or a volitional act, this description corresponds to common Victorian usage. It was normal to accept determinism and voluntarism as mutually exclusive statements of whether a person was or was not free to choose one course of ideas or movements rather than another. Maudsley wrote, 'medicine deals with matter, force, and necessity; law deals with mind, duty, and responsibility'.[27] Political individualism ensured that the concept of responsibility remained closely tied to the belief in voluntary actions. This tempts one to assume an equivalence between legal discourse and public opinion. Viewing the law as the practical embodiment of this opinion would further encourage such an assumption. However, there is nothing immutable about this equivalence, and it is usually more profitable to describe the opinion of recognisable groups rather than public opinion in general.

Modern western society construes 'the will' as a mental function or faculty, which is a defining trait of human nature. (It is not the point here that this is philosophically and psychologically naive.) Mental terms describe a supposedly *universal* existential reality. By contrast, 'natural' terms describe a reality, the experience of which is increasingly *restricted* to specialist groups. 'Mind' is a resource for general interests, while 'nature' is a resource for group interests. Nineteenth-century criminal law aimed to enforce order, to represent public feeling, and to embody values which transcended any particular interest. In pursuit of these ends, jurisprudence explicated criminal responsibility in terms of the presence or absence of specified states of mind. The absence of a state of mind capable of 'knowing' rendered a defendant no longer definable as a person. Alienists on the other hand, argued for the explication of criminal responsibility in terms of the presence or absence of disease. To them disease meant something physical (i.e. natural). And they claimed a unique expertise in this physical dimension. The restrictiveness of medical discourse therefore posed a substantial threat to the universality of legal discourse.

The final chapter argues that legal and medical discourses can, nevertheless, be treated as polarities (with others, notably the mind-body relation) within a unified thought system. Ultimately, we should be concerned not with the arbitration of competing medico-legal claims, but with the discourse of controversy itself.

CHAPTER TWO

MEDICAL CRITICISM AND
PENAL PRACTICE

1 *Alienists and Criminal Responsibility*

Lunacy reform reached a peak in the 1840s; it was marked by a burst of specialist literature and the first medico-psychological journal. At the same time, parliament repealed the last remnants of the 'Bloody Code', thereby greatly restricting the range of the capital sentence. The Law Commissioners struggled to impose some order on criminal law statutes and their administration. A Select Committee on Legal Education (1846) advocated important reforms in the legal profession. There was widespread debate about extending the police along metropolitan lines; and Pentonville opened in 1842, followed by a wave of prison construction.[1] There was also a climate of unprecedented interest in a rational collective response to miscreants. A considerable literature on criminal insanity was therefore to be expected.

Criminal lunatics posed a sharp problem in the rational differentiation of miscreants. This chapter describes their ambivalent social position between patients and criminals. The term 'criminal lunatic' became a formal administrative category, designed to resolve this ambivalence. In one sense, criminal lunatics were merely a problem of management specialisation. After all, lunatics and criminals shared much in common: they were isolated, incarcerated, surveyed and disciplined.[2] The utilitarian theory accepted by some of the most active reformers argued for this. Nevertheless, in spite of their successes, utilitarian reformers did not achieve political dominance. A majority continued to think in terms of judgement and punishment; even utilitarian practice contained within itself unresolved contradictions between assigning blame and manufacturing improved citizens.[3] There was therefore no question of just simply reducing what to do with individuals to a problem of management. As the insanity plea exposed the problem of responsibility in stark terms, it became everyone's resource for debating the changing patterns of social order.

Alienists believed that the lunacy legislation gave them authority and made it their duty to speak out on responsibility. During the 1840s at least, it appeared as if much informed opinion would concur. However, nobody agreed about the proper range of this authority. The Commissioners in Lunacy included barristers, and justices continued to oversee certification and county asylums. Even among alienists there was little agreement: superintendents of county asylums, proprietors of private madhouses, private practitioners, Commissioners, and university writers on psychological medicine, had varied interests. The situation was fluid. There was every reason to campaign for one's views: few positions were so secure as not to need defence, and few practices so entrenched as not to appear remediable.

Formal solidarity began among alienists in 1841 with the founding of the Association of Medical Officers of Asylums and Hospitals for the Insane (it became the Medico-Psychological Association in 1865).[4] The Association was not initially an effective pressure group; individual London practitioners exercised more influence. Of these, Dr John Conolly became a figurehead.[5] The owner of two private London asylums, Dr Forbes Winslow, independently founded the first specialist journal in 1848.[6] At the end of the 1850s, this publication lost ground to the *Journal of Mental Science*, which the provincial Association had launched under Dr John Charles Bucknill, Superintendent of the Devon County Asylum, in 1852.[7] Bucknill and the joint succeeding editors, Henry Maudsley and C. Lockhart Robertson, contributed to alienists' sense of unity by emphasising the universal scientific goal of truth. Maudsley was a brilliant and arrogant man, who went on to stake out the strongest claims for scientific approaches to social problems (while earning a great deal of money in private practice). He also held the chair of Medical Jurisprudence at University College, London, a prestigious vantage point from which to advocate psychological medicine. Maudsley had little time for the low-status public asylums, believing that the interests of psychological medicine were better served by investment in scientific research.[8] The split between London and the provinces, and between private and public medicine, runs through alienism as through the profession at large right from the beginning. This might have been counterbalanced with the appointment of the provincial Thomas Laycock to the chair of the Practice of Medicine at Edinburgh in 1855. He was an outspoken advocate of psychological medicine, but his writings were often obscure, and local political in-fighting left him somewhat outside the medical establishment.[9]

Striking evidence for the alienists' inability to provide themselves with a secure social basis comes from the absence of distinct training. In spite of individual lecturers like Laycock and Sir Alexander Morison, visiting physician to Bethlem 1835–53, the general practitioner remained ignorant of medico-psychological thought.[10] Alienists believed this seriously damaged the cogency with which evidence for insanity could be presented.[11] In particular, it meant that there was no procedure for consolidating a common viewpoint on medico-legal questions. As Dr David Skae, Physician to the Royal Edinburgh Asylum, lectured his colleagues: 'If I had told you that our College did not require their students to study mental diseases, there was no further explanation required for the differences of opinion among medical witnesses in questions about insanity.'[12] The implication was that opposite sides could always balance a non-specialist practitioner against an expert.

Sometimes alienists addressed the public over the heads of their medical colleagues. Most decisions about who was insane were taken in private. At a trial, however, an alienist might hope to make a spectacular display of authority and humanity. Professional claims came forward every time alienists appeared in court. They justifiably believed that the acceptance of their evidence would indicate that they did possess the professional position to which they laid claim. When the evidence was rejected, alienism – and the cause of science – lost. 'The most scientific witness may be cross-examined as if he were a fraudulent bankrupt, and every effort made to render his evidence unintelligible to the jury or unworthy of evidence.'[13] The degree to which practititioners felt themselves to be on trial is indicated by how many of them wrote on the subject.[14]

But why was it that they were so enraged by the criminal law? In part it was the problem of their social status. Another factor, which must be explained at length, lies within the law itself. It appeared to many that existing law, with its variable verdicts, embodied a *lack* of science; in other words it epitomised social reaction and unreason. The criminal law reached different verdicts about insanity between 1800 (Hadfield) and 1843 (M'Naghten).[15] Hadfield's acquittal was due to the brilliance of defence counsel (to which he was specially entitled having been indicted for treason) rather than to a new attitude to medical opinion. It was only with two major trials – of Oxford in 1840 for treason and M'Naghten himself – that the use of medical evidence led to demands for clarification. The resulting Rules were a failure and different verdicts continued to be reached. But the Rules were law, and were cited as such by jurists. They also became an immediate focus for opposition to a legal system uninformed by the medical viewpoint.

Daniel M'Naghten shot and killed Sir Robert Peel's private secretary while believing himself persecuted by the police, supposedly on instructions from the Tories. He was found insane at the direction of Lord Chief Justice Tindal. Perhaps in order to divert criticism from the actual course of justice, while conceding the degree of anxiety felt, Lord Lyndhurst, the Lord Chancellor, led the Lords in formulating a set of questions which were to be answered by the judges appearing together before the House. This was an unusual procedure; it could even be doubted whether its results had formal standing.[16] Answers to the questions were finally forthcoming; these constitute the M'Naghten Rules.

The questions were more a direct response to M'Naghten's trial than a well thought-out presentation of the issue in general. The difficulties following from this were reflected in Tindal's introductory remarks to the answers. '[We] have forborne entering into any particular discussion upon these questions, from the extreme and almost insuperable difficulty of applying those answers to cases in which the facts are not brought judicially before them. The facts of each particular case must of necessity present themselves with endless variety, and with every shade of difference in each case.'[17] Judges normally established the law through individual trials; they were not adept at answering questions not directed to particular facts. One judge, Mr Justice Maule, gave a dissenting opinion, because he objected to the generality of the questions. Everybody knew that in fact the questions did have a particular case in mind but this could not be admitted because it would constitute an interference in M'Naghten's case. Maule also showed insight in stating that these formalisations 'may embarrass the administration of justice, when they are cited in criminal trials'.[18]

The judges' answers added little to existing law. In effect, they restated the 'right-wrong test': a man was not responsible for his criminal deed if, at the time of committing it, he was unable to know that the deed was wrong.

> We have to submit our opinion to be, that the jurors ought to be told in all cases that every man is to be presumed to be sane, and to possess a sufficient degree of reason to be responsible for his crimes, until the contrary be proved to their satisfaction; and that to establish a defence on the ground of insanity, it must be clearly proved that, at the time of the committing of the act, the party accused was labouring under such a defect of reason, from disease of the mind, as not to know the nature and quality of the act he was doing; or, if he did know it, that he did not know he was doing what was wrong. The mode of putting the latter part of the question to the jury on these occasions has generally been, whether the accused at the time of doing the act knew the difference between right and wrong: which mode, though rarely, if ever, leading to any mistake with the jury, is not, as we conceive, so accurate when put generally and in the abstract, as when put with reference to the party's knowledge of right and wrong in respect to the very act with which he is charged.[19]

This statement left certain expressions unclear (such as 'the nature and quality of the act', not to mention the moral and legal ambiguity of the word 'wrong') but it did provide judges with a phraseology which was to be repeated in many trials. Interpretation was another matter. 'It is doubtful whether there is any field of law in which there has been as much confusion and variation in interpreting the very same words of a seemingly simple legal formula as there has been in the courtroom operation of the *M'Naghten* rules.'[20]

The judges' legalistic formulations aroused bitter opposition from

Victorian alienists. Modern psychiatrists in turn consider the Rules eroded through subsequent progressive court decisions which were responsive to the medical viewpoint. Medical critics have argued that the Rules assumed a narrow identification of insanity with disordered reason, a view compatible with jurisprudence but incompatible with naturalistic descriptions of insanity as disease. The law created 'artificial lines, untrue to Nature'.[21] Alienists criticised the Rules for acknowledging incapacity following intellectual, but not emotional or volitional, disorder.

> The objections of doctors with experience of mental disease have remained in substance unchanged throughout the last hundred years. Briefly, they have contended that the M'Naghten test is based on an entirely obsolete and misleading conception of the nature of insanity, since insanity does not only, or primarily, affect the cognitive or intellectual faculties, but affects the whole personality of the patient, including both the will and the emotions. An insane person may therefore often know the nature and quality of his act and that it is wrong and forbidden by law, but yet commit it as a result of the mental disease.[22]

In brief, the Rules incorporated the 'right-wrong test' and rejected the idea of 'irresistible impulse'.

There were really two criticisms, though they were normally not distinguished. First, that the law ignored the recent and most reliable medical findings. This could be put down to ignorance, prejudice, or other contingent factors. Second, that the law was not in any way based on scientific medicine. This was the naturalistic argument that natural facts provided the only valid basis for the rational ordering of human affairs. From this viewpoint the law appeared burdened with the irrationality of historical tradition; value-free knowledge could only be derived from science.

The judges certainly had not taken into account medical opinion when formulating the Rules. It is unlikely that it would have occurred to them to look outside the law and what they considered its social function. They sought above all to disabuse people of an impression 'that the impunity accorded to the insane by the practice, if not by the principles, of the law, had been carried further than was consistent with the safety of society'.[23] The legal criteria of criminal lunacy were defined as states of mind and not as symptoms of insanity. 'The jury are not impannelled to try whether or not the prisoner is mad, but whether or not he is a wilful and malicious murderer.'[24] It was not the judges' job to consider medical categories. 'They have laid down no test of madness whatever. They have laid down tests of responsibility, or, more strictly speaking, have specified facts from which, when juries have found them, Judges are to infer malice; but it is no part of their duty to say how far particular diseases affect the relation of persons to such tests.'[25]

Statements of this sort did nothing to clarify which medical evidence about which states of mind was to be taken as indicating that the law might find a lack of responsibility. Alienists thought they should be consulted at this point, and many jurists later agreed. However legalistically the Rules were interpreted, judges could not in practice avoid implying that certain signs indicated a lack of responsibility. But the classification of signs, or symptoms, was exactly the activity which medical practitioners claimed for themselves. Alienists wanted the language of medicine, rather than that of law, to operate in decisions about insanity. Conflict reached a head when symptoms, about which alienists felt confident and enlightened, were not treated as signs in court. This occurred with the recently described symptoms of emotional and volitional incapacity and, most acutely, with the symptoms of 'impulsive insanity'. 'It is against the dangerous ignorance of morbid mental conditions which the law thus evinces that we desire again to record our protest. A monomaniac with perverted emotions and homicidal tendencies cannot, says science, control his conduct, and cannot therefore be held responsible for his acts. The law says he can and shall be.'[26]

In the medical discourse there was a tendency towards conflating tests of insanity with tests of responsibility; alienists talked as if the fact of disease meant a lack of responsibility.[27] This, however, was definitely not the case in law: 'Mental illness should not itself be an independent ground of exculpation, but only a sign that one of the traditional standard grounds – compulsion, ignorance of fact, or excusable ignorance of law – may apply.'[28] The legal view dominated in practice. When disease itself became exculpatory, it was not through the insanity defence but through administrative changes leading to the medical viewpoint prevailing outside the court.

The question whether disease affected responsibility belonged to medical discourse. Here disease had a determinist form, which entailed consequences, whatever the 'state of mind' might be. This logic meant that movements influenced by disease could not involve responsibility. While alienists rarely made such extreme claims for the irresponsibility of all diseased individuals, critics often interpreted their writings as leading in that direction. This suggested a *reductio ad absurdum* argument that doctors exonerated anyone touched by disease. If the determinist logic of medical knowledge were taken seriously, it was easy to portray the medical argument as dismissing the possibility of responsibility at all. Whether or not it was a logically valid argument, medicine acquired a certain notoriety because it sometimes seemed to render responsibility meaningless.

While the Rules did little to clarify practice, it was not clear that the alienists, in claiming that they could provide empirical criteria for reaching a decision, helped either. First, their empirical criteria were remarkably vague; second, empirical criteria could not of themselves solve a problem of evaluation; and third, if it were the logic of determinism that exculpated lunatics (as alienists falsely thought) then perhaps responsibility did not exist at all.

Two Acts in the 1880s might have offered scope for amending the legal responsibility of lunatics. The Trial of Lunatics Act (1883) altered the wording of the special verdict to 'guilty but insane'. This phrase responded to the Queen's concern, following an assault upon her, that the verdict of 'not guilty on the ground of insanity' was not a deterrent. The new verdict upset legal minds because it found both guilt and a lack of *mens rea*. The Criminal Lunatics Act (1884) changed the Home Secretary's power and obligations to the criminally insane.[29]

Some limited developments in Scotland and the United States are customarily cited as harbingers of medical influence, though it is improbable that they created such influence. The Scottish judge Lord Deas allowed a finding of culpable homicide in Dingwall's case (1867) where the accused had murdered his wife while intoxicated. This is sometimes considered precedent for the plea of 'diminished responsibility'. However, this phrase was not in use at the time. The case is more rightly interpreted as an illustration of Scottish law's greater flexibility about the boundary between murder and lesser crimes involving killing. In Fraser's case (1878), a Scottish jury decided that the man had killed his child but that he had done so when he was unconscious by reason of somnambulism. This was treated as a special case; the decision reached was not due to medical evidence for impulsive movements and it was not an important precedent. Fraser was dismissed but not acquitted, after undertaking never to sleep in a room with any other person.

Strong retrospective claims for precedent in a medically informed decision, that insanity had led to impulsive crime, have been made for two New Hampshire cases in 1869 and 1871. Judge Doe, a New Hampshire state judge, sought out the views of a leader of one faction of the American alienists, Isaac Ray. Ray's *A Treatise on the Medical Jurisprudence of Insanity* (1838) was much read as a statement of the scientific objections to the limited tests of responsibility approved by the law. Doe's sympathy with Ray's views influenced Chief Justice Perley's opinion, in State v. Pike (1869), that if 'the killing was the offspring or product of mental disease' the defendant should be acquitted and that the presence of disease was a fact to be determined.[30] This expressed exactly what some alienists wanted: the law's recognition of a factual relationship between disease and deed which exonerated responsibility.[31] Yet not all state courts or all alienists agreed with this (as Guiteau's trial made clear). At no stage were there clearly understood coherent alternatives between which courts could decide.

The continuing American debate came to a head in the Durham

decision passed down by Judge Bazelon in the District of Columbia in 1954. He stated that 'an accused is not criminally responsible if his unlawful act was the product of mental disease or mental defect'.[32] This has been the cause of much confusion. Psychiatrists and some judges believed it established medicine's right to provide categories for classifying criminal deeds. However, Judge Bazelon intended his statement to help legal procedure by forcing medical witnesses to give clearer evidence, which could be better subjected to the adversary process.[33] This was not what psychiatrists were looking for. The alternative medical and legal readings given to Durham sharply illustrates the persistence of medical and legal discourses. Durham did not produce the results that Bazelon wanted; since 1972, variations of the words in the American Law Institute's Model Penal Code have been used. No section of opinion seems completely satisfied.[34]

No decision comparable to Durham exists in England. Rather decisions were overtaken by the 1957 Homicide Act which introduced a plea of diminished responsibility, reducing murder to manslaughter.[35] (The argument for this plea began in the nineteenth century, with Scottish law providing a model.) The effect has been to reduce the courtroom conflict between psychiatrists and lawyers. Nevertheless, the question of defining the necessary mental element in crime and of specifying exculpatory mental conditions is still very puzzling.[36] In most cases, medical considerations now enter in the pre-trial period, when psychiatrists are not subject to either the adversary process or publicity.[37] This administrative change has largely withdrawn the issue from public attention.

It is a medico-legal commonplace to remark on the number of different interpretations given to the Rules. Medical spokesmen have often considered this flexibility objectionable, for three reasons. First, such latitude has allowed judges and juries, not medical experts, to assess the consequences of disease. Second, this has denied to defendants the humane consequences of medical knowledge. Third, it is a tacit denial of the medical philosophy that knowledge of nature decides courses of action. Some lawyers have also disliked the Rules' flexibility, but for the different reason that it implies the law is unclear and operates irregularly.

Yet it can be argued that the Rules were valuable specifically because they were vague. They therefore allowed the boundary of criminality and insanity to be continually reassessed. I argue that this reassessment is important in its own right. 'The advantage of the words "nature and quality of the act" is that they are elastic. They can be construed narrowly or widely. The M'Naghten Rules leave the jury untrammelled to use their common sense in looking at the facts of the particular case to decide whether the accused should be held criminally responsible for his actions.'[38]

2   *Criminal Lunatics*

Decisions at the crime-insanity boundary have, over the last century, become a function of administrative procedure. These procedures are now relatively private and controversy is proportionally diminished. The administration of criminal lunatics developed during the nineteenth century, an early example of centralised state responsibility. The historical significance of Hadfield's trial was that it precipitated the formal terminology and segregation of criminal lunacy. Subsequent developments exemplified social change towards government administration of miscreants, differentiation of deviant classes, and investment in specialist institutions. For the first half-century, however, government acted reluctantly, still torn between a passive and an active role. After the mid-century, legislation set a pattern of intervention which inevitably affected criminal lunatics.

Though Hadfield was not convicted, he was held in custody as a dangerous person (as civil law allowed) while a bill was rapidly enacted.[39] The resulting Criminal Lunatics Act provided for a verdict of not guilty on the ground of insanity and required defendants so found to be held in custody at His Majesty's pleasure. The special verdict's wording reflected the tradition that the sovereign embodied the realm's justice and mercy. The Act made criminal lunatics a formal species in 1800, since when they have created discussion and problems out of all proportion to their numbers. At times (as in 1843), they have even appeared to be the main problem of regulating lunacy.

> The subject of insanity, and numerous questions connected with it, have of late, owing to a variety of causes, occupied more than usual attention. The appalling attempts on the lives of persons high in office and dignity, and other atrocities, in excuse or extenuation of which the plea of insanity has been urged, have excited a strong interest, and have given rise to inquiries as yet scarcely answered to the satisfaction of the public.[40]

Yet few people outside legal and penal administration had a clear idea of either who criminal lunatics were or how many of them existed.

Though persons acquitted by the special verdict were a clearly identifiable group, they did not include all those who might be called criminal lunatics. This became increasingly the case as the century advanced. The 1800 Act formalised a proceeding which previously had been used in various ways. If a person was found insane on arraignment by a special jury empanelled to determine sanity, or, if during a criminal trial, a jury found insanity, then the court could order the person to be kept in custody without a verdict being reached. The ground for this was that a defendant had certain rights, such as the right to challenge jurors, and if the defendant had no understanding of these rights then he or she was unfit to plead.

The judges, rather than statute, dictated how juries were to decide this issue which, of course, continued significant after 1800. The legally authoritative definition of fitness to plead was given by Baron Alderson in 1836: is the accused 'of sufficient intellect to comprehend the course of proceedings on the trial, so as to make a proper defence – to know that he might challenge any of you to whom he may object – and to comprehend the details of the evidence ?'[41] In addition, judges decided legal technicalities, such as the latest stage at which it was possible to raise unfitness to plead, and where the burden of proof for this unfitness lay.[42] The practical effect of these questions varied with provision of counsel for the defendant and with the role of other officials in pointing out possible insanity.[43] Officials who met the accused before the trial increasingly influenced his or her subsequent history. Prison officers, and particularly prison doctors, became more sensitised to the possibility of insanity in those temporarily in their custody. As Walker remarks, 'the key to this escape route for the insane offender has been in the hands of the prison doctor ever since such an official came into existence'.[44] He relates this argument to the proportion of persons found unfit to plead. The number was larger for persons indicted for murder (and therefore liable to a capital sentence) than for other offences. The gravity of murder – both the crime and its penal consequence – attracted attention to the possibility of insanity. Walker concludes that there is a jump in numbers correlated with the 1865 Prison Act.[45] This Act regularised prison administration and ensured that the prison surgeon inspected every new arrival, which perhaps increased the chances of finding insanity.

After 1840, criminal lunatics included another group besides those found unfit to plead or insane. The Insane Prisoners Act in that year formalised the transfer of insane prisoners to asylums, and this included prisoners awaiting trial as well as those convicted. The 1816 Criminal Lunatics Amendment Act had provided only for the transfer of insane convicts (though not those awaiting hanging) to asylums. The 1840 provision led to some awkward consequences; it meant that a certificate of insanity signed by any two justices and any two medical men gave the Home Secretary discretion to put an untried prisoner into an asylum. In theory the trial was merely postponed, but in practice it never took place. Several cases in which judges objected to this were followed in the 1880s by a Home Office standing order that the practice should normally be avoided.[46] In retrospect one can see that these statutory provisions were the foundation for acceptance of the medical viewpoint.

The Insane Prisoners Act also enabled convicted prisoners to be transferred to asylums and allowed for them to be certified between the trial and the punishment. This meant that it was possible for hanging to be side-stepped by certification, even if insanity had been rejected at the trial. The murderer Townley 'escaped' in this way in 1863, leading to a new law. The Insane Prisoners Amendment Act restricted the justices who could sign a certificate of insanity to those officially appointed to the place where the prisoner was confined and at the same time made it obligatory (instead of discretionary) for the Home Secretary to act on a properly obtained certificate. By 1884, because local prisons had come under central control, the Home Secretary had taken over the justices' duty of appointing doctors to examine prisoners whose sanity was in doubt. In consequence, certification of a prisoner came under the central control of specialists in the Home Office or in the Commission of Lunacy.[47]

These changes illustrate the general way in which the Home Office developed administrative control in social problems. The details were increasingly left to a specialist body delegated to perform a custodial function. Criminal lunatics became part of an organised system instead of anomalies who belonged nowhere.

Around 1800 most criminal lunatics remained in gaol, though Hadfield was sent (until he escaped) to Bethlem, the medieval charity hospital which was then in a dilapidated building in London's Moorfields. The 1808 County Asylum Act sent criminal lunatics to Bethlem, or to a gaol, house of correction, or private madhouse if other accommodation was not available. Criminal lunatics confined in prisons and workhouses round the country were gradually centralised and supported by government funds.

Meanwhile, much needed new buildings for Bethlem were completed in Southwark in 1815. At government expense, two blocks were added in 1816 as special male and female criminal wings. The hospital exercised domestic control, though inmates were financed by the government. The initial accommodation was for fifteen women and forty-five men, but overcrowding was the rule; by the 1850s there were about a hundred inmates, mainly lunatics considered to be violent.[48] In 1843 there were 257 criminal lunatics in England, with eighty-five in Bethlem, thirty-three in gaols and the rest in public and private asylums.[49] Many of those not in Bethlem were persons indicted for larceny and minor assaults who had been dealt with under the 1840 Act. They were perceived more as a problem to the efficient running of the institutions to which they had been sent than as a social danger.

Bethlem's move in 1815 coincided with a Select Committee investigation of the conditions for lunatics which made Bethlem notorious. The Committee's report emphasised the cruelty of the confinement, feeding and other domestic facilities, as well as the lack of medical involvement. Conditions improved a little in the new buildings, but the institution's aristocratic governership continued and external controls were resisted. At mid-century, Dr Bucknill described Bethlem's criminal wings: 'It is not a modern prison, for there is no corrective discipline; it is not an hospital, for suitable treatment is impossible; it is not an asylum for the relief and protection of the unfortunate, for it is one of the most gloomy abodes to be found in the metropolis. It is simply a *receptacle*; into which the waifs of criminal law are swept, out of sight and out of mind.'[50] Bethlem finally came into line with all other asylums after an investigation by the Commissioners in Lunacy in 1852 which resulted in the Lunatics Care and Treatment Amendment Act. At the same time, a new and resident Medical Superintendent, Dr W. Charles Hood, attempted to initiate a new regime which incorporated some of the better values of custodial care.[51]

Overcrowding in Bethlem's criminal wings led to the construction of a special wing at a private asylum, Fisherton House at Salisbury, in 1849.[52] Parliament considered on several occasions what to do with criminal lunatics because of danger from overcrowding and because of their nuisance in ordinary asylums; there was also concern about the insanity plea.[53] The Criminal Lunatics Asylum Act (1860) finally provided for a new purpose-built institution (already in the course of construction) which became Broadmoor. Inmates from Bethlem and Fisherton House were transferred there from 1863. A small number of other lunatics who were considered to be dangerous and who were still accommodated in a variety of places round the country were also transferred.[54] Broadmoor was administered by a medical superintendent from the outset. Though it had a state imposed custodial duty, the earlier lunacy legislation ensured that an attempt was made to reconcile this with medical goals.

People entered the criminal wings at Bethlem, Fisherton House or Broadmoor under warrant from the Home Office. They stayed there until the Home Secretary, advised by the Commissioners in Lunacy, on the recommendation of the medical superintendent, authorised their discharge.[55] This was the meaning of retention 'at His Majesty's Pleasure'. (Prison inmates refer to 'pleasure men'.) In practice a warrant of removal to a criminal asylum usually meant a permanent removal. It was extremely difficult to attribute 'recovery' to someone who had shown potential for violence. There were certainly no specific treatments or regimes which were claimed to cure criminal lunatics. Medical superintendents accepted their custodial role; although recovery was seldom possible, they felt that medicine provided an appropriate ameliorative framework for such people. Whether this was the case from the inmates point of view – given the grouping together under extremely secure conditions of individuals sharing only a violent past and a social stigma in common – was another matter. Many inmates stayed until they died, and this could be a long time: Hadfield was inside for forty-one years, M'Naghten for twenty-three, and the artist Richard Dadd for forty-three.

Nevertheless, releases were authorised. Bethlem records suggest that those discharged included women who had murdered their children and some men who, while distressed, had murdered their children or close relatives. There were also a few odd cases such as Bloomfield, who had killed in a drunken frenzy but had been quiet and industrious at Bethlem. Among those admitted under the special verdict (or perhaps found insane on arraignment or found unfit to plead) between 1816 and 1864, a percentage of 10·4 men and 27·2 women were released at some stage.[56] As Bethlem and Broadmoor held the most violent criminal lunatics, it was only those whose violence had been closely circumscribed who were released. Infanticidal women were a special case since their crime was both limited in its victims and unrepeatable once they had passed child-bearing age. These women did not so much recover as pass out of the time of danger. Other inmates were sometimes discharged when it was deemed that murder had occurred in special circumstances, when it was restricted in scope, and when the individual conformed with the ideals of sane and moral conduct set in the asylum. Bethlem's case records suggest how quietness, industry and co-operation with the day-to-day domestic arrangements were valued. These indeed were the criteria of mental health; those who exhibited these qualities could be described by superintendents as sane, in contradistinction to the description which had placed them there in the first place.[57]

When a release was authorised, the case notes terminate with the word 'pardoned'. Technically, it does not make sense to pardon someone who was found not guilty. The use of the word indicates an understanding of the inmates' deviant status and of the penal consequences of the special verdict. Deviance, even when medically labelled, can indeed be pardoned.

3 *Punishment and Moral Order*

By the 1860s, legislation had equipped the Home Office with machinery to protect society from criminal lunatics, while conforming with the view that lunacy required medical superintendence. But an administrative orderliness was belied by judicial, medical and press comment, often in terms far from temperate. Though there were special procedures for criminal lunatics, critics abounded – often contradicting each other. Some believed that these procedures enabled criminals to 'escape' via a medical label, others that penal rather than medical solutions were still operating.

The criminal lunatics at Bethlem and later at Broadmoor were mainly murderers. Other crimes, notably bestiality and arson, were represented in small numbers (later on, the number of transferred convicts increased). The insanity plea was inextricably bound up with indictments for murder, when the statutory capital sentence made a vital difference to its meaning.

Murder and hanging were deeply symbolic acts. 'Morality and im-morality meet at the public scaffold, and it is during this meeting that the community declares where the line between them should be drawn.'[58] Executions were public in England until 1867. Criminal statute law reform in the first half of the century was preoccupied with hanging.

Parliament debated its first motion for complete abolition in 1840. A literature ranging from utilitarian dreaming to fairground drama flourished. It is not surprising therefore that the decision about a murderer's guilt or insanity aroused public concern. On many occasions the questions of insanity and of hanging were hopelessly confused. Or, rather, what appeared as confusion illustrated the inseparability of descriptions and values.

Alienists agreed that hanging deeply exacerbated medico-legal conflict. 'The difficulties with which administrators of justice have to contend in distinguishing crimes from the result of insane impulse will never be entirely removed, but they will be rendered much less important when the good sense of the community shall have produced the effect of abolishing all capital punishments.'[59] Maudsley went even further: 'Abolish capital punishment, and the dispute between lawyers and doctors ceases to be of practical importance.'[60]

The profusion of capital offences typical of late eighteenth-century England was gradually reduced between 1823 and 1837. By the 1840s it was limited to murder, treason, unnatural offences, arson or burglary endangering life, arson in royal dockyards or arsenals, and piracy.[61] This was in effect a restriction to murder. However, it was widely understood that the existence of the sentence was not the same as its execution. Under the 'Bloody Code' some juries refused to convict, and often hanging was not carried out. Penal reformers had in mind both a more humane and a more orderly system of enforcing 'a just measure of pain'.[62] But reformed or unreformed, the system balanced punishment and mercy, the latter perhaps symbolising that the law pursued values transcending the secular power.

Mercy was the prerogative of the sovereign. By the nineteenth century, this power was passing to the Secretary of State. After Victoria's accession capital sentences were no longer reported to the Crown.[63] The Home Secretary could review any case, and one of the more common reasons for doing this was possible insanity. In addition, judges acquired the power to record, instead of pronounce, the death sentence in murder cases (a power in existence for other felonies). This ensured commutation, as in Westron's case in 1856. The Criminal Law Consolidation Act (1861) removed this judicial discretion (it had become redundant under new legislation) thus giving the Home Secretary a monopoly.[64] This was yet another example of the centralisation of decisions. While many capital sentences were reported to the Home Office, and while petitions and recommendations were often forwarded, the practice of automatically reviewing every capital sentence was not introduced until some time between 1865 and 1882.

The Home Secretary might act in two ways in relation to convicts whose insanity was at issue. The first was to accept a certificate of insanity (which was always done following the 1840 Insane Prisoners Act) and warrant a transfer to a criminal asylum.[65] The second, in the case of capital offenders, was to commute the sentence because insanity might have been a contributory factor in the crime. Both actions sometimes aroused opposition from judges and newspapers because it appeared that a Secretary of State was interfering with justice.[66]

If penology was to be orderly and just, then it was anomalous to have a place for mercy. The two approaches – reformed and unreformed – to punishment were never really reconciled. It was strikingly inconsistent that a guilty verdict, following an unsuccessful insanity plea, was often followed by mercy on the ground of possible insanity. A discourse common to the new penology and medicine – the discourse of science – raised expectations of a more objective and mechanical procedure. In addition, to alienists this process of mitigation was evidence that the legal tests of responsibility were anachronistic and hence perpetuated bad law.

> We see prisoner after prisoner sentenced to be hanged – in conformity with legal dogmata, as they are pronounced by our learned judges, but in spite of scientific protest that such prisoners are insane – and we see the sentences subsequently revoked, by appeal to the Home Secretary, who acts upon the advice of scientific referees, and of the judge who presided on the trial; the former often simply repeating what had been urged in the evidence for the defence; the latter agreeing in the judgment which he was bound, legally, to oppose.[67]

Anger at this state of affairs hinged on the tacit assumption that law should produce 'natural justice', by which alienists meant a correspondence between justice and nature. This was characteristic of the medical approach. By contrast, it was arguable that the existing procedure was not bad law but efficient social control, reconciling contradictory feelings about guilt and mercy.

The existence of statutory penalties for crime meant that the insanity plea was pre-eminently used by those charged with murder. It was of course not exclusive to murder, but there had to be peculiar circumstances before defence counsel would risk having their client 'shut up for life in an asylum, which is generally much worse than what he would get otherwise'.[68] In one case of assault (Reynolds 1843) the defence raised the plea but was persuaded by the judge to drop it in the best interests of the accused, who received eighteen months in prison instead of possible life in asylum. It followed that the insanity plea was intimately connected with arguments for and against hanging. 'When insanity has been pleaded in answer to a charge of murder, upon the issue of the trial has depended whether the prisoner should be merely treated with Indian hemp by the doctors, or submitted to the Russian hemp of the ultimate executive.'[69] Opponents of capital punishment were quick to exploit the insanity defence where life and death was at stake.

Alienists shared aspects of the reforming ethos. Penal reformers and insanity specialists both pictured a historical transition from eighteenth-century barbarism to nineteenth-century humanity in regulating miscreants. A Christian zeal for the value of human life was also common to both. Once the earlier objectives of restricting the death penalty had been achieved, this zeal fed into a movement for abolition, not always supported by alienists. Abolitionists furthered their moral stand with vivid examples of the disorder at public executions, the possibility of error, and the existence of mitigating circumstances (such as insanity). They petitioned the Home Secretary about individual cases and were instrumental in the establishment of a Royal Commission in 1864.[70] Ironically, the Commission's recommendation to make executions private resulted in abolitionists losing their most eye-catching argument.

Alienists were acutely aware of the drastic consequences implicit in the insanity plea: their ethical perception of these consequences certainly influenced them. It was not a very great step from the Hippocratic oath to the Christian ethic, requiring the preservation of life in court as well as in hospital. William Wood, the Medical Officer at Bethlem, expressed this sentiment: 'Every benevolent mind would shrink with horror from the thought of adding to the misery of that awful affliction which, in the providence of God, is visited upon our race, and punishing the wretched sufferer, already oppressed beyond human endurance, for the consequences of a malady over which he has had no control, which, humanely speaking, he has done nothing to deserve.'[71] Reformers tended to believe that the quality of society was expressed by the quality of its benevolence, and that the law was therefore justified only by utility. The Glasgow alienist J.M.Pagan conceded that it might be logical to execute an insane criminal for retribution, but since that view of justice was invalid, it was in reality just cruel.[72] It was both barbaric and useless to punish the insane if they were unable to help what they did.

An insanity plea was at the same time a plea for the life of the prisoner. The general argument in favour of the insanity defence could also be an argument for abolition. Nevertheless, the alienist's legal duty was to give medical evidence, even if in practice it was not possible to separate this from sentiments about hanging. Professor Taylor commented: 'It is on this point that medical witnesses seem to me to lose sight of their true position – they too frequently look to results.'[73] Most alienists were not abolitionists, but they certainly were against hanging if there was the slightest possibility of insanity.

> If a *prima facie* case of mental derangement be established in favour of an accused person, the testimony of a scientific expert, although necessarily speculative, is legitimate and admissible. His object is to save human life, by affording the prisoner the benefit of any doubt

that may have been raised as to his sanity and responsibility when the overt act of crime was committed.[74]

This same confusion existed when juries considered their verdict in the light of the probable sentence. 'We cannot doubt that many of the criminal patients now confined in our asylums would, had the punishment of death been abolished, have been convicted of guilt, and sentenced to transportation.'[75] One reaction was to suggest that there should be degrees of punishment related to degrees of responsibility in cases of murder. This was mooted, for instance, after the controversial acquittal of Mrs Brough in 1854 for multiple child murder.

> The feeling against capital punishment is spreading among the class of men from which common juries are taken; and sooner or later the executive will be compelled to devise the means of inflicting severe secondary punishment. We entertain the strongest conviction, that had the jury been able to find Mrs. Brough guilty with extenuating circumstances, so as to escape capital punishment, but to ensure the infliction of perpetual imprisonment, they would have found that verdict. As it is, the punishment of perpetual imprisonment will be ensured by the legal fiction that she is insane.[76]

Rule-minded people – whether jurists supporting the objectivity of social laws, or medical men supporting the objectivity of natural laws – objected to juries behaving in this way. One cannot know whether the practice was common, but it would have served to reflect public feeling in individual cases.

Attacks on the Queen were another element which linked discussion of hanging, insanity and degrees of responsibility. Most of these attacks were outrageous rather than dangerous.[77] By the 1840s it was considered incompatible with public feeling to hang people for this kind of offence, even though the Queen was repeatedly attacked and there was need for deterrence. These cases focused attention on the need for flexible middle ground between the extremes of insanity and acquittal or conviction and hanging.

The most famous of Victoria's assailants was the earliest. Edward Oxford was clearly conscious of the nature of his act when he shot at the Queen in 1840. But medical evidence of insanity, supported by good evidence of insanity in his family, was accepted. He was acquitted. Then, as later, this was considered a liberal interpretation of the law. John Francis also fired at the Queen; though his pistol was loaded only with powder, he was found guilty.[78] However, his sentence was commuted to transportation for life. Soon after, William Bean fired a pistol-load of tobacco and paper at the Queen. Between Francis's and Bean's trials, the government responded with new legislation to the dilemma of either hanging the weak-minded or stretching the insanity verdict to cover cases where the accused knew what he was doing. The 1842 Treason Act differentiated between a serious attempt to kill or harm the sovereign and 'high misdemeanour' which merely involved pointing firearms, throwing things, and such like. Bean received eighteen months imprisonment. The legal device of high misdemeanour was thus a convenient means of side-stepping conflict between medical and legal views of treasonable conduct.

The 1864 Royal Commission considered all these topics. Significantly, however, it felt unable to devise a better formula than existed in the Rules. The issue was left for practice to resolve. This was very unsatisfactory for those who believed that objective knowledge could provide a foundation for decisions.

The question of murder and hanging was inseparable from crime in general. Many Victorians believed there was an overall increase in crime. Urban overcrowding, casually employed unskilled labour, and fluctuations in factory and out-work employment, all related to this alleged increase.[79] It was accepted that most offences were against property and were of a petty (if often repeated) nature. But crime conjured up the general potential of the labouring masses for violence and for breaching the political order.

Most crimes committed by those using the insanity defence were crimes against the person. In addition, the victim was most probably a near relative or closely associated with the accused. Legal discourse considered responsibility in individual terms, and medical discourse treated such crimes as the product of individual disorder. This individualistic language diverted attention from any possible social content – overt or symbolic – in the violence. Medical discourse portrayed diseased conduct as having meaning only in terms of the disease itself. However, crimes clearly conveyed other meanings. For example, Forrester killed his children when financially distressed, Townley murdered his fiancée because he considered her 'his property', Brixey killed her employer's child to preserve its innocence, and Oxford shot at the Queen. To say that these crimes were 'caused by' insanity was to restrict their meaning. The non-medical symbolism was intrinsic to them, as public concern about criminal lunatics demonstrated. The possible increase in acquittals owing to insanity, the possible role of the insanity plea in encouraging murder, and the effect of commuting capital cases because of insanity, were therefore natural topics for judicial and journalistic alarm.[80]

Such fears reached their high point in relation to M'Naghten. 'The public mind was in considerable alarm on this subject. The public had been inundated by medical books calculated very much to mislead juries in the case of future trials of a similar kind. Those books spoke of what they were pleased to call a homicidal propensity.'[81] It was not uncommon to talk of those acquitted on the ground of insanity as 'escaping', a term which exposed a deep split between different social responses to miscreants. As Professor Guy wrote: 'I believe that I do not misrepresent the

tendency of public opinion when I state, that, those who have experience
of the insane show a growing disposition to attribute many acts of cruelty,
violence, and fraud to unsoundness of mind; while those who have no
such experience turn from these views with suspicion and aversion.'[82]
Dr Hood gave critics of the insanity defence ammunition when he stated
that, out of seventy-nine patients acquitted of murder and sent to Bethlem between 1852 and 1858, 'in several cases no symptom of insanity has
been evinced during the period of residence in the asylum . . . the jury
acted upon the evidence of the medical witnesses, who had formed erroneous opinions of the cases'.[83] He had in mind patients like Charles Forrester who killed his two children in 1857 because he was afraid they would
starve. Forrester's case notes stated that 'there is nothing to remark in the
mental state of this man than that he is of sound mind'.[84]

Alienists rightly feared that a few cases in which insanity was falsely
found (or even only falsely put forward) jeopardised their authority.

> As a matter of fact, too, it can admit of no question that the unjust
> law with regard to what shall constitute legal insanity, would have
> been abrogated before this, but for the mischief done by those
> scandalous cases which have now almost entirely destroyed the value
> of medical evidence of insanity. It is full time that an effort was made
> to purge ourselves of the discredit which we suffer by allowing, in
> silence, the reckless attempts made to implicate the whole profession
> in the support of ill-grounded and unscientific theories, and in the
> ministering to individual vanities and interests.[85]

These remarks reveal the seriousness of medical disagreements in
individual cases. They also reveal the public image which alienists
thought they had. Finally, they show the way a group lacking power tried
to rectify that position through identification with dominant values. The
key tactic was to separate good and bad science and to show that good
science 'really' supported these dominant values.

In order to answer critics who considered the insanity defence a social
danger, Guy examined the effect of lunacy acquittals on the incidence
of murder. He concluded that the insanity defence was not the danger
which many people assumed: there were between two and seventeen
insane homicides a year, and no increase occurred after notorious cases
(M'Naghten, Brixey, Buranelli, or Townley).[86] He later extended his
analysis to include the effect of executions on the incidence of insane
offences. Once again he declared there was little effect.[87] But this time
his figures suggested that there had been a jump in the number of
insanity verdicts, as well as certifications following conviction, between
the periods 1839 to 1848 and 1849 to 1874. He concluded that if there had
been some cause for alarm, that period was now over; the last twenty
years had seen little change in the plea's success.

It is unlikely that Guy's figures could have done much to remove emotional opposition. The insanity defence *symbolised* a loss of social control. Only a party of educated reformers believed that statistical facts were the proper grounds for social action; Guy himself had been Secretary of the Statistical Society for a quarter of a century. Other opinion continued to employ intuitive knowledge. Guy's conclusion contrasted with that of the judges who continued to express concern about an increase in the success of the plea.[88]

Another way to reassure medical critics was to assert that it was unscrupulous lawyers rather than self-interested alienists who pressed the insanity plea in unsuitable cases.

> These acquittals on the ground of insanity, contrary to public opinion, are often erroneously ascribed to the crotchets of medical experts. They are, I believe, more commonly due to the powerful and impassioned addresses of counsel, who in civil as well as in criminal cases simply fight for victory wholly irrespective of any abstract ideas of justice. Medical opinions are brought forward or suppressed in order to complete a sensational picture.[89]

Taylor's point was undoubtedly valid, though it did tend to devalue the authority of medical expertise. He therefore coupled these remarks with a call to eliminate the adversary position of expert witnesses.

Alienists committed to the insanity defence emphasised that they supported the social order. 'The inducements to self-control must not be weakened; and society must be protected.'[90] The most obvious way they could make this clear was to stress that an acquittal on the ground of insanity was, in many cases, an incarceration for life. They pointed out that the carceral response to both illness and criminality meant that physical control was not going to be lost. Winslow even described the confinement of criminal lunatics as a form of punishment.

> To talk of a person escaping the extreme penalty of the law on the plea of Insanity, as one being subjected to no kind or degree of *punishment*, is a perfect mockery of truth and perversion of language. Suffer no punishment! He is exposed to the severest pain and torture of body and mind that can be inflicted upon a human creature short of being publicly strangled upon the gallows. If the fact be doubted, let a visit be paid to that dreadful *den* at Bethlehem Hospital . . . where the criminal portion of the establishment are confined like wild beasts in an iron cage![91]

The crucial difference was that the ill were not hanged, and this revealed a real underlying difference in opinion. Asylums and prisons both ensured management. But the law had a second function, to exact retribution, and medicine threatened this meaningful ritual.

Medical men reversed the usual scare tactics by arguing that murders occurred because lunatics were still at large.[92] They claimed that prejudice against the insanity plea was also responsible for resisting early incarceration of potentially dangerous lunatics; there was a symmetry about allowing people to kill and allowing them to hang. Medical logic suggested that society's safety would be best achieved by the early diagnosis of insanity. 'The triumph of science, whether natural or social, is prevision; and in no instances do we see more melancholy examples of its neglected application than in the criminal acts of lunatics.'[93] This was a strong form of medical discourse, firmly identifying social control with technology. It was a dream, not a reality, since singular failures in prevision occurred.

James Pownall, a magistrate and a medical practitioner, suffered from short periods of violent mania. In 1859 he was released from Northwoods, a private asylum near Bristol, showing no sign of insanity. He was allowed to go and stay with another practitioner in a village where, three weeks later, he murdered a servant. He was acquitted. But at Bethlem, where he was sent as a criminal lunatic, he again showed no sign of insanity. Alienists insisted that society needed their expertise to protect itself. At the same time, they quarrelled among themselves as to which party (Northwoods' superintendent or the Commissioners in Lunacy) had made such an error in releasing a murderer.[94]

This tragedy illustrated the alienists' ambivalent social role. They were eager to prevent violence, and in this role they were ahead of the public in the sense that they wanted to facilitate certification. But when they tried to reclassify violence as illness, after the event, they themselves were considered a danger. This ambivalence stemmed from an incomplete social change from a strategy favouring direct rule-making to one favouring indirect management.

It is now common to refer to 'medicalisation' as a social process underway in the nineteenth century. The term refers to the way in which events previously the subject of moral judgement have become the object of medical practice. This change is usually linked to a sociology of professional medical interests, though it should also be correlated with secularisation, scientific naturalism, and the rise of the social sciences. The very limited medical impact on the insanity defence in the nineteenth century restricts the generality of the medicalisation thesis. The thesis does, however, provide terms for understanding the alienists' claim that medical discourse, including the insanity defence, enhanced rather than weakened moral order.

The key concept was management. Victorian mental scientists equated health with virtuous moral choice and development of character. They described moral values as facts of nature. In health, a person was responsible for self-management. With disease, this self-management had to be replaced by external management – the institution and the medical man. But disease was an extremely ambivalent concept. It was both a product of self-mismanagement (i.e. of vice) and an objective natural fact. The first correlated with the alienists' self-perceived moral duty, the second with their therapeutic and managerial position. The body was a resource for both moral exhortation and managerial expertise.

This argument is illustrated by many studies of Victorian medical views on masturbation and masturbatory insanity.[95] These views, now so obviously 'false', have been a gift to the argument that medicine is social control. Roger Cooter extends this in his interpretation of popular physiological writings in the second quarter of the century.[96] He argues that the body was used symbolically to express middle-class values in the light of changing social conditions. Medical writing on masturbation and bodily health sought to make readers internalise class values.

Medical discourse on the insanity plea incorporated a similar dimension, thereby legitimating the alienists' sense of their moral contribution. Winslow ardently believed in this moral vocation. He interpreted his role in a religious manner, holding that health was that state in which the mind was receptive to moral truths. Thus he believed that the tyranny of a Nero or a Robespierre might be 'undetected, unperceived, unrecognised mental disease, in all probability arising from cerebral irritation or physical ill-health'.[97] His logic implied the medicalisation of all crime and the elimination of all tyranny by a good system of medical policing. This was extreme, but it indicated the direction in which the insanity defence led. It proposed the creation of a society in which evil and retribution had no meaning. Few Victorians were prepared for this. Even the alienists, Winslow among them, were caught in the tension between morality and management. But in their eyes, the scientific study of nature provided an objectively valid way forward. Opposition to hanging, criminal lunacy, and medical criticism of the Rules came together in the strategy for a new moral order.

The proposal to medicalise crime cannot be seen as just medical entrepreneurship. As Foucault points out, the philosophy of the penitentiary also involved making the criminal a natural object to be observed, learned and changed.[98] Crime and illness shared qualities in common; both had a latent naturalness which became more openly acknowledged as the century advanced. The criminal, as an offender of the law, and the lunatic, as an offender of mental normality, became objects of scientific study, disciplinary regulation, and technical manipulation. Those who resisted the use of the medical label were therefore likely to be equally resistant to criminology. It is perhaps no coincidence that the judiciary sometimes opposed both the insanity defence and the penal administration. Both treated miscreants in ways that lessened the importance of judicial retribution. The insanity defence became visible with social changes highlighting miscreants as objects for naturalistic study, about which scientific truth could now be formulated.

CHAPTER THREE

THE MEDICAL VIEWPOINT

I *Descriptions of Lunacy*

Criminal lunatics had an uneasy existence between prison and asylum, between discourses of guilt and disease. The tension between these oppositions lay in both the penal and the lunacy systems, but criminal lunatics brought it inescapably into the open. They therefore seemed to encapsulate the whole paradox of moral control in the name of humanity. Many alienists claimed that there need be no paradox. Inconsistency and disorder existed, they argued, because society would not base its decisions on laws of nature. The criminal law disregarded scientific truth; they were anxious to point this out in detail. Alienists expended much effort on theories of madness; they were fascinated by a scientific naturalism of abnormality. They observed, classified, explained and theorised to such an extent that they were quite unable to perceive the lack of givenness in what they had constructed. In short, alienists possessed an elaborate discourse, part of which was the insanity defence.

Medical theorising needed to reconcile many disparate elements in an alienist's world: daily confrontation with abnormality, institutional administration of a faceless mass, sensitivity to mainstream clinical medicine, and a literature of experimental neurophysiology. Alienists occupied a unique social position in which all these elements were present. This meant that they did have an experience that could not be duplicated. Medical theory gave this experience abstract form. However, it did not follow that psychological medicine had the standing that alienists themselves attributed to it.

A sense of history was a leitmotiv with alienists. The fact of progress justified confidence while preserving modesty. It conveyed a sense of knowledge against a background of ignorance, a faith in healing when little could be done. 'A glance at the past will show how great a step forward has been made, and may yield some reason for congratulation; a glance at the present, showing, as it cannot fail to do, how small a proportion the gains bear to what remains to be acquired, will prove that as yet we have rather discovered the right path than made much way on it.'[1] The name of one man, Philippe Pinel, symbolised a break with the eighteenth century and the founding of psychological medicine. He was associated with three terms – observation, the brain, and humanity – which represented what alienists offered to the law. 'Humanity' became the key word of the asylum movement, and particularly of 'moral treatment' (attention to living conditions and the psychological environment, as opposed to medical intervention).[2] Observation and the brain comprised the intellectual resources which sustained medical evidence of lunacy in criminal trials. Alienists claimed that clinical observation established sound knowledge of madness in all its varieties, and that neurophysiology was researching its causal basis. Both developments were considered novel. This atmosphere of progress gave alienists hope and confidence; the break with past ignorance objectified the moral value of their enterprise.

British descriptions were deeply influenced by French example. Medicine in France, reorganised under the Republic, institutionalised a pattern of clinical knowledge.[3] Hospital clinicians began to study symptoms in large numbers of cases, to elaborate life histories of different diseases, and to localise disease sites ('lesions') via autopsy. About the same time, the brain and nervous system emerged uncontested as the site of mental life. It was decisive that clinical medicine developed alongside an explanatory medicine accounting for disease as localised physical change.

These connections were exemplified by general paralysis of the insane (GPI). A.L.Bayle's and L.F.Calmeil's descriptions of the syndrome of GPI in the 1820s linked morbidity in brain membranes with a picture of progressive insanity.[4] In theory, this description differentiated a large group of asylum inmates who suffered from a definable disease (even though its cause was unknown). In practice, its historical significance is difficult to determine. It has been suggested that descriptions of *dementia paralytica* existed before 1822 and that the disease itself changed.[5] Further, after the 1820s, individuals with GPI were not always identified and separated from other lunatics.[6] A modern view that GPI provided a model for understanding insanity (by standardising the natural history of a disease and then linking it to physical disorder) must be applied with caution to the nineteenth century. But there is no doubt that physicians believed in an abstract model of progress along these lines.

Pinel was a self-conscious Baconian in developing a natural history of disease. His ideal of a descriptive classification (or nosology) of lunacy in all its forms, which would correspond to nature and be independent from explanatory fashion, remains a major theme in psychiatry. When nineteenth-century alienists referred to their practice as scientific medicine, they meant primarily that they pursued this ideal. The value of the knowledge they produced is a vexed question; answers to it depend upon resolving the conflict between modern psychiatry and anti-psychiatry. But this question can be put on one side.

Nosologies of insanity were legion in the nineteenth century. The alienists' failure to achieve consistency or consensus indicates the precarious nature of their knowledge. Yet certain areas of agreement were stabilised, and one of these was again traced to Pinel. He argued (and the historical truth of this was not then questioned) that the only species of insanity recognised in the eighteenth century was intellectual disorder. John Locke's brief statements about madmen were repeatedly blamed for this narrowness.[7] Be this as it may, Pinel became the *locus classicus* for disease descriptions featuring emotional and volitional disorder. His attention was first drawn to these disorders in inmates exhibiting periodic insanity. He observed that intellectual clarity persisted in the midst of paroxysms, even those leading to 'automatic atrocity'. He therefore described a disease called 'manie sans délire' (lucid mania or mania without delusion).[8] Contradictory remarks suggest that he was undecided about the relations between mania and delusion, believing that the former was 'scarcely ever without some change or perversion of the functions of the understanding'.[9] This emerged as a major medico-legal difficulty.

Pinel became less equivocal about describing mania without delusion. He named a phenomenon which later bedevilled relations between alienists and the courts.

> Finally the nervous affection gains over the brain, and then the lunatic is dominated by an irresistible desire for violence; and if he can seize a sharp instrument, then he is led with a kind of rage to sacrifice the first person who gets in his way. He exhibits, however, in other respects, the free exercise of his reason, even during his outburst. He replies directly to questions which one puts to him, and he lets slip no incoherence of ideas or sign of delusion. He feels deeply all the horror of his situation; he is racked by remorse as if he reproached himself with this frantic tendency.[10]

It was a very peculiar human whom Pinel described, so peculiar that most people without direct experience were reluctant to accept it. General scepticism was reinforced by the law's view of what it was to be human, which excluded such possibilities. Other medical practitioners were also sceptical. J.L.Casper, the leading German forensic specialist, rejected Pinel's category outright, declaring that one of his report's 'may well be termed a horrible newspaper anecdote, but scarcely a medical observation!'[11] Casper argued that 'impulsive insanity' was merely symptomatic of a more fundamental disorder which a physician less concerned with classification than Pinel might have discerned. But Casper worked within a medical metaphysics (comparable with German jurisprudence) in which good and bad principles were inherent in human nature.

Pinel's period of leadership was followed by that of J.E.D.Esquirol, a major figure in campaigns for public hygiene, medical jurisprudence, and social intervention by medical expertise.[12] Esquirol's group in part inspired, and had many connections with, a parallel British movement. Many workers ignored Pinel's disaparagement of a constant relation between nervous lesions and mental disorder and instead pursued a rigorous programme in morbid anatomy. They also re-examined Pinel's nosology. Esquirol's own scheme became the most influential one in the first half of the century.

Esquirol modified his scheme between earlier and later writings. This illustrates just how difficult it was to stabilise knowledge enough to be convincing. In an 1818 article on 'manie' he re-examined Pinel's description of 'manie sans délire' and renamed it a species of 'monomanie' in which some delusion would be present.[13] Monomania was insanity focused on one area of perception or action, in some cases accompanied by extensive lucid periods. It existed nosologically between 'lypémanie' (or 'mélancolie') and 'manie', the apathetic and furious poles of lunacy. Monomaniacs acted with great intensity about one idea or small group of ideas; in this state they were extremely dangerous. Homicide, to Esquirol, was the characteristic act of a monomaniac.

In a later mémoire on 'la monomanie-homicide', Esquirol added his authority to Pinel's category of purely affective disorder, thereby creating a medical orthodoxy that insane violence might be accompanied by some rational and moral awareness.[14] Esquirol called insane conduct without delusion 'monomanie instinctive', a term originally introduced by E. J. Georget.[15] 'There are other monomaniacs, who slay from an instinctive impulse. These last, act without consciousness, without passion, delirium [i.e. delusion] or motive. They destroy, in consequence of a blind and momentary disposition, independently of the will. They have an attack of monomania without delirium.'[16] Alienists contrasted this knowledge with eighteenth-century ignorance, an ignorance which they accused the law of perpetuating.

A phrase in common use confusingly cut across these terms. Medical and non-medical writers referred to 'partial insanity' as a legally problematic area. This term could mean either insanity coming and going (with lucid intervals or sane periods) or insanity limited to certain mental faculties. Given that responsibility was a unitary concept, it was a severe problem to determine the responsibility of the partially insane. Thus Lord Brougham introduced a discussion of M'Naghten's case in the House of Lords by referring to the legal problems of partial insanity or monomania.[17] The two categories were not medically identical, though a person exhibiting monomania (especially delusion or impulsive conduct about one idea) exemplified partial insanity. 'Partial insanity' was merely a general term indicating that many lunatics were not totally abnormal.

Alienists argued that partial insanity correctly characterised impulsive deeds of rare homicidal maniacs. Elsewhere they stated that the mind as a whole was affected by 'partial' insanity. The latter argument enabled them to attribute non-responsibility to anyone touched by insanity, making such people proper objects of full medical attention. The result was a tension between finding non-responsibility while rational intelligence persisted, and finding non-responsibility because rational intelligence must succumb in the face of emotional or volitional insanity.[18] These alternatives mirrored the problem whether the rational faculties were ever completely unaffected by impulsive insanity.

The new topography of lunacy was not uniquely French, though French authorities influenced English and American discussions, such as those by James Cowles Prichard and Isaac Ray. Esquirol's views 'more or less modified, are adopted by all writers on the medical jurisprudence of insanity'.[19] Prichard's extensively cited writings contained most of the points which were to crop up when mid-century British alienists tried to assert their claims in court.

Prichard was a Unitarian Bristol physician, anthropologist and philologist who became one of the first Commissioners in Lunacy.[20] He distinguished two classes of insanity, corresponding to the intellect and to the emotions and will. Intellectual insanity, recognised in the eighteenth century, comprised three sub-divisions: monomania or partial insanity, mania or raving madness, and incoherence or dementia. For the other 'nineteenth-century' forms, Prichard used the term 'moral insanity'. His division followed the traditional lines between the 'intellectual' and the 'active' (emotional and volitional) powers of mind.

> In cases of [moral insanity] the moral and active principles of the mind are strangely perverted and depraved; the power of self-government is lost or greatly impaired; and the individual is found to be incapable, not of talking or reasoning upon any subject proposed to him, for this he will often do with great shrewdness and volubility, but of conducting himself with decency and propriety in the business of life. His wishes and inclinations, his attachments, his likings and dislikings have all undergone a morbid change.[21]

Prichard's much used (and confused) term 'moral insanity' provided a focus for existing discussions about emotional and volitional lunacy.[22] Prichard went on to say that 'there is in this disorder no discoverable *illusion* or *hallucination*' and admitted that 'it is often very difficult to pronounce, with certainty, as to the presence or absence of moral insanity, or to determine whether the appearances which are supposed to indicate its existence do not proceed from natural peculiarity or eccentricity of character'.[23] Thus he recognised two of the key medico-legal problems which the notion of moral insanity created: the possibility that cognitive disorder was not necessarily present in insanity, and that insanity and eccentricity were continuous. The recognition of moral insanity 'brings with it many inconvenient results, since it takes away the opportunity of resorting to the most decisive, and the more easily discoverable criterion of the existence of madness; I mean the presence of hallucination or illusion: and it seems in some cases to confound insanity with eccentricity, or natural singularity of character.'[24] Prichard somewhat restricted the range of his category by trying to discriminate disorders resulting in impulsive movements from those modifying the emotional tone. The former were called, by other writers, 'instinctive madness': 'In this disorder, the will is occasionally under the influence of an impulse, which suddenly drives the person affected to the perpetration of acts of the most revolting kind, to the commission of which he has no motive. The impulse is accompanied by consciousness; but it is in some instances irresistible.'[25] Instinctive madness characteristically produced physical assault of the kind done by Burton (at Maidstone) or Dr Pownall.

Such cases brought home Prichard's remark that 'there is scarcely an act in the catalogue of human crimes which has not been imitated, if we may so speak, by this disease'.[26] The qualifying phrase 'if we may so speak' was necessary, since it was precisely because 'moral insanity' did 'imitate' crimes that judges accused it of being an unacceptable redescription. Prichard was well aware of the problem of distinguishing between irresistible and unresisted impulses; in practice he used the presence or absence of motive and the evidence of character change as criteria. Nevertheless, he asserted that observation, as well as the authority of Pinel, Esquirol and Hoffbauer, proved this illness a fact.[27]

Prichard's conclusion that all lunatics were emotionally unsound was the general medical view. Accordingly, in contrast to the Rules, it was not delusion but 'the moral state, the disposition, and habits of the individual concerned that the principal account ought to be taken'.[28] As the physiologist W. B. Carpenter said, the primary fact in insanity was a *'deficiency of volitional control'*.[29] But it was such 'facts' that exacerbated the problem of responsibility, since moral states and habits were precisely what made a person liable to punishment.

The medical debate, whether there could be volitional insanity without some vitiation of reason, continued throughout the century. Since intellectual disorder might well be hidden, it was not possible to confirm this one way or the other.[30] It was an issue which encouraged opinions based on theories of mind. Robertson, when superintendent of the Sussex Lunatic Asylum, argued that to accept an impulse to homicide without any other medical symptoms 'would be contrary to our belief in the responsibility and freedom of the human will'.[31]

All alienists would have agreed nonetheless with the review of Prichard's 'moral insanity' written by Daniel Hack Tuke half a century later: 'But when all is said that can fairly be urged against moral insanity, it remains a clinical fact, however rare, that there are certain persons who are insane and unaccountable, but in whom there is no disorder of the intellectual faculties which can be regarded as sufficiently marked to establish the fact of insanity or imbecility in the eye of the law.'[32] This 'clinical fact' created much of the controversy over the insanity defence.

Alienists did not have the requisite standing for the public acceptance of 'clinical facts'. Further, 'clinical facts' were not necessarily relevant to 'legal facts', and the latter by definition prevailed in court.

Many alienists could not accept that different orders of facts existed. They lived in a period of heroic optimism in science as unique truth.

> Now we have an immense mass of cases related by men of unquestionable competence and veracity, where people are *irresistibly* impelled to the commission of criminal acts while fully conscious of their nature and consequences; and the force of these facts must be overcome by something more than angry declamation against visionary theories and ill-judged humanity. They are not fictions invented by medical men . . . for the purpose of puzzling juries and defeating the ends of justice, but plain, unvarnished facts as they occurred in nature.[33]

An ethos of inductivism was extremely strong in mid-Victorian scientific and medical circles. The facts of irresistible impulse were upheld by the consensus of authority; their validity compared with any other item of natural history. Medical evidence stemmed from a rational approach to knowledge, but the law gave such knowledge merely contingent status. This was a point of conflict between legal and medical discourse which only power could resolve.

2   *Insanity as Physical Disease*

Alienists collected examples of human abnormality from their natural world. These objects came from a web of relations; judgements about them could not be separated from explanatory theory, which was predominantly 'physicalist'. Insanity existed as physical disorder in the nervous system, thus providing the logical justification for medicine's view on responsibility.[34] Medical discourse required a person's exculpation when physical disease produced determinism in conduct. At the same time, physical explanations were the prerogative of scientific medicine; physicalism was therefore also central to claims for medical expertise. 'Unless insanity is *a disease*, a disease of the brain affecting the mind, I do not see what we have to do with it more than other people: but if it is a disease, I maintain that we are bound to know more about it than other people.'[35]

Alienists reiterated at every opportunity the fact that insanity was a physical disease. '*No mind can properly be considered to be "unsound" or "insane" which is not subject to actual disease,* the "insanity" or "unsoundness" being invariably the products – the effects – the consequences, of some deviation from the healthy condition of the brain, its vessels or investments, disordering the mental manifestations.'[36] Such assertions increased in vigour in the mid-century, but they were not new. Scull points out the role that physicalism played in earlier polemics about the medical administration of asylums.[37] It had also been common for eighteenth-century medical men not to distinguish between mental and physical illness in their treatment of patients. But clinical medicine, coupled with experimental neurophysiology in the mid-century, gave new confidence that physicalism was becoming systematically empirical. The hope was not fulfilled, but it was a disappointment that alienists shared with the best experimental researchers.

The constant repetition that insanity was brain disease contained pre-scriptive meanings. In part, the reiteration reflected the alienists' view that non-medical opinion still considered insanity a spiritual state. 'Insanity has been considered to be a spiritual malady – a functional disease; to be an affection of the immaterial essence; to be a disorder of the soul, and not simply the result of a derangement of the material instrument of mind interfering with the healthy action of its manifestations.'[38] Spiritualist theories of insanity were denigrated by association with therapeutic pessimism.[39] By contrast, physicalism linked progressive humanitarian practice with progressive objective knowledge. 'To that principle and its applications must be attributed the rescue of the insane from that state of degradation and the cruel usage of which they were the victims at the close of the last century . . . it will be more and more developed, for to recede would be to reverse medical progress, and stop all the large advance in mental science made of late years.'[40]

To describe insanity as brain disease was to recommend a particular discourse. The statement was not the culmination of empirical know-ledge; it was the advocacy of the form of thought and the institutional power which would, it was argued, make such knowledge possible.

Physicalism also integrated into mainstream science a new and ill-defined group working in an area of admitted complexity, confusion and stress. This was a source of confidence. Experimental science was entering a period of self-sustaining growth in prestigious institutional settings. The professional scientist, along with a novel conception of 'pure science', emerged in the first half of the century. Science, particularly in the German ideal of *Naturwissenschaft*, became a value in its own right. Though only a piecemeal institutional basis for science existed in Britain until late in the century, the ideals worked deeply on individuals.[41] Medical men formed by far the largest group influenced by science. For them, physicalism was the intellectual means for coupling their necessarily mundane practice with the ideals of a new age.

The new descriptions of insanity (emphasising emotional and volitional elements) and physicalism belonged also to a broad reorientation of psychological theory. John Stuart Mill and Alexander Bain argued that complex affective elements, not just pleasures and pains analytically comparable with sensations, influenced human action.[42] Few psychologists still maintained that knowledge could be considered a psychological state which was (without emotion) sufficient to cause action. It looked as if the Rules presupposed an outdated psychology by choosing the presence of knowledge as the criterion of responsibility.[43] Mental scientists also showed a new concern with physiology, as well as with animal, racial and morbid psychology. An enthusiastic group of writers claimed that physiological psychology ('mental physiology') would transform theories of mind.[44] This hope was frustrated, but it did establish the mind as an object of scientific research. It was also one foundation for the later discipline of experimental psychology. Alienists were closely involved with these movements, and their *Journal of Mental Science* explicitly promoted the physiological approach as a new psychology. This was the background to claims like Dr Davey's that 'as there is a true and a false religion, so there is a medical psychology and a legal psychology'.[45]

The inconsistency and complexity of nineteenth-century medico-psychological causal theories makes generalisation dangerous. It is no wonder that sceptical physicians called for modest aims, purely descriptive study, and a utilitarian attitude. Dr Mayo berated medical philosophers who 'reason upon these mental properties as if they were the subject of experiment; as if we could practice upon them the "separatio naturae", which discovers causes, instead of contenting ourselves with the process of observation, which must often content itself with developing laws'.[46] As elsewhere in science, tension existed between this scepticism and explanatory speculation. It was a more sophisticated scientific stance to claim that clarity and therapeutic progress would emerge only from causal understanding of insanity. But understanding was ideal rather than real, with important implications for practice. 'Did we possess a perfect knowledge of the physiology of the organ of the mind, we should naturally, as in other diseases, endeavor to adapt our terms to the *structure* affected; but, in the absence of this knowledge, it would seem reasonable to adapt them to the affected *function*.'[47] In other words, researchers continued to describe mental functions. Thus alienists returned to a non-esoteric language to portray morbid minds, even though their ideal was both explanatory and esoteric.

A tension in descriptive and explanatory methodologies, added to indecision about mental and physical language, fostered the formation of schools and the conflict of personalities. Alienists developed a stable body of knowledge and practice in a few areas, particularly when specific neurological symptoms were evident (e.g. the different types of epilepsy). But they failed to achieve this in relation to the legally most problematic categories, notably moral insanity and irresistible impulse. The most cautious researchers therefore tended to distance themselves from such topics.

The long, almost arbitrary, lists of the causes of insanity attest to the field's instability.[48] 'Psychological' causes, such as occupation, vice or religious anxiety meshed in with physicalism. Medical aetiology was strikingly incoherent in its language of mind and body. Prichard, for instance, defined insanity as illness of the mental faculties, described faculties as functions of the brain, and then related the brain to the body as a whole. He did not specify what he meant by these relationships.

Alienists used a language which intermixed mental, physical and social categories. 'Nay, so dependent is the immaterial soul upon the material organs, both for what it receives and what it transmits, that a slight disorder in the circulation of the blood through different portions of nervous substance, can disturb all sensation, all emotion, all relation with the external and the living world.'[49] This reflected a contradiction between an awareness of human wholeness and a groping towards scientific analysis. A Conolly or a Prichard was not able to differentiate satisfactorily between social, moral and physical causes of insanity, between proximate and predisposing causes, and between mental and bodily symptoms. These were merely terms in a vocabulary; they could be rearranged to suit the immediate purpose.[50] No single scheme was possible. This was a significant drawback in getting public acceptance for medico-psychological views.

Alienists over-simplified when they divided themselves up into schools advocating the 'somatic, the psychic, and the somato-psychic' theories.[51] No alienist believed that the mind could be disordered independent of the body. At the same time they were receptive to the importance of psychological disturbance. A commitment to an extreme somaticist position, however, encouraged reliance on physiognomical or cranioscopical diagnostic techniques. It also led to the claim that all mental illness reflected a brain lesion which could be detected by a post-mortem examination. Conversely, it was sometimes said that the frequent failure to detect lesions demonstrated the psychological level of causation of certain insanities. There were some links – with endless permutations – between psychological theories and moral treatment, and somatic theories and physical treatment. But there was little consistency in practice.

Though causal theories were so flexible, this does not invalidate the argument about the significance of physicalism. As long as the diseased *state* took a physical form, the *causes* might be of any kind, and the social and medico-legal implications of physicalism would follow.

Physicalism had many sources and was supported by many arguments; it was certainly not restricted to insanity specialists or academic mental scientists. One broadly based source was the phrenology movement. F. J. Gall's and J. C. Spurzheim's work in the period from 1800 to 1820 stimulated medico-psychological theories; their phrenology treated mental faculties as localised brain functions. This influenced British insanity specialists until the mid-century by offering a coherent theory of human nature with a place for both reformist humanitarian sentiment and medical physicalism.[52] Phrenology supplied a language for talking about mental faculties and brain activity simultaneously. It served as a linguistic and conceptual bridge in the transition to physicalist views. Further, phrenology offered extremely practical prospects for the identification of lunatics. It was widely accepted that physiognomy (which merged with the more narrow cranioscopy, and persisted long after the latter was discredited) would help establish a science of disease signs. Practitioners hoped that as the science developed it would delve beneath the surface to hidden levels of physical causation.

Gall had correlated lunatic types with the improper development of parts of the brain and their corresponding mental faculties. This became common currency in Britain during the 1820s through Spurzheim and the leader of the British movement, George Combe. Combe tied physiological and pathological concepts to distinctively British political, educational and religious preoccupations, thus giving phrenology a place in reform-minded middle-class circles. These were the same circles which produced many of the new asylum superintendents, and phrenology's mixture of progressive thought, scientific physiology and practical physiognomy attracted them. As Roger Cooter observes: 'The doctrine certainly harboured a set of social values and beliefs with which they could identify and through the science itself these values could be justified.'[53] George Combe's brother, Andrew, elaborated a phrenological basis for insanity, and leading alienists, such as Conolly in England and Ray in the United States, were inspired by it for their social programmes of medicalised care.[54]

The most important empirical argument for physicalism came from post-mortem examinations of brains, surrounding membranes and connected blood vessels. 'In the great majority of persons dying insane, the cerebral organs present distinctive appearances which can be readily appreciated by a person experienced in this department of pathology.'[55] Some authorities, Esquirol among them, were sceptical of the amount of knowledge acquired in this way, but many asylum medical men regularly carried out autopsies. The autopsy was considered the key to integrating alienism and scientific medicine. The reason why medicine attached such value to autopsies was obvious; only with death could the physical basis of disease be made visible. Disease in the living body was known by signs. That the signs of insanity were so diverse made autopsies all the more necessary.

However, it was by no means clear just what was visible. Reports of brain alteration were made regularly, but the criteria for assessing alterations were not comparable with each other nor with a healthy norm. Records of colour, solidity, weight, and so on, were influenced by uncontrolled variables. But instead of rejecting such work as hopeless, alienists argued that the failure – sometimes even to observe alteration – should be taken as an index of ignorance rather than evidence that insanity might not have a physical basis. Bucknill believed that 'the indications of physiology point to our imperfect powers of observation, and assure us that cerebral lesion, although in some cases inappreciable to our senses, must exist in every instance of disordered mind'.[56] He drew on an existing medical theory to speculate that the disorder might be in the pattern of brain cell replacement and growth rather than in anything visible.[57]

Another element in aetiology was the disease's progress from functional to structural change; only the latter produced visible brain damage. Sometimes the function/structure division was an analogue for psychological/physiological causes; at other times, the division supported physicalism when empirical correlation between signs and morbid change was weak.[58] Functional theories were usually expressed in a mixture of psychological and physiological language. By mid-century, however, it was most usual for psychological factors to be dressed in physical garb.

Theories about what brought on insanity commonly described the proximate cause in terms of altered blood supply or irritation to the brain, the assumption being that blood vessels and nerves exposed the brain to disequilibrium. 'In abnormal conditions of the circulation, this uniformity of distribution [of nutritive material] no longer exists; and, in anaemic or hyperaemic conditions, the functions of a compound organ are thrown into a state of unequal excitement or depression.'[59] The obvious influence of drugs or alcohol – 'Alcohol yields us, in its direct effects, the abstract and brief chronicle of the course of mania' – provided a model.[60] The last remnants of the Galenic humoral tradition were also evident. In addition, alienists dressed up everyday-views about over/under-excitement leading to deficit/surplus of mental energy (correlated somehow with nervous forces) in various parts of the brain.

> The physiological principle upon which we have to build a system of cerebral pathology is, that mental health is dependent upon the due nutrition, stimulation, and repose of the brain; that is, upon the conditions of the exhaustion and reparation of its nerve-substance being maintained in a healthy and regular state; and that mental disease results from the interruption or disturbance of these conditions.[61]

This was a medical system of infinite possibility. It invoked explanations in terms of altered blood supply, nervous energies, nutrition, mental work, attention, emotional disturbance, and so on. Not coincidentally, it used a language of checks and balances essential to the individual's relation to society and to the economy.

The bodily economy, physicalist aetiology, and the diagnosis of living and dead signs were elements of a common discourse. Throughout the nineteenth century, neurophysiology supplied a unifying theoretical basis for these themes: during the first part of the century rigorous experimental techniques and training became institutionalised in France and Germany; the mid-century was a period of heroic optimism in medical ability to exploit neurophysiological concepts; by the end of the century, self-conscious criticism of 'brain mythologies' began to be apparent.

In addition to providing the scientific authority in medical discourse, neurophysiology had two other important implications for the insanity defence. First, complex knowledge of central and reflex action supplied idioms for describing human movements in automatic terms, and hence in terms not entailing responsibility. These neurophysiological idioms were most prominent in evidence for 'irresistible impulse'. Second, neurophysiological theory employed a hierarchical language appropriate to both nervous functions and personal conduct. This conceptual hierarchy represented values associated with being in control and being controlled; such knowledge was in part constructed from the division between being in control (responsibility) and being controlled (disease) which featured in the insanity defence. Neurophysiology thus objectified meanings associated with different forms of human conduct.

Reflex nervous theories became more precise in the 1830s, when the functional concept was related to the sensory, central-organising, and motor components of the nervous system.[62] Research then proceeded in two directions. First, experimentalists and anatomists searched for the centres and pathways of different functions. Second, less rigorous investigators explained behavioural phenomena which seemed to occur without conscious direction. Such speculative explanations were commonly used in Britain for animal instincts, human reverie, somnambulism, unconscious skills, and habits, as well as for activities like mesmerism, table-turning and spiritualism. The reflex also proved useful in mental pathology, for example for explaining hysterical phobias. The theory systematised by Marshall Hall and Johannes Müller had differentiated between lower areas of the nervous system, where reflex concepts were appropriately applied, and higher areas where they were not.[63] The new applications called this into question; physiologists suggested that the whole of the nervous system could and should be analysed in terms of similar units of structure and function, namely sensory-motor connections and reflex processes. This theory of nervous continuity, fully established in the 1870s, is fundamental to modern neurophysiology.[64]

Mental physiologists and alienists, notably Laycock, made a considerable contribution to the theory of nervous continuity. Laycock began using reflex theory for interpreting complex abnormal movements in studies of female hysteria while house surgeon at York County Hospital.[65] His clinical observations led him to claim that the higher part of the brain, as well as lower levels, linked between sensory impressions and motor responses without conscious intervention. He argued that complex movements, though conscious, could occur without volition – or even in opposition to volition – when mediated by brain reflexes. He elaborated a clinical syndrome of automatism, exemplified in the following case reported by a colleague.

> I am now attending a lady who evinces the reflex visual and auditory phenomena very strikingly. The shadow of a bird crossing the window, though the blind and bed-curtains are closed, the displacement of the smallest portion of the wick of a candle, the slightest changes in the fire-light, induce a sudden jerking of the spinal muscles, extending to the arms and legs when violent, and this without the slightest mental emotion of any kind beyond a consciousness of the movement. At times, the vocal organs are implicated, and a slight cry, quite involuntary, takes place . . . Her mental powers are good, and she can exert considerable control over herself . . . In answer to your inquiry, whether the patient is conscious of any *painful impression* on the eye or ear, when the reflex movements take place, I should say decidedly *not*. The sensorial impression and the motion consequent upon it, appear irrespective of any painful sensation or mental emotion, and are only noticed by the patient in consequence of the resulting movement.[66]

The patient appeared in control of herself except in the physical circumstances described, when her conduct was apparently quite unintended and uncontrollable.

Hysterical and epileptic automatisms provided the strongest clinical evidence for disorders displaying a lack of mental control and were therefore an important adjunct to discussion of moral and impulsive insanity. Conolly asserted that a lunatic's morbid feeling 'appears in some cases to be as little within the control of the patient, as the muscular movements are in a fit of hysteria or epilepsy'.[67] Laycock translated this medico-psychological commonplace into a neurophysiological conclusion with an objective foundation.

Laycock's predilection for metaphysics made for uneasy relations with practical medicine. But he believed that his philosophy was the necessary background to understanding his courtroom evidence. It lay behind his arguments in trials such as Bryce's and Clark's, when he argued that the brain reflex system had produced anti-social conduct which the accused could not have controlled. When courts rejected his evidence, he took it both as a personal insult and as a rejection of the discipline of medical psychology. He became one of the strongest critics of legal prejudice, claiming that lawyers employed an anachronistic psychology hidebound by introspective mental categories and ignorant of physiology.

The potential of sensory-motor neurophysiology for understanding insanity was supported by prestigious European specialists. Wilhelm Griesinger became the leading advocate for giving medico-psychological research an institutional basis in the universities. His success led to the dominance in medical psychology enjoyed by Germanic countries at the end of the century.[68] An early reputation as a theoretical systematiser was built around his account of the reflex concept. Like Laycock, he claimed that reflexes explained both movements in general (accompanied by consciousness) and specific morbid events.[69] Like Laycock again, he saw the relevance of reflex theory to the belief that some aspects of insane conduct could not entail responsibility. Philosophy of mind, experimental science, and medical practice – each was held to be of unprecedented value to the others. Psychology included a cluster of topics which interested the speculative alienist.

> Accordingly, in looking over the more recent attempts which have been made to advance and to fructify psychological research, we find that a very large proportion of them come either from the side of physiology, or from the practical necessity of seeking more definite knowledge in the treatment of insanity. A series of facts have thus come to light in connexion with the structure, functions, and diseases of the nervous system, which have already begun to carry the precision of the positive sciences into the region of psychological research.[70]

Easily observable psychological states – normal and morbid, from reverie to delirium tremens – were the principal subject matter of the new mental physiology. Medico-psychologists were, with reason, daunted by the complexity and experimental difficulties of neurophysiological research; observations which were equally accessible to the non-specialist therefore remained highly valued. Britain also lacked an institutional basis for elaborate experimentation.[71] The physician Sir Henry Holland asserted:

> Dreaming – insanity in its many forms – intoxication from wine or narcotics – and the phenomena arising from cerebral disease, are the four great mines of mental discovery still open to us; – if indeed any thing of the nature of discovery remains, on a subject which has occupied and exhausted the labours of thinking men in all ages . . . By the curtailment or suspension of certain functions, by the excess of others, and by the altered balance and connexion of all, a sort of analysis is obtained of the nature of mind.[72]

An extensive literature, both expert and popular, related insanity to everyday experience of the balance between mind and body. This was an important point of contact between medical discourse and commonsense.

Factors like habit, dreaming, and the effect of chemicals suggested a two-level model in which mind (and its instrument the brain) controlled lower-level automatic operations. Drunkenness suggested that when the controlling system was diminished or removed, the lower automatic level worked more freely. Physiologists therefore argued that the higher level exerted an 'inhibitory' function over the natural tendency of the lower level to transform sensation into movement.[73] It followed that a break-down of inhibition was the common factor in 'morbid' mental states, whether dreaming, reverie, hysteria, epilepsy, or lunacy. Inhibition became a key element in late nineteenth-century neurophysiology. It provided support for the alienists' claim that emotional and volitional disorder – the uninhibited expression of lower nervous levels – was characteristic of insanity. This claim was dramatically reinforced by some spectacular, pointless and horrible crimes.

Laycock and Griesinger wrote for medical colleagues and students. Similar ideas reached a wider audience through moralistic and educational writings. There was also concern about hypnotism, spiritualism and alcoholism, states which illustrated that people could perform complex movements without mental control. This was an incentive for some mental physiologists to popularise an idea of human automatism modelled on reflex theory. At the same time they linked this phenomenon with criminal lunacy.

Mesmerism had existed since the 1780s as a fringe medicine allied with utopian hopes for curing individual and collective ills.[74] Mesmerised subjects exhibited real peculiarities which required explanation. A Manchester surgeon, James Braid, coined the term 'hypnotism' in 1843. He described how the hypnotist made a 'peculiar impression directly . . . on the nervous centres, by which the mind is for the time "thrown out of gear"'.[75] This 'out of gear' condition showed many analogies to the fixed and uncontrollable movements of lunatics. Hypnotism, as well as the spiritualist seances and table-turnings which were fashionable from the late 1840s, was interpreted in terms of automatistic psychological states.[76] 'All the phenomena of hypnotism and electro-biology . . . point to a great automatic centre, which can mould human action with the most perfect adaptation to definite ends, without being controlled by the will, and which may be excited, moreover, to do so either by impulses directly from without, or by strong ideas operating downwards upon it from within.'[77] Mental physiologists regarded mesmeric and spiritualist enthusiasms as unhealthy; movements without mental control were a danger. They argued that spiritualism, like insanity, was 'due to an automatic action of the brain'. Laycock considered spiritualists 'morbid mono-ideists', and he cited a case in which the seance state became permanent, in other words, a state in which insanity took over.[78] Medical men argued that pre-existing – even unconscious – ideas and beliefs were responsible for experiences like table-turning. Their basic point was confirmed by Michael Faraday's apparatus which recorded hand pressure on a table prior to its rotation during a seance.[79] Participants denied in good faith that such pressure had been applied. Not surprisingly, scientists failed to establish their explanation with devotees; this determinist form of scientific explanation conveyed precisely those values which spiritualist practice sought to evade. Devotees were looking for ethical guidance not the devaluation of their personality.

The best known demystification of spiritualism was provided by the physiologist and London University Registrar W. B. Carpenter.[80] About 1850 he concluded that in some normal conditions (routine muscular movements) and in some abnormal ones (movements under hypnosis or during a seance), ideas stimulated movements automatically. He termed the reflexes producing these movements 'ideo-motor' and localised their centre in the fore-brain or cerebrum.[81] Carpenter argued that much everyday behaviour was mechanical, in the sense that it followed from sensations or ideas activating structural patterns laid down in the brain. People did not bear *direct* responsibility for such behaviour; however, they did bear *indirect* responsibility for brain reflexes because these were acquired through growth and experience. It was therefore imperative to develop right habits because, after a certain time, all habits became automatic. The mind controlled the automatic movements of the future through the conscious exercise of attention in the present. Reflex theory integrated with a moralism of character.[82] Carpenter wanted to show how scientific knowledge could direct education; this was his programme for a better society, a programme to make people comprehend the true dimensions of their responsibility. He expressed the results of modern science in everyday language, putting them into the context of everyone's experience of the relative power of will and habit.

All the elements of Carpenter's mental physiology were contained in his reaction to drink.[83] He was a teetotaller who used science to argue that drink made people into automatons. To reduce mental control, to reduce the inhibition of lower reflexes, was a personal and social recipe for disaster. Drink left the body without purpose, the individual without value, and society without order. Moderation did not suffice; teetotalism was necessary to close any opening for the automatism of habit.

Everyone compared excessive drunkenness and madness; both exemplified a loss of personal control. But to alienists it was more than a comparison. Alcohol in the bloodstream altering the brain's nutrition was a model for the proximate cause of all forms of insanity. It was also accepted that excessive drinking led to insanity, in the first and in subsequent generations. Drunkenness demonstrated in the clearest possible way the significance of time and habit on human character. It was a truism that initial choice was decisive in a drinking bout or alcoholism (a syndrome described clearly by 1850).[84] The truism became a moral fable: everyone was morally responsible for their future character and conduct. Even people with a predisposition to insanity could give themselves resisting habits. Responsibility was inescapably a matter of time. 'What he ever at any time has done, that he *is* now; and, when his name is called, nothing which has ever been his can be absent from that which answers to the name.'[85]

Nevertheless – and this was crucial to medico-legal issues – medical men argued that at some point, in both alcoholism and insanity, disease set in. From then on, they claimed, responsibility did not exist for deeds. However, this point could not have been objectively defined, even if insanity were an entity whose presence could be determined by tests (which it was not). Common moral discourse, which alienists fervently shared, assumed a continuity of responsibility through time; strictly speaking, insanity and alcoholism were self-caused. Medical discourse was logically incompatible with this. Value-judgement, and not just observation, was required to exchange discourses. For the most part, medical practitioners did not question a moral description of states of health and disease, even though a determinist logic was also important to their discourse. This reveals substantial incoherence.

Drink was, of course, perceived as a drastic social problem. 'It is obvious that if drunkenness were to be readily admitted as a defence, three-fourths of the crimes committed in this country would go unpunished.'[86] Habitual drunkenness stood for many people as a symbol for the brutal, uneducated, labouring and unchristian lower classes. Conversely, the middle classes also saw it as a symbol of the aristocracy's unfitness to rule. Temperance became an important vehicle for propagating evangelical values.[87] It was not coincidental that many medical men joined in this movement; they shared the morality which attempted to bring about social reform at the level of individual habits, and they were constantly face to face with the extreme effects of drink. In addition, the conditions which reformers claimed promoted drunkenness were the same conditions which alienists claimed promoted insanity. Alienists had in mind causal links of the most destructive kind between drink and insanity:

> Were men with one consent to give up alcohol and other excesses – were they to live temperately, soberly, and chastely, or what is fundamentally the same thing, holily, that is healthily – there can be no doubt that there would soon be a vast diminution in the amount of insanity in the world. It would be lessened in this generation, but still more so in the next generation.[88]

As an increasing number of alienists in the second half of the century became pessimistic about therapy, they turned their attention to mental hygiene or prevention. This again united a concern with madness and drunkenness.[89]

The conception that lunacy involved the 'functional disturbance of nervous centres' was a flexible formula for objectifying evaluations of human nature. Laycock, Carpenter, Daniel Noble, Robert Dunn, Bucknill and D. H. Tuke wrote to attract medical students and practitioners to mental physiology. Knowledge of the hierarchy of functional levels in the

nervous system gave alienism a scientific basis. Maudsley put the programme in its strongest form in his *Physiology and Pathology of Mind*
(1867), cited as authoritative throughout Europe even though Maudsley's
physiology was entirely derivative. It was a *tour de force* for the discourse
which turned a lunatic into an 'organic machine automatically impelled
by disordered nerve-centres'.[90] This was not just metaphor; it was also
a programme for social action in which the insane, like machines, required
maintenance.

Reference to unconscious ideas had little to do with Freud's later
development of the dynamic psychological concept of 'the unconscious'.
Victorian medical psychologists referred freely to unconscious mental
elements. Mental physiologists referred to nervous activity as the unconscious side of psychological life ('unconscious cerebration' as Carpenter called it).

A French admirer of Laycock's and Carpenter's work claimed that it
showed that 'there is no mode of mental activity which may not be produced under its unconscious form'.[91] 'We have thus in the reflex action
all that constitutes the psychologic act except consciousness.'[92] Maudsley
illustrated how this way of thinking made 'irrational' morbid events
comprehensible: for example, a mother's sudden impulsive attempt to
kill her daughter.

> The idea which arose in the mind as the motive impulse of her
> singular deeds came not by any regular process of conscious
> association; it appeared as the result of cerebral activity in the
> recesses of the unconscious mental life; the unconscious nature, as
> so often happens in every one's life, surprised and overpowered the
> conscious life. The idea thus starting automatically into sudden
> activity appeared to her verily as a revelation from heaven or an
> impulse from Satan; and the action which it dictated was scarcely
> more within control than the sudden spasm of chorea, or the con-
> vulsion of epilepsy.[93]

Nor was this idea of unconscious activity an esoteric one. Educated lay
interest in unusual and mysterious mental manifestations created much
discussion about circumstances in which the thinking mind might be
absent.

Theories of unconscious activity became controversial only when
alienists pressed the law to recognise them. But, as Maudsley pointed out,
this recognition was a medical *sine qua non*: 'The fundamental defect in
the legal test of responsibility is that it is founded upon the consciousness
of the individual. And while this is so, it is admitted in every book on mind
published at the present day, even by pure metaphysicians, that the most
important part of our mental operations takes place unconsciously.'[94]
The law defined humans as being conscious of the mental elements preceding movements, and this was precisely what the new physiological

psychology questioned. The law was intellectually reasonable, given a metaphysics of mind as conscious being, but unreasonable if mental life could contain unconscious nervous events.

Philosophical alienists like Laycock and Maudsley believed that a reformation in social attitudes to insanity required a metaphysical reformation of theories equating mind and consciousness.[95] Maudsley denounced contemporary idealistic psychology, grouping together J. S. Mill and Sir William Hamilton for this purpose. 'The advances which in recent times psychology has made, have been actual appropriations from the physiologist.'[96] 'Metaphysical' mental science relied on an introspective method which was of necessity blind to unconscious psychological life. His attacks on legal ignorance assumed it was based on the same false method. 'On considering the uncertain state of popular and scientific opinion with regard to homicidal insanity, it will appear that the confusion is due mainly to the influence of the method of studying mental phenomena, to the false foundation upon which psychology rests. The method is subjective, whereas it should rightly be objective.'[97] By subjective method he meant introspection and *a priori* definitions of the relation between mental states and actions; by objective method he meant neurophysiology and *a posteriori* acceptance of the facts of uncontrollable movements.

This was the theoretical side of alienists' practical response to violent and irrational crime. Homicidal mania, according to Dr J. Crichton Browne, revealed reflex functions out of control:

> The manner in which some of these impulses are experienced leads us to regard them as allied, in their nature, to reflex actions of the muscular system. They are not only sudden and invincible, but they pass on to action, almost without consciousness on the part of their subject, and they are excited only by certain definite stimuli, resembling in this, those types of reflex action dependent upon impressions conveyed by nerves of the special senses.[98]

Maudsley described a girl in his care as 'a most mischievous little machine' and 'an automatic machine incited by sensory impressions to mischievous and destructive acts'.[99] Lunatics suffered from either centrally or peripherally initiated impressions which, like the switch on a machine, started pre-determined conduct.

These physiological alienists knew *a priori* that moral and impulsive insanity existed. Science underwrote these clinical categories. 'The generalisations of a positive mental science . . . might, in truth, enable us to predicate, apart from experience, that such a form of disease must sometimes occur.'[100] In scientific discourse, impulsive deeds were as explicable as they were natural. 'The medical psychologist, who studies mental function by the physiological method . . . does not experience the same difficulty [as the public] in realising the probable state of mind in impulsive insanity, and in conceiving an explanation of it.'[101] Medical nosology and aetiology reinforced each other. For alienists this was a strong basis on which to organise an insanity plea. But it was a basis which judges and jurors did not share.

The medical discourse also contained extremely influential hereditarian assumptions. All historians have been struck by the strength of late nineteenth-century theories of heredity.[102] Physical inheritance of mental incapacity constituted the strongest element in medicine's argument that it, rather than the law, should assess conduct. Further, the recognition that actions became habit, and habit became inheritance ('the inheritance of acquired characteristics'), gave new urgency to the physiological approach. It also exacerbated perhaps the most difficult problem for the insanity plea, namely, the assessment of responsibility and irresponsibility when the balance between them changed over time.

A hereditarian component of insanity was accepted throughout the nineteenth century. As the French psychologist Ribot observed: 'The transmission of all kinds of psychological anomalies – whether of passions and crimes . . . or of hallucinations and insanity . . . is so frequent, and evidenced by such striking facts, that the most inattentive observers have been struck by it.'[103] Hereditarian theories did, however, gain more emphasis after 1850. Heredity became a principle around which the understanding of insanity was organised. The directional sequence of succeeding generations provided a biological analogue for hierarchical classification of incapacities. It also rationalised both aetiology and prognosis. This ordering in turn was part of an evolutionary *Weltanschauung*. Hereditarian theories also removed weaknesses in the alienists' earlier discourse, such as why there was a differential liability to disease in the same environment, or why asylums produced poor therapeutic results.

It was again Maudsley who wrote most insistently about heredity's contribution to insanity. There was little new, however, in his conclusion. Prichard had already noted that 'a natural predisposition may be inferred to have existed in every instance in which the disease has appeared'.[104] An emphasis on heredity also followed from the enthusiasm for physiological psychology. Gall and the phrenological alienists in Britain, such as Conolly and Andrew Combe, deduced that normally and abnormally developed mental faculties must be inherited along with their physical analogues. In the 1840s Laycock discussed the continuity between reflex and intelligent functions, not just in the individual, but in the inheritance of later generations.

Physiology provided a theoretical basis for alienists interested in rationalising their claim that insanity ran in families. Mental physiology supported such claims because it treated the mind like other bodily functions; it was not questioned that these were to a large extent innately determined. 'Since the direct cause of insanity is some morbid affection of the nervous system, and as every part of the organism is transmissible, clearly the heredity of mental affections is the rule.'[105] Medical writers and popularisers also accepted some degree of inheritance of acquired characteristics. When a particular mental trait turned into habit, it became embodied in the structure of the nervous system; this acquired structure was passed down to following generations.[106]

One clinical observation which seemed to confirm the dominating influence of hereditary taint was the link between epilepsy and insanity. It was claimed that epilepsy in close relatives was as useful for diagnosing a tendency to mental weakness as insanity in more distant relatives. 'There is a kinship between nervous diseases by virtue of which it comes to pass that they undergo transformation through generations. The two diseases most closely related in this way are insanity and epilepsy.'[107]

The emphasis on heredity in the second half of the century belonged with extremely wide-ranging directionalist theories of humanity, race, economy and society; reference to specific theories of progress or evolution is too limiting. Victorian society portrayed moral and economic progress in a range of social, medical, anthropological or biological theories, each of which presupposed directional change as the norm and interpreted individual discrepancies as deviations. It was commonplace to draw analogies between non-western races, the insane, criminals and the uneducated working class, all occupying a place off the path of progress. Languages of pathology and savagery were interchangeable. Thus one writer listed 'the absence of all *moral sense* . . . loss of *self-control* . . . absence of *decency* . . . *criminal* impulse', and so on, as the '*bestial phenomena of human insanity*' which 'resemble those of human idiocy'.[108] Many medical men, such as Prichard and Holland, were also interested in anthropology, in which theories provided two alternative ways of describing deviation from the progressive norm. Deviants were either survivals from an earlier period or degenerates reverting back to an ancestral stage (or merely away from the present stage). The way of writing varied with different intellectual traditions, but the underlying similarities were more important than differences in detail. Two particularly strong intellectual currents after 1860 encouraged hereditarian views in relation to an overall scheme of progress: Herbert Spencer's evolutionary philosophy, and French theories of degeneration, re-expressed systematically by Benedict Augustin Morel.[109]

Maudsley, after describing three women who exhibited moral insanity, commented: 'They are examples illustrating the retrograde metamorphosis of mind. The moral feeling has been slowly acquired in the course of human cultivation through generations as the highest effort of mental evolution; and in the course of family degeneration, we find its loss mark a stage in the downward course.'[110] It followed that the forms of insanity were not disease entities; rather, they were stages of degeneration from a standard which medical men agreed should be partly defined in social terms. It also followed that disease conditions and anti-social conduct were comparable and associated reversions; this made it unnecessary to distinguish between depravity and moral insanity. Maudsley argued that the identification and isolation of lunatics and criminals was basic to social hygiene: 'The social fabric is held together by moral laws; but we have here a being who, by reason of his inability to recognise them, is outlawed from the social domain.'[111]

Physiologists hoped it would become possible to observe degeneracy by comparing normal and progressively diseased nerve elements. Objective tests would then exist for judging responsibility and its decrease over time and generations. In reality of course this was not possible; medical evidence continued to be expressed by insanity in relatives and by degeneration signs.

It was rarely seen that demarcating responsibility on the ground of disease was, in terms of its logical structure, comparable to demarcating responsibility on the ground of social background and upbringing. Dr Mayo rightly recognised that it was as just to punish the insane as to punish those born into crime or poverty, if the law was primarily utilitarian.[112] Neither circumstance could in one sense be avoided by the individual. In Mayo's opinion, however, this could not be allowed to affect society's need to safeguard its interests; he therefore continued to attack the insanity defence. Maudsley accepted Mayo's logic, but to him it entailed the opposite social consequence. While Mayo wished to punish the insane, Maudsley wished to extend medicine to criminals. They both treated insanity and criminality as divergencies from acceptable conduct. But whereas Mayo supported a punishing legal system, Maudsley looked forward to a society in which doctors acted as technological experts, isolating and caring for degenerate elements.[113] Maudsley's approach came to be dominant in criminology at the end of the century.[114]

3 *Diagnosis in Theory and Practice*

Medical discourse integrated a scientific ideal and a moralistic practice. While the discourse contained many esoteric elements, it also reformulated everyday concerns. Its strength lay in a capacity to rationalise so much within its frame of reference. It was at its weakest when forced to confront specific problems. The law therefore exposed its great weakness: could medicine say something uniquely persuasive and meaningful about a *single* criminal deed?

The answer depended on two things: medical practice in diagnosing insanity and the courtroom presentation of this diagnosis. Alienists had limited success in communicating their new science. They sought to define insanity by observable physical criteria, enabling objective truth to draw the boundary between depravity and insanity. This was a category mistake: they confused the boundary between discourses with the boundary between the terms of one discourse. The mistake was compounded by dissension over disease types and by difficulty in providing physicalist descriptions of individual lunatics.

Alienists' 'explanations' for homicidal attacks did not specify the physical causes which constitute their basis. They could only have faith that the details would someday emerge and that physiology meanwhile provided the relevant conceptual framework. Maudsley said that 'the physician who studies insanity as a disease finds, then, that he has mainly to do with the reflex action of the spinal cord, of the sensory ganglia, and of the ganglionic cells of the cerebral hemispheres'.[115] This was an assertion, not a 'finding': neurophysiology was the language not the occupation of alienists. Yet both belonged to the same discourse.

It was a common strategy to argue the resemblance between insanity and the less problematic related diseases like epilepsy or alcoholism. This was one way to convince the public of the insanity specialist's role. Ultimately, however, alienists needed to develop detailed physicalist theories and observations of lunacy itself. Hence they turned their attention to reflex action theories, theories about automatic and controlling levels in the nervous system, and theories relating blood supply to nervous energies. Such knowledge provided a framework for the identification of categories like moral insanity.

> Now, it is always the principles of a science which guide observation and correct experience, and it is therefore the principles of medical psychology which would guide us in this as well as other instances ... If Townley was, or is, or has been insane, he had or has disorder or defect of brain-function of a nature and induced by causes which medical psychology expounds, or ought to expound.[116]

The key issue was whether alienists could demonstrate a 'defect of brain-function' in offenders like Townley to the satisfaction of anyone else.

Brain defects were invisible. They remained hidden behind symptoms until the post-mortem, and even then their visibility was hazy. Occasionally some evidence emerged. Mrs Brough killed her six children in 1854 and received an acquittal which many people thought unjust. When she died in Bethlem eight years later, the post-mortem revealed blood clots in the brain, which Dr Hood correlated with a partial paralysis evident before the crime.[117] Such data (mostly collected with the non-criminally insane) supplied the most convincing support for medical expertise.

General as well as specific empirical findings entered into medical decisions about criminal lunacy. Alienists approached each case with a classification of movements structured by neurophysiology; they looked for signs to see where in this scheme the accused belonged. Symptoms were explained in general terms by neurophysiology, and the explanation

was then used to validate the description. The objective status of neurophysiology in general was thereby transferred to the individual description. It is possible to interpret this as circular argument, especially if one
claims induction as the scientific method. Nevertheless, this medical
argument was not particularly weak or unusual. Dividing the world up
into a scheme, and then circularly locating particular events within it, is
common social practice.

Historically, however, alienists shared the British scientific community's empiricist ethos: they tried to express their conclusions about
an individual's conduct in empiricist language, and they claimed to argue
inductively. This left them exposed to criticism from laymen who looked
too closely at the state of knowledge concerning the brain and lunacy.

The jurist Fitzjames Stephen, during the 1870s, undertook to draft
a criminal code. He studied the latest thinking about insanity and
responsibility, hoping that medicine would provide facts to assist this
work. But the links he found between theory and description were too
weak for his purposes.

> I have read a variety of medical works on madness, but I have found
> the greatest difficulty in discovering in any of them the information
> of which I stood in need; namely, a definite account of the course of
> symptoms collectively constituting the disease. Most of the authors
> whose works I have read insist at a length which in the present day I
> should have supposed was unnecessary on the proposition that
> insanity is a disease, but hardly any of them describe it as a disease
> is described. They all, or almost all, describe a number of states of
> mind which do not appear to have any necessary or obvious con-
> nection with each other. These they classify in ways which are
> ultimately admitted to be more or less unsatisfactory.[118]

Stephen's search for a usable medico-legal formula was frustrated. He
hoped that medical men would supply him with scientific facts which
could become legal facts. But alienists did not have this kind of knowledge.

> If medical men could tell lawyers precisely how A's mind was
> affected in relation to a particular act by the mental disease under
> which A was labouring when he did that act, the lawyer could tell
> whether or not the act was a crime; but this is just what medical
> men cannot tell. Generally they can only say that A did in fact labour
> under a particular disease with the nature of which they are very
> imperfectly acquainted, but how that disease may have been related
> to any particular action of A's in most instances they cannot tell at
> all.[119]

While Stephen's comments were valid, this did not prevent alienists
from arguing that their general knowledge had consequences for the
insanity defence. This explains the continued emphasis on insanity as

brain disease, which puzzled Stephen.

Alienists, as well as their critics, were aware that they used a circular argument in identifying criminal lunatics. 'Thus, we infer unsoundness of mind because of the character of the acts; and, on the other hand, it is because we think there is disease of mind that we pronounce the acts insane.'[120] Sometimes this circularity looked more like self-evidence; thus Winslow exclaimed (about Mrs Brough): '*The act itself bears insanity stamped on its very face !*'[121] In this sense, to define was to know. Much of our knowledge is of this kind. But Winslow and his colleagues did not see it that way; they continued to look for a non-circular method of diagnosis.

This was a central hope invested in physicalism; alienists trusted that physical events would provide the objectivity needed to break such circularity. 'The phrase *moral insanity* in no way conveys a true or adequate idea of these mental states. In the majority of them there is disease of some nerve-centre, recognizable by those who study such diseases, though they will hardly convince a jury of it.'[122]

Medico-psychological practice and language did not correspond to the ideal of expertise. The discrepancy between ideal and real was evident, for example, in a number of textbooks. Bucknill and Tuke's *Manual of Psychological Medicine* (1858) had separate sections on 'Diagnosis of insanity' and 'Pathology of insanity'. The former was couched in psychological language, the latter in physiological language; practice and theory were separate and the latter's physicalism did not illuminate the former. Bucknill acknowledged that insanity required peculiar diagnostic techniques. 'The diagnosis of almost all other diseases depends principally upon weighing the evidence afforded by physical signs and symptoms, upon evidence addressed to the senses; but in mental disease, it is, for the most part, dependent upon evidence which is cognizable by the intellect alone, and upon data which the senses furnish to us only at second hand.'[123] Maudsley published *The Physiology and Pathology of Mind* in one volume, but it divided into two halves corresponding to physiology and insanity. The two halves were even published separately in the third edition.[124] J. L. Casper's internationally respected handbook of forensic medicine took pains to distinguish scientific 'hypotheses' concerning the anatomy and physiology of the nervous system from the 'empiric-psychological' method which had to be used in medico-legal cases.[125]

There was nothing unique about the insanity specialism in this regard. Many aspects of nineteenth-century 'practical medicine' were only tenuously related to experimental physiology and physico-chemical knowledge put forward as 'scientific medicine'. Science constituted a programme for medicine, but it did not necessarily constitute its practice. In a similar way, the physiological approach to psychology was scarcely realisable. J. S. Mill made this point when, while enthusiastically welcoming Bain's physiological associationism, he said that far more knowledge was still available from the traditional introspective methods.[126] Even at the heart of experimental physiology, in German universities, there was the same discrepancy between physico-chemical theory and the less reductionist reality.[127] To single out the alienists for pursuing theory at odds with practice is therefore to ignore the intellectual context in which physicalism was applied to all living systems, not just the mind, during the nineteenth century.

As Stephen noticed, alienists continued to describe 'states of mind' when faced by prisoners awaiting trial. How, then, did they make decisions ?[128] First and foremost was the interview. This lasted anything between a few minutes and a couple of hours and was conducted by a local practitioner or a visiting specialist. Physicians were unhappy with the *ad hoc* pre-trial facilities for medical examination; they looked forward to a time when such facilities would be built into the system.[129] The prison surgeon had more opportunity to observe over a longer period of time, but he was less likely to be acquainted with the literature of mental pathology or to test systematically for insanity.

During the interview the alienist closely observed physiognomy and expression: 'Look upon the cunning lear of a lunatic, the savage glare of a maniac, lack-lustre eyes of a splenetic, or the meaningless stare of an imbecile; such things cannot be counter-feited.'[130] Contemporary engravings in textbooks, and photographs, such as those from Bethlem in the 1850s, bear witness to the enormous significance of visual signs.[131] 'No physician can practise his art satisfactorily and successfully unless he is [a good physiognomist].'[132] The cranioscopical techniques of phrenology were, as far as practical diagnosis was concerned, only a more precise development of this ancient tradition.

Details of interviews were rarely recorded, but statements made in court imply that prisoners were asked a series of questions to test their reasoning faculties, their perception of reality, and above all their emotional response to the alienist's 'healthy' view of the circumstances in which the accused had lived and offended.

The interview also involved the same kind of examination which any medical man would make when confronted by a potential patient. General bodily health – the pulse, the state of breathing, dryness of the mouth, action of the bowels, smell, bodily injuries – was considered relevant. Temperament and circumstance were also considered. Alienists were particularly eager to uncover 'habits', especially indulgence in drink or sexual vice (such as masturbation). The results were then considered in relation to forebears and relations. Given the assumption of hereditary disposition, insanity in near relatives was good evidence (independent of the person's own conduct) for insanity in the prisoner. Again, this was orthodox medical procedure at the time, though perhaps it was taken further by alienists than by other groups.

In practice, the best evidence available to alienists was that which their critics also accepted: cognitive disorder (often termed 'delusion') and character change. The interview usually uncovered delusion, thus often providing grounds for a successful insanity defence. Jurists approved of delusions as evidence since, unlike evidence about lack of control, it was open to normal standards of examination. 'It is of the essence of the plea of insanity that the ground of exemption should be generally recognised, and capable of satisfactory proof.'[133]

Sudden change in a person's habits and temperament also provided legally accepted criteria. Supposedly insane conduct could be compared with earlier conduct, and witnesses could be called to confirm this life history. 'As a general principle, we must be guided in our opinion, by instituting a comparison between the manifestations which prevail at the time when the mind is supposed to be disordered, and the previous mental condition of the individual in its natural and habitual state.'[134] In order to signify exculpatory insanity, character change obviously could not be self-inflicted. Robert Handcock and Richard Dadd exemplified these conditions: they were moral and relatively successful men who broke their habitual mode of life for no apparent reason, and certainly not because of vice. Bucknill accepted that 'perhaps the only diagnostic symptom between mere vicious propensities and moral insanity, is the mode of causation', meaning that in a truly insane person the cause came from outside.[135] He readily conceded the danger of admitting impulsive insanity without such evidence: 'As a rule, in the absence of other symptoms of insanity, it will be well to insist that homicidal impulse only can be admitted, upon proof that an efficient cause of mental disease has been followed by a notable alteration of disposition and habits, and that the overt act has not been instigated by criminal motive.'[136]

These considerations were impracticable when alienists claimed to identify congenital moral insanity (as Laycock did with George Bryce or Winslow did with Townley). The circularity was then very evident, as other medical men indicated by distancing themselves from such cases. It is hardly surprising that descriptions of depravity were preferred. Sometimes alienists failed to describe adequately a difference between insanity and eccentricity, as in Dr Conolly's evidence about Lieutenant Pate (who had attacked the Queen with his cane): 'It seemed to me that he has a very small share of mental power, without object or ambition, and unfit for all the ordinary duties of life. In conversation he would undoubtedly know the distinction between a right and a wrong action, but I should say that he would be subject to sudden impulses of passion.'[137] This evidence failed to convince because Conolly gave no decisive grounds for preferring the language of disease to that of eccentricity, and no means to escape the circularity of his description.

When medical men decided someone was ill because they behaved out of character or in disregard of circumstances, they used the commonsense criterion that when someone behaves 'irrationally' there is something wrong with them. Similarly, when they used physiognomy their criteria were open to public inspection. One reason why phrenology had become popular was the shared medical and lay assumption that character could be read in physique and expression. 'Motivelessness' was another lay criterion for abnormality which alienists used as a signal to look closely for insanity. What did separate alienists from the public was physicalism and 'experience'. But 'experience' was hard to demonstrate; an altered blood supply, uncontrolled reflex actions, or nervous lesions, offered little in the way of communicable facts. Critics then, as now, mark the discrepancy between the theory and practice of diagnosis.

That alienists used publicly accessible observations for distinguishing moral insanity is shown by their lists of diagnostic symptoms. Prichard claimed homicidal insanity revealed itself in a marked disturbance of character and health, in the lack of motive, in the number of victims killed and the frequent subsequent attempts at suicide, in the lack of accomplices and escape plans, and in the close emotional ties with the victim.[138] These characteristics certainly were found in one class of murderers, but it was not clear that expertise was required to identify them. Esoteric physiological knowledge seemed irrelevant to diagnosis; rather, possessing such knowledge implied a willingness to recognise homicidal mania as a distinct phenomenon.

Since alienists used commonly available criteria, many laymen assumed they could practice diagnosis on equal terms. Judges like Baron Bramwell certainly took this view. He emphasised the jury's competence to subject medical testimony to critical commonsense. He insisted that the jury, rather than experts should decide because it knew the difference between insanity and depravity and bore in mind the law's retributive and utilitarian functions. As a Scottish judge stated: 'Soundness or unsoundness of mind is a fact which is to be judged of not merely or mainly as a question of law or of science, but on the ordinary rules which apply in daily life.'[139]

One commentator did not see how *anyone* could fathom the human mind, let alone determine whether or not an act could have been controlled.

> To send for a physician ... to 'examine,' as it is called, 'into the mind of the prisoner,' is to call upon him, as if he were a psychological engineer, and the intellectual and moral faculties and motives of human action as palpable objects for his inspection, as the wheels, levers, pulleys, and screws of a steam-engine. The mysteries of the human mind are not patent to these specialists any more than to any other branch of the [medical] profession.[140]

It was therefore only right that common people should make the decisions about insanity; such was the essence of justice.

Alienists were accused of being biased in favour of finding insanity and of being deceived by simulation. They replied that knowledge and experience enabled them to discern insanity where laymen were biased not to find it; they were also capable of telling real from feigned symptoms. 'The insane are so peculiarly special in their words and actions that it requires much initiation and some experience to distinguish between the workings of disease and the utterances of a troubled conscience.'[141] Each side was biased, according to the opposite viewpoint, because each side applied its own discourse to the problem.

Historians who argue whether medical evidence was correct in any particular case themselves partake of the discourses they study. In certain cases, nineteenth-century alienists described syndromes like puerperal mania and GPI which are instantly recognisable to modern doctors as post-partum depression and tertiary syphilis. Observations cluster into groups and there is much continuity between nineteenth-century and modern views. But these are not grounds for a lack of responsibility; agreement about diagnosis does not validate an insanity plea. We must have something more than the physician's diagnosis, namely, the same values, in order to accept the conclusion drawn from it.

Another cluster of symptoms included temporary paroxysms, depression, hallucinations and sensory disturbance. These symptoms appeared insignificant beside the subsequent apparently unprompted murder, though they were important signals to an alienist who had met them before. But they were poor evidence in court because they relied on the accused person's own 'special pleading'. The symptoms remained the subjective experience of the accused, however dramatically reported: 'a suddenly arising hallucination or delusion which has accompanied the act; a loud roaring sound in the ears, or a redness as of fire or of blood before the eyes, or a sulphurous smell in the nostrils, testifying to the disorder which has seized upon the sensory nerve-centres'.[142] One example of this was the case of Samuel Wallis, who had stabbed his wife in a frenzy. Judge and jury focused on the crime's motivelessness. Medical evidence, however, emphasised Wallis's earlier melancholy and his delusion of 'a fearful thundering noise' in a disused colliery and 'trains . . . running up and down as fast as they could' on a railway line where no trains were running.[143] The jury found him guilty but recommended him to mercy, and his capital sentence was commuted.

The subjective sensations of defendants were considered important evidence by alienists. Mrs Brough described being oppressed by a 'black cloud' when she killed her children and tried to cut her own throat. Alienists linked this feeling with earlier symptoms of partial paralysis and later post-mortem observations of blood clots in the brain. In another case, Mrs Vyse provided Dr Hood with subjective evidence which he used successfully in her defence.

> When worried by her business transactions she suffered from a painful sensation seated in the interior of the cranium, on the surface of the brain, and which she spoke of as 'perspiring of the brain' – a symptom often complained of by patients who suffer from mental disease, as giving a creeping, irritating feeling, but never more graphically described than by Mrs. Vyse. It is indicative of morbid action or secretion of the membranes of the brain, which is very manifest by examination after death.[144]

This might well have described a very real experience. The problem for the court was to evaluate its accuracy when the only guarantee lay in the defendant's report and in the doctor's expertise. Jurists thought it would be improper to defer to either of these sources. Medical evidence in such cases was not necessarily the reason for the acquittal. Juries also took into account commonsense factors.

The prevalence of commonsense language was demonstrated when Maudsley, the most outspoken physicalist, fell back on it to list the characteristics of homicidal mania: 'the paroxysmal nature of the actual violence', 'the mighty relief which the patient feels directly he has done the deed', the frequency of the attack being upon near relatives or anyone at hand, and the indifference displayed to the deed since it was 'done when he was *alienated* from himself'.[145]

Unlike lawyers and the public, alienists lived with lunatics. Such institutional intimacy with disease constituted the fundamental perceptual difference. 'This power of recognition becomes by experience a tact not easily communicable in words, but sufficiently certain in practice.'[146] Since society had gone to great lengths to institutionalise lunacy, it was reasonable to expect it to listen to those appointed to administer the results. Alienists sometimes reacted bitterly. 'Many a gibing sneer and ill-timed jest at medical testimony in courts of justice would be spared if those who utter them so glibly were to spend a few months in an asylum.'[147] It was Victorian society, not the alienists, which created the problem of the insanity defence.

Alienists thought the public needed educating. 'It will be a hard matter for those who have not lived among the insane and so become familiar with their ways and feelings to be persuaded, if, without such experience, they ever can.'[148] Dr Robertson recorded the case of G. T., a patient at the Sussex Lunatic Asylum with a history of occasional vicious attacks interspersed with long periods of intelligent conduct and clear moral understanding. His attacks always involved a sharp pointed instrument ('this man has never attacked with his fists in the fair English fashion'), were made without warning, and were extremely dangerous.[149] G. T. even agreed that he should be kept under restraint. He was soon transferred to the greater security of Fisherton House. Robertson was in no doubt about the insanity and lack of responsibility shown by the attack made at Sussex: 'It was made without provocation; indeed, in return for unvarying kindness and attention. It was done before witnesses and without the slightest chance of escape.'[150] He pointedly remarked that G. T. would have been found guilty had he been indicted. But because he was already institutionalised, no charge was considered. Robertson concluded that 'the previous history of this case, at once points to the existence of some deep-seated moral perversion, or lesion of the will more likely, or perhaps both, it is hard to say, from which these homicidal attempts resulted'.[151] This description was revealing. Robertson described a real experience which laymen were unlikely to have. At the same time he used commonsense psychological language, with unhelpful gestures towards medical theory ('lesion of the will'), which hardly carried conviction of expertise.

Robertson described another man, with a history of auditory hallucinations (especially when drunk) leading to homicidal attacks. G. C. had been in and out of both asylums and gaol. He had been tried and convicted for the manslaughter of a fellow prisoner while in Maidstone gaol. This was not his first assault. Robertson believed that the hallucinations had appeared subsequent to the violence. 'Beyond these auditory hallucinations and the impulse to homicide under an admitted delusion in Maidstone Gaol, no trace of mental disease exists. The patient is perfectly conscious of right and wrong, and able to appreciate his duties and relations in life.'[152] If he killed again he would be guilty of murder, according to the Rules, though he was insane enough to be in confinement.

Maudsley also used clinical experience to illustrate the insufficiency of the right-wrong test. He described a thirty-one-year-old married woman who repeatedly experienced what she felt to be an overwhelming suicidal impulse and she had to be forcibly restrained. She was at the same time tormented by her belief that suicide was evil. 'In face of such an example of uncontrollable impulse, what a cruel mockery it is to measure the lunatic's responsibility by his knowledge of right and wrong!'[153]

The practical result of the alienists' experience was the aphorism that 'every case should be examined on its own merits'.[154] They were well aware of the endless variety of the abnormal human mind. Insanity in general was never satisfactorily defined; it followed that it should be defined anew to meet the conditions of each individual. The only answer was to treat the question 'practically, in the only way in which it can arise in the courts, and to consider briefly, not what is the general limit of moral responsibility in the abstract, but in what cases such responsibility ceases to exist'.[155] However, this cautious approach called into question both the general nosology and the physicalist theory which was supposed to turn psychological medicine into a science. The contrast between generalised theory and individual diagnosis was a major weakness.

Diagnostic pressures, administrative rules, scientific theory, and professional aspirations, were all inextricably tangled in the alienist's lived experience. These interactions were the medical discourse, creating the position which the 'mad doctor' took for granted in court. Medical discourse, like that of the law, was deeply embued with Victorian moral values. But medical and legal strategies of moral ordering were opposed: indirect or delegated intervention conflicted with direct or representative punishment. Medical discourse had to struggle to exist in the juridical social world.

CHAPTER FOUR

LAW AND RESPONSIBILITY

I *Lawyers, Rules and Jurisprudence*

Medicine espoused an ordering of human affairs derived from the order of nature; the physical objectivity of health and disease was its justification for claiming social importance. Medico-psychological language, however, was strikingly similar to everyday descriptions of conduct. The very real weaknesses in cogency and coherence were hardly hidden by incantations about 'scientific truth'.

These weaknesses were compounded when medical opinion had to be elaborated in legal contexts. The law's lineage and power meant that it was medicine, rather than law, which had to justify itself. Because the law's approach to miscreants was entrenched, it appeared natural (devoted to 'natural justice') and self-evident. Further, judiciary and counsel had unquestionable professional autonomy compared to the alienists' questionable social authority. Within the context of the insanity plea, there was little shift in this lop-sided distribution of power during the nineteenth century. The law tolerated the plea in certain circumstances, but these circumstances were rarely defined by medical criteria alone.

It is important therefore to divest the legal discourse of self-evidence, relate it to the meaning and operation of the insanity verdict, and describe the legal rules which controlled the court. Judges and legal men also had group interests, as well as views on their social role. A look at the legal background makes it much easier to understand the basis on which different parties offered contrasting descriptions of the same crime.

The lunacy reformers' campaigns were, from the very beginning, directed towards legislative change and their achievements were correspondingly legalistic. They used a legally constituted bureaucracy to extend state responsibility, the centre overseeing every local institution and each individual lunatic. Statute took over – and transformed – the sovereign's ancient responsibility for the madman and his property. But there was also historical continuity between the law's concern with the rights of 'freeborn Englishmen' (such as the right to disposal of property and to *habeas corpus*) and the legal form of the new powers to certify. Once the asylums became national policy, legal sanction obliged counties to finance them and local officers to support their pauper inmates (through a system integrated with the New Poor Law).[1] It was the law's role to prevent false confinement in pursuit of gain and to extract money from recalcitrant authorities to cover asylum costs. A continuing legal presence in lunacy was ensured by insisting that three out of the six full-time Commissioners in Lunacy were barristers. This legal expertise employed itself on two main tasks: ensuring that local financial and administrative responsibilities were fulfilled, and ordering the affairs of private lunatics with property. As in all interactions between central and local government, there was continuous financial argument, sometimes reaching the courts. Reports in the *Law Times* (a weekly founded in 1843) referred to lunacy more in this connection than in any other. Several compendiums of the lunacy laws were written in an attempt to clarify administrative complexities.[2]

Though the legal profession as a whole was resistant to change, it was also deeply divided, with some factions actively engaged in internal reform. The Inns of Court maintained their ancient autonomy and class separation from solicitors, opposing recommendations from a Select Committee (1846) and Royal Commission (1854) that qualifications should be standardised by a regular system of education. Solicitors, however, achieved a powerful voice by establishing the Incorporated Law Society in 1843.[3]

There were only fifteen puisne common law judges in 1850, forming a powerful elite appointed by the Lord Chancellor from the bar. It was argued that their quality and independence was guaranteed by restricting numbers and by making them answerable only to legal opinion in the Inns of Court.[4] That judges expected to exercise real power was evident in their administration of the insanity defence. Though structured by statute and precedent, judicial pronouncements had a degree of latitude ultimately controlled only by the opinion of their colleagues. Judicial practice was in part determined by each judge's interpretation of the balance between statute and common law. This interpretative scope increased in an area as vague as the insanity plea, even after the judges collectively formulated the M'Naghten Rules. Indeed, it is arguable that the Rules gave even more scope to the interpretative-minded judge (e.g. Baron Alderson in Crouch 1844 and Francis 1849).

Though lunacy was primarily the preserve of the civil law, medico-legal procedure also had implications for the criminal law. Criminal and civil laws both altered a person's legal status. The 1845 Lunatics Care and Treatment Act perpetuated a distinction between pauper and private patients. Paupers were confined following notification to a magistrate by a relieving officer or overseer; two signatures were required, that of the magistrate (who was meant to see the pauper) and a doctor. This procedure usually aroused little public interest since it concerned people with neither status nor money. A private certification required a reception order signed by someone familiar with the lunatic, accompanied by a certificate signed by two doctors who had conducted independent examinations and who had no connection with the receiving institution.

It was also possible to be found insane by inquisition, a practice re-organised in the 1853 Lunacy Regulation Act. Relatives or heirs of a propertied person petitioned the Lord Chancellor for the proper administration of the estate. The Lord Chancellor then issued a writ *de lunatico inquirendo* and a jury was empanelled to try the case. Those found insane under this procedure were known as 'chancery lunatics' and had their property supervised by the crown as represented by two of the Commissioners in Lunacy. The lunacy inquisition aroused some controversy; it was perhaps the most direct way in which a finding of insanity was used as an instrument of control. Barristers argued that 'no one can be incarcerated as a lunatic except one who is dangerous to himself or others'.[5] Alienists, by contrast, sought greater powers of intervention, as in Windham's case in 1862.[6]

The 1845 legislation (and later amendments) was very careful to lay down precise procedures for certification, as well as for monitoring asylum admissions and administration. The property of those certified was subject to special legislation which treated the person as a minor and placed the property in trust to the state. Despite these safeguards, there was an undercurrent of resistance to the authority medicine had in reclassifying persons and their property. Aggravation was not un-common; in 1858–9 and 1876–7 there were 'lunacy panics' about false certification, both times resulting in Select Committees. There were several well-publicised cases in which 'lunatics' sued for false certification or relatives tried to certify a profligate in order to protect their own financial interests.[7] Civil libertarians who had opposed the 1845 Acts formed the Alleged Lunatics Friends Society, which campaigned for certification only when a person was dangerous and for the right of lunatics to a jury trial to determine their condition.[8] The system of private certification was opposed by the Society in the 1852 inquiry into Bethlem and in the 1859–60 Select Committee on the care and treatment of lunatics. By the 1860s, however, though the alienists had come under attack in a few well-publicised cases, the substance of medical control was unquestioned.

The law's role in settling the property of the insane was further developed in relation to testamentary capacity.[9] The acrimonious wrangling endemic to contested wills took another twist in allegations that the testator had composed the will while not in full control of his faculties, as was often the case in old age. Medical opinion was employed and apparently well rewarded in such testamentary hearings and civil lunacy inquiries. Critics insinuated that reward was also the motive for alienists who gave evidence in criminal trials. Medical men considered it easier to persuade a court of the existence of insanity in testamentary cases than in criminal trials. This provoked some resentful comments about society's greater concern with property than with people.[10] It is difficult to say whether there was an increase in the use of medicine to decide property matters. A considerable body of entailment law also existed to protect an estate against profligacy or eccentricity, so that medicine was by no means the sole avenue of approach.

The lunacy statutes gave medical men special rights and duties to certify insanity. Logically speaking, the same powers should have existed in the criminal law: if civil law accepted that alienists had valid empirical means of identifying insanity, then the same resources existed for the criminal law. However, this deduction was not often drawn, not even by alienists. Jurists certainly treated lunacy legislation and criminal law as having different existences without comparable internal logic and procedure.

There were many nineteenth-century attempts to rationalise the sources of criminal law. Though various committees looked into codification, they achieved little beyond various consolidation acts. At any rate, common law practice improved as the system of law reporting became more extensive and more accurate. In the mid-century, law reporting was competitive and unofficial, though the *Law Reports* began their attempt to establish a monopoly after 1865. Little substantial change took place in the practice of the superior criminal courts themselves.[11]

People indicted for felony were sent for trial before the judges on circuit at the county assizes, or appeared at the Old Bailey or Central Criminal Court (enacted in 1834). The vast majority of cases were apparently cut and dried. Defendants with money, active relatives, or a concerned benefactor, engaged an attorney (or solicitor, as they preferred to be called) to work on their behalf. Not until 1836, when defence counsel was permitted for felonies, did judges relinquish their standing as guarantors of the defendant's rights.[12] The lawyer's decision to enter an insanity plea was a strategy *in extremis*. One can only speculate how they reached such a decision; it certainly varied with local circumstances. Nor has research been done to uncover the social network through which solicitors or barristers approached medical experts.[13] Judged by frequency of appearance in court, certain specialists became well known, either for their zeal in supporting the plea or for their familiarity with the law. Drs Winslow and Conolly appeared in the former capacity, and Professor Taylor in the latter. The prosecution often called on medical evidence – from ordinary practitioners, prison surgeons, or forensic experts – to oppose an insanity plea. All in all, both the defence strategy and the court procedure developed in an *ad hoc* manner. The custom of bringing in experts evolved slowly, through experience.

Other countries shared the problem of defining criminal lunacy. Scotland was proud of its independent legal system; its common law, statute law and administration differed from that of England at many points. Much United States practice developed as an offshoot of English law. Throughout the nineteenth century English and American lawyers and alienists kept a close eye on cases on either side of the Atlantic; key English decisions were sometimes cited in America.

Custom and informal networks characterised the English legal profession; there was a corresponding casualness in legal theory or jurisprudence. English lawyers and judges have often been sceptical about theory, believing that law *is* its practice. Case law, or law as the product of historical evolution, makes the Anglo-American system distinctive. This compounded an indifference to the development of theoretical jurisprudence, which had no official status in the academic world.

In continental Europe, by contrast, legal discourse was also theoretical. The French criminal system operated under the Napoleonic Code, inaugurated in 1810. This code, and the rationalist approach to society which it expressed, encouraged a formalistic rather than evolutionary approach throughout Europe.[14] Codified law reflected and supported jurisprudence as an academic discipline. Particularly in Germany, jurisprudence was raised to the status of objective knowledge.

To Europeans, English law appeared both underdeveloped and unscientific since a grounding in first principles had not been established and the results incorporated into practice.[15] In the first half of the century, English law summaries existed only as 'commentaries'.[16] Utilitarians hoped to change this by reconstructing the law along systematic lines; Jeremy Bentham's work was influenced by the French physiocrats, and shared a common conceptual world with the instigators of French codification. His follower John Austin published lectures on legal theory; these did not deeply influence practice, but they did provoke thought about non-utilitarian elements in the law.[17] The general absence of sustained theoretical reflection on English law was partly remedied in the second half of the century.[18] Sir James Fitzjames Stephen's clear and incisive work is still cited, and is invaluable to medico-legal history.

The 1800 Criminal Lunatics Act required juries to record a special verdict of 'not guilty on the ground of insanity' when they found a person to have been insane at the time a criminal deed was committed. Jurists accepted (though it may have been a logical error) that the lack of guilt followed from the absence of *mens rea*.[19] The law required two kinds of factors to establish guilt: the deed must be done by the accused (*actus reus*) and the deed must be preceded by a certain mental state (*mens rea*). How exactly to define a guilty state of mind is a complex problem, inseparable from philosophical questions about the meaning – and possible introspective knowledge – of mental action and intention. Stephen argued that only a deed accompanied by intention was properly called an 'act'.[20] The law judged acts.

Stephen assumed that the *mens rea* concept specified something psychological: it 'means no more than that the definition of all or nearly all crimes contains not only an outward and visible element, but a mental element'.[21] Jurymen, who had the task of deciding whether the *mens rea* requirement was satisfied, certainly interpreted it in psychological terms; these were the terms of the 'common man'. This psychological approach permitted empirical statements to be made about guilty minds. Medico-legal conflict was therefore inevitable, since alienists also claimed to make empirical statements about minds, but theirs were 'scientific' and not 'common'. It appeared as if law and medicine were vying with each other to describe psychological facts. A different jurisprudence, however, might argue that it was a *legal* (not psychological) fact that excusing conditions operated in certain cases; finding these conditions was independent in principle of medical reality.

The *mens rea* concept has been accepted for many centuries. Jurists argued that raving madmen ('wild beasts'), children, wives accompanied by husbands, and people compelled by physical force, could not be proper objects of punishment.[22] Criminal law textbooks assumed that the mental conditions leading to exemption were simple and self-explanatory: 'Those pleas and excuses must be founded upon the want or defect of *will* in the party by whom the act has been committed. For without the consent of the *will*, human actions cannot be considered as culpable.'[23] Stephen examined the question more closely, though he too avoided philosophical questions about the nature of mental events and free will. He proposed a pragmatic description of the mental events which normally lead to an act entailing responsibility.

> The reasons for and against . . . courses are the motives. They are taken into consideration and compared together in the act of choice, which means no more than the comparison of motives. Choice leads to determination to take some particular course, and this determination issues in a volition, a kind of crisis of which everyone is conscious, but which it is impossible to describe otherwise than by naming it.[24]

Volition was simply that state of mind in which a preference for a particular course of action passed over into that action. Stephen's description was close to utilitarian psychology: Austin had defined 'will' as the event in which a desire results in an action.[25] But whereas utilitarians argued that the law's function was to exert sanctions against individual desires, Stephen argued that its function was to publicly demonstrate whether mental volition had or had not been present.

Stephen's rather sophisticated definition was unlikely to describe what most jurymen meant by volition. 'Victorian' is almost synonymous with 'will power'; a genre of popular writing exhorted readers to exercise their innate mental power over thoughts and acts.[26] Responsibility resulted when this power was, or might have been, exerted. Individual wills were facts to Victorians: 'Every human creature attaches to the words "to will," or their equivalents, as vivid a meaning as every man with eyes attaches to the words "to see".'[27] It was therefore the jury's responsibility to decide whether the will had been, or could have been, used in each case.

Theological and metaphysical tradition, which placed limits on the will in terms of its knowledge rather than its capacity, supported the view that the will was an irreducible power. Medical opinion considered this anachronistic metaphysics: 'The present view of the law seems to have originated partly from ignorance of the more obscure phenomena of insanity, and partly from the metaphysical conception of a will whose freedom is only limited by its intelligence.'[28] Alienists found support among utilitarian psychologists, who argued that volition as a causal power had been debunked once and for all in Thomas Brown's discussion of causation; 'this same "*will*" is just nothing at all'.[29]

Stephen also provided a classic interpretation of the law's social function. He argued that existing practice could not be explicated solely in terms of its utility to the public good. This anticipated Durkheim's definition of crime as conduct which offends the collective conscience. 'We can . . . say that an act is criminal when it offends strong and defined states of the collective conscience' and that 'crime shocks sentiments which, for a given social system, are found in all healthy consciences.'[30] Further, because alienists tried to redefine the objects of the collective conscience, they too were guilty of 'crime'. This at least was the view of some critics.

To Stephen, good law represented the consensus of public feeling. The law was both a literal and a symbolic enforcement of accepted values. This was the implication in his famous statement that 'the sentence of the law is to the moral sentiment of the public in relation to any offence what a seal is to hot wax'.[31] Commentators on murder trials considered public sentiment a relevant factor, even when this sentiment conflicted with reformist opinion. Thus, because they were supported by public opinion, the judges in Burton's and Haynes's trials exercised the full rigour of the law, though there was a question of insanity.

Judges defended their role with the utilitarian argument that rigorous punishment was the best deterrent.[32] This argument gained extra strength from the ritualistic quality of trial and punishment in separating immoral from moral. Ritual and utility were mutually reinforcing. 'Great part of the general detestation of crime which happily prevails amongst the decent part of the community in all civilized countries arises from the fact that the commission of offences is associated in all such communities with the solemn and deliberate infliction of punishment wherever crime is proved.'[33] It was Stephen's achievement to demonstrate that these retributive feelings could be incorporated into rational jurisprudence.

Recent work in both the sociology of deviance and the philosophy of law (particularly that of H. L. A. Hart) supports the view that the law is inherently concerned with moral ordering. Hart argues that the *mens rea* requirement cannot make sense in terms of utilitarian theory; in utilitarian terms it might well make sense to punish people who clearly cannot help what they do.[34] (This does occur under laws presupposing strict liability.)[35] Instead, our criminal law allows state of mind and presence of choice to be operative factors in deciding whether sanctions should apply. It is the supposed absence of the appropriate state of mind which, in the nineteenth century, justified finding the insane not guilty. This is reasonable if we concede that justice embodies a collective representation of values whose meaning alters with an accused person's mental state.

These arguments were little developed in the nineteenth century, but they enable us to explain the strong resistance of judges and parliament to medically inspired proposals for changing the law. It is not surprising that such proposals were greeted with suspicion and scepticism; they threatened to relocate the symbols of the moral order.

A utilitarian theory of punishment was as likely to support as to oppose retribution. Though Austin argued that the insane should not be punished when they could not be influenced by sanctions, almost everyone *was* influenced by some kind of sanction.[36] The utilitarian argument therefore led Baron Bramwell to state that the law should make sanctions even more severe for those who had difficulty being influenced: 'The unhappy madman is a person who requires the threat more than anybody else, because, from the condition of his mind, he is more likely to have some temptation to commit the offence, and less intelligence to deter him from doing it.'[37]

The philosopher F. H. Bradley understood the relationship between the idealist theory of willed human action and the inherent retribution in punishment. Though hardly a 'popular' writer, he captured a pre-eminently Victorian mentality. 'When you treat their will as a something physical, and interpret its action by mechanical metaphors, [the vulgar] believe that you do not treat it or interpret it at all, but rather something quite other than it . . . you ignore the centre of their moral being, that which for them means freedom, and *is* freedom.'[38] Bradley agreed with what he took to be the general view, that the freedom to make moral choices was what defined humanness. The law was therefore correct to resist medicine's attempts to upset this. Punishment, for its own sake, was a corollary of a bad moral choice and the legitimate purpose of a legal system.

> Punishment is the denial of wrong by the assertion of right, and the wrong exists in the self, or will, of the criminal; his self is a wrongful self, and is realized in his person and possessions; he has asserted in them his wrongful will, the incarnate denial of right; and in denying

that assertion, and annihilating, whether wholly or partially, that incarnation by fine, or imprisonment, or even by death, we annihilate the wrong and manifest the right; and since this . . . was an end in itself, so punishment is also an end in itself.[39]

The intrinsic value of punishment explains emotional opposition to medical evidence. To dismiss it as prejudice is to misunderstand its social importance. The point requires emphasis because of the shift away from retributive penal theory since about 1950. To many modern reformers, Bradley's scathing comment that 'punishment to Mr. [J.S.] Mill is "medicine"' would seem a compliment.[40] No one observing the capital punishment debate can doubt, however, that Bradley's view is still apt. Yet modern reformers, unlike their Victorian counterparts, have gained considerable power, both in legislation and in professional autonomy.

Judges and prosecuting counsel understood their role as delegates of public morality. Legal men jealously guarded the discourse in which human action was a proper object of judgement. The judiciary's considerable social prestige, as well as the power and independence of the Inns of Court, required an image as society's guardians. Medical criticism attacked the law at several levels. Most obviously, it fostered competition in the administration of deviance. More profoundly, it proposed to undermine the theoretical rationale of the legal process, by substituting scientific for legal modes of thought. Medicine also had the appearance of destroying the law's retributive and utilitarian social functions: a standard reaction to a successful insanity plea was to assert that it would encourage crime. The emotional temperature naturally rose when the crime was murder and the deterrent, hanging, unenforced.

Legal discourse did accept that the insanity defence was sometimes valid but assumed such occasions were rare. Jurists knew there would inevitably be pressure from defence counsel, falling back on insanity as a last resort in murder cases; they therefore insisted on rigorous tests for the absence of a guilty mind.

It was extremely difficult – perhaps impossible – to determine a state of mind prior to a criminal deed. The only direct evidence was the defendant's subjective report, and this was not legal evidence. Lawyers were understandably sceptical about evidence for states of mind except where it was supported by witnesses subject to the adversary process. Even then it was necessary to decide what constituted a normal mental state preceding willed conduct. People commonly used concepts such as 'motive' and 'intention' and asked whether such factors were present.[41] But as Stephen observed, 'the only possible way of discovering a man's intention is by looking at what he actually did, and by considering what must have appeared to him at the time the natural consequence of his conduct'.[42]

In practice, courts tried to avoid tortuous questions about states of mind. Instead, they relied on commonsense questions about what a 'reasonable man' would know, feel and do under similar circumstances. But this had the important implication, as Hart says, that 'no simple identification of the necessary subjective elements in responsibility with the full list of excusing conditions can be made'.[43] This was a stumbling block to any clarification of the law, either by codification or, as alienists recommended, by scientific knowledge.

When the judges formulated the M'Naghten Rules, they responded to immediate pressures and did not argue from first principles. These Rules did not justify, but took for granted, the jurisprudence linking a knowing mind, criminal intent, criminal action, and guilt. Hence they described exculpatory insanity in terms of a lack of knowledge. What the Rules' phrasing meant still arouses discussion, but most nineteenth-century judges assumed the meaning was clear enough in the context of specific trials. Judges had to explain to a jury what they were to decide. An absolute of English law was that it was the jury which should find the facts; one such fact was the presence or absence of the mental state necessary for guilt. Judges therefore instructed the jury to determine whether the accused did not 'know the nature and quality of the act he was doing; or, if he did know it, that he did not know he was doing what was wrong'.[44]

The distribution of power between judge and jury was (and is) important in political debate. Juries decided facts, but judges had considerable power to influence this decision. First, the judge operated the legal rules which controlled onus of proof and presentation of evidence. Second, the judge, instructing the jury before it retired to consider the verdict, discussed evidence and established the legal framework of the jury's task. Sometimes judges made it very clear where they stood on an insanity plea. It was Lord Chief Justice Tindal's implied direction to the jury to acquit which caused much of the outrage about M'Naghten. Conversely, in Dove's trial, Baron Bramwell scorned the medical evidence. The Rules were therefore concerned as much with evidence and judicial instructions as with the criteria for distinguishing exculpatory insanity.

The onus of proving insanity belonged to the defence, and it was therefore the defence that normally produced such evidence.[45] There was no established procedure, however, about how medical evidence should be given:

> The extraordinary medical evidence that was given upon M'Naghten's trial has made a strong impression upon the members of the medical and legal professions. Apothecaries and surgeons, without experience in insanity, volunteered their evidence; and physicians and proprietors of lunatic asylums – *who had never seen the man until after he knew he was to be tried for his life* – were allowed to give evidence which excited the greatest surprise.[46]

Evidence was not simply a juridical problem to be solved by new precedents or rules; its use indicated deep differences between medical and legal discourse. These questions may be separated under six headings.

(1) The expert witness. This was someone who, by virtue of special knowledge, experience or skill, was allowed to offer opinion on the basis of facts before the court. (Ordinary witnesses were supposed to state only facts.)[47] This role grew considerably during the century; courts were aware that they were establishing new precedents. It was the judges who decided whether a witness should be allowed expert status; the occasions on which this was appropriate were gradually clarified. The concept of the expert witness originated with the use of court appointed advisors (especially in civil cases) and perhaps also with special juries. Some experts were already used widely, e.g. engineers in industrial injury cases and medical men establishing time and mode of death. This was not the case, however, for insanity specialists; though they considered themselves expert, in the legal sense, courts did not always accord them that status. Further, jurists and laymen alike argued that insanity was not an expert (or 'scientific') question, but a commonsense one, like any other matter of fact. The young physician of nervous diseases, J. Russell Reynolds, even argued this point against alienists: 'The standard by which sanity is to be tried is the common sense of humanity, and not the opinion of a few scientific men.'[48]

(2) Expert evidence as opinion. When a medical witness was allowed to state his conclusion about the meaning of observations made by himself or other witnesses, the court treated it as opinion and not fact. This devalued his objectivity in the specific case and, by implication, called into question the scientific standing of medicine in general. Medico-psychologists claimed that scientific truth was by nature universal; it was therefore nonsensical for the court to call it 'opinion'. When the courts persisted, alienists accused the law of antiquated metaphysics and the judges of reactionary prejudice. From the legal point of view, alienists were ignorant of the court's duty to find legal facts. In short, alternative legal and medical 'truth' existed.

(3) Expert evidence did not decide responsibility. It was quite clear in law that evidence was given to determine facts, and that the jury's verdict about these facts decided responsibility. The forensic specialist Professor Taylor understood this, but in the heat of the moment an alienist might give an opinion, or even state facts, about the accused's responsibility. The judges would then interrupt: 'We do not want your opinion as to the prisoner's responsibility. Simply give your opinion from what you know, and from the evidence you have heard, as to the state of her mind.'[49] Confusion was understandable; the alienist's social *raison d'être* was his ability to diagnose irresponsible people requiring certification under the lunacy laws. These laws existed because parliament considered

it proper to delegate the power of finding civil non-responsibility; but the criminal law put non-responsibility on a different footing.

(4) General and specific opinion. Because of the zeal with which judges protected the rights of juries, the courts sometimes insisted on a technical point which separated opinions of a general kind from those about the specific case. Strictly speaking, expert opinion was general opinion about the meaning of hypothetical facts. Evidence was not 'factual' until decided on by the jury. This issue caused some disquiet after M'Nagh- ten's trial. In a later trial (Francis 1849) Baron Alderson rejected a question put to a medical witness about whether the accused was at the time of the crime of unsound mind: 'I am quite sure that decision [to allow such a question at M'Naghten's trial] was wrong. The proper mode is to ask what are the symptoms of insanity, or to take particular facts, and, assuming them to be true, to ask whether they indicate insanity on the part of the prisoner. To take the course suggested is really to sub- stitute the witness for the jury, and allow him to decide upon the whole case.'[50] Prosecution and defence counsel have therefore perfected the art of the 'hypothetical question', in which the evidence before the court is disguised in the form of a hypothesis; this ritual seems to have been practised less well in the nineteenth century.

(5) Type of evidence. Judges had discretion to allow or prevent the hearing of different types of evidence. A feature of M'Naghten's trial which disturbed both lawyers and journalists was that evidence was given by medical men who had not seen M'Naghten before the trial. Suspicion of a medical conspiracy against natural justice was perhaps understand- able in the circumstances. The practice was avoided thereafter. There was another anomaly in M'Naghten's trial: defence counsel reading from medical texts. This was procedurally embarrassing because courts were supposed to hear evidence from witnesses who could be examined, not authorities, or hearsay. Baron Alderson, once again, prevented medical extracts from being read.[51] In an earlier case (Greensmith 1837) the judge ruled out evidence about insanity in near relatives; he also discredited other medical evidence in his instructions to the jury. Bramwell was the judge best known for using his discretion to tip the balance against medicine. But perhaps he was only more open than other judges in revealing the power of his position.

(6) The adversary process. Medical experts certainly found the adversary process the most substantial and offensive legal aspect of a court appearance. Many scientists are still shocked at the way their knowledge is attacked in court; for Victorian alienists, it was even worse. First, they were extremely sensitive to their lack of social status and scientific credibility; second, their philosophy of scientific truth meant that cross-examination was a wholly illogical proceeding. Such is the power of the pure science ethos that a new breed of expert has had to

evolve, one able to reconcile scientific truth with legal questioning. Few Victorian alienists were willing to compromise their scientific values in this way. Rather, they felt morally bound to persuade the courts to accept science as objective truth. Judges and counsel, by contrast, felt morally bound to treat all evidence as evidence for or against the accused, leaving it to the jury to decide the truth. If alienists were disturbed by the experience, they were even more disturbed by the result; common jurymen decided matters which were matters of science.

This was a basic conflict between medical and legal discourse. Was truth the obscure objectivity of nature or the plain commonsense of jurymen? Was truth best determined by sober deliberation or by emotional cross-examination? The alienists' response was that insanity should be decided by a neutral panel of experts appointed by, and answerable to, the court.[52] This, they said, would reinstate scientific knowledge in its rightful place. Courts should be laboratories equipped to interrogate nature. However, as Stephen pointed out, in law 'the result to be reached is not truth simply, but such an approach to truth as the average run of men are capable of making, and that this result is more likely to be found in the opinions of common than in those of scientific jurors'.[53]

The choice between common or scientific truth would determine the form of social authority. Alienists interpreted the 'natural' in 'natural justice' as a reference to 'nature'; jurists, by contrast, interpreted 'natural' as a reference to the 'reasonable man'. Nature and the reasonable man were mythologies of alternative moral orders.

The tenacity of the legal viewpoint is illustrated by reactions to Stephen's review of the insanity plea in the 1870s. In the 1850s Stephen had argued that the existing law was adequate; later on he admitted that the Rules excluded certain forms of exculpatory insanity. He therefore proposed (to a Select Committee on homicide in 1874 and a Royal Commission on indictable offences in 1879) that a lunatic, while knowing what he was doing, might be prevented from 'controlling his own conduct'.[54]

Stephen's suggestion was unacceptable both to the Royal Commission and to other judicial witnesses. Jurists presupposed the reality of a freedom to act wilfully. It was considered impossible to distinguish between willed passionate acts and the equally passionate products of disease. It was better for the law to avoid creating untenable boundaries which might result in the acquittal of those who were ungoverned rather than ungovernable. 'The test proposed for distinguishing between such a state of mind and a criminal motive, the offspring of revenge, hatred, or ungoverned passion, appears to us on the whole not to be practicable or safe, and we are unable to suggest one which would satisfy these requisites and obviate the risk of a jury being misled by considerations of so metaphysical a character.'[55] Even those who felt some sympathy with

Stephen's proposal considered it unsatisfactory to rewrite the test of criminal insanity just for homicide.

Stephen's proposals formed part of a projected criminal code. Codifiers assumed that legal rules could and should be formulated by objective standards – by deduction from first principles or by correspondence to natural reality. It was this latter point which gave legal and medical discourses a common element. To go further into this it would be useful to have a comparative history of medico-legal issues; but, as yet, nothing exists along these lines.[56]

French law provided a contrast to that of England throughout the nineteenth century. The 1810 Code Pénal (or Napoleonic Code) attempted to create a criminal legal system independent of historical conditions. Book 11 dealt with 'persons punishable, excusable or responsible for crimes and misdemeanors' and Article 64 discussed exculpatory conditions. 'If the person charged with the commission of a felony or misdemeanor was then insane or acted by absolute necessity, no offense has been committed.'[57] Viewed out of context, this article appeared to make liberal provision for the insane since it allowed insanity itself, not just particular forms or consequences, to qualify as an excusing condition. The Code apparently treated insanity as a natural fact. However, it was by no means either so clear-cut or so liberal in practice. French alienists in the 1820s and 1830s had the same struggle to establish their viewpoint as their English colleagues slightly later. But whatever actually happened in France, British alienists made unfavourable comparisons between the wording of the conservative English Rules and the liberal French Code. British alienists thereby suggested that Article 64 was a model for reform.

English alienists made similar polemical comparisons between English and French administration. The French court could appoint expert witnesses to give evidence about the accused's state of mind without this evidence being part of the prosecution or defence case. This appeared to make science neutral and alienists expert. English alienists compared this to an English model which they also favoured: the Admiralty Court in which four Masters of the Trinity House could be called on in expert questions involving navigation.[58] The French examining judge was not, however, compelled to call for or take notice of reports from medical examiners, and the history of individual trials shows that controversy was also endemic in France.[59]

In 1871 the newly unified German nation adopted a criminal code based on existing state codes, which in turn were influenced by French law. The new code described exculpatory mental states in terms of the power of will rather than causation by disease. 'There is no punishable act, if, at the time of doing it, the actor was in a state of unconsciousness or of morbid disturbance of the mental faculties which excluded the free determination of his will.'[60] German jurisprudence hinged on the question of freedom of the will, encouraging a very different style of medico-legal discussion. Nevertheless, the problem of the boundary between crime and madness crossed all such national differences.

2   *Responsibility with Time*

Criminal trials were ·occasions for displaying guilt and innocence. To substitute insanity for guilt confounded the exhibition. Jurists, as the actors, and citizens, as the audience, had an investment in this display. Insanity was a potent symbol for a new and not always welcomed set of power relations; abnormality was becoming a hidden object of scientific study rather than a visible object of the law. The transition was neither smooth nor complete. To remove the visible signs of power required trust in the new social groups which were exercising power on the basis of knowledge. Victorian alienists had great difficulty arousing this trust. When they did acquire some authority to assess criminal insanity, this occurred outside the trial, within administrative frameworks (concerning public health, poverty, and the prisons) which had already opened the way to 'expert' management.

From the juristic viewpoint, which favoured an overtly judgemental view of abnormality, there was a fatal flaw in the medical discourse: the logical necessity for a mechanistic view of *all* human actions. Some medical writing invited attention to this point:

> It is certain, however, that lunatics and criminals are as much manufactured articles as are steam-engines and calico-printing machines, only the processes of the organic manufactory are so complex that we are not able to follow them. They are neither accidents nor anomalies in the universe, but come by law and testify to causality; and it is the business of science to find out what the causes are and by what laws they work.[61]

If lunatics and criminals were 'manufactured', the implication was that the law, being drama rather than technology, was superfluous. It was a small logical step to claim that not only legal judgement but also moral judgement was superstition. Jurists therefore attacked the insanity defence as a slippery slope to moral and political anarchy.

> Even those physicians who argue that there is no distinction in nature between crime and insanity, and who blame organism for all errors, do not, so far as I know, assert that there should be no such thing as government . . . That being so, why should any different method of procedure be adopted in relation to the insane, than that which is adopted in relation to the sane ? The state exists for the sake of healthy men, and not for the sake of those who are diseased.[62]

Interestingly enough, Maudsley agreed with this sentiment. But the point at issue was not the political result, but the political means; responsibility for all, or technology for all. This stark polarity has re-emerged through the work of Thomas Szasz, who has done more than anyone to make psychiatric judgement – rightly – a contentious issue.[63]

In fact, most alienists, at least before 1870, employed a dualism between the free moral actions of health and the determinism of disease. This made the jurists' accusations false. But such imputations did expose a serious unintelligibility in the medical discourse. Some doctors later resolved it by boldly opting for a universal determinism. The long-term consequence of this is 'the therapeutic state', the beginnings of which were already noted with concern in the mid-nineteenth century. 'The medical art is not, as formerly, limited to the cure of specific and definite disease; its application is extended widely over our habitual and ordinary state.'[64]

The insanity defence dramatised the switching between languages of moral choice and determinism, both between medical and legal discourses and within the medical discourse itself. The difficulty was exacerbated by the problem of earlier responsibility for later conduct; the boundary of crime and insanity became a question of biography.

Lay and medical moralists alike emphasised the cultivation of good mental habits to ensure that when the reasoning faculties were diminished (for instance, during emotional stress), thought and conduct would still be moral. Through habits 'every man becomes, in an important sense, the master of his own moral destiny'.[65] This was the view which W. B. Carpenter represented in a physiology of nervous reflexes and habit, and Maudsley translated into hereditarian theory. In a sense they merely reformulated the assumptions of parents and educationalists. The longer a habit was indulged, the more difficult it was to dislodge. Every thought and every act therefore required prudence, however peripheral it might seem at the time. 'And hence it is said with truth, that none but a person of confirmed virtue is completely free.'[66] If anything, physiology reinforced this theory of character: it portrayed habits becoming built into the body's fabric and thus impossible to eradicate or even to control. 'Possibility of compulsion should make us see more clearly the need of so strengthening our will for good as to make that compulsion impossible for us, except in theory.'[67]

Important consequences for the concept of responsibility followed from this. This was equally true for medical and legal discourse. However unthought-out or even unintended a habit might be, it existed because of earlier thoughts and acts. Responsibility ensued, not necessarily because any particular movement was intended, but because a chosen life history led to that movement. It was generally accepted that very angry or severely distressed people had little control over themselves. But the moralist's attention was not limited to the present; it illuminated the past when the possibility of immorality began. Responsibility existed in the light of what the past revealed. When Stephen agreed that certain diseases might lead to uncontrollable movements, he nevertheless added a qualification: 'I think that the general rule that a person should not be liable to be punished for any act done when he is deprived by disease of the power of controlling his conduct should be qualified by the words, "unless the absence of the power of control has been caused by his own default".'[68] This was basic legal sense, and many alienists would have concurred.

Depravity theories emphasised *continuity* between the criminal's past and present; it was right to find responsibility and to punish, since past actions could have been avoided. Medical theories, by contrast, emphasised *discontinuity* between past responsibility and present conduct. Disease cut across a person's life. Alienists shared the general moralistic outlook, but they interpreted the disease as a sign that concepts of criminal responsibility had ceased to be appropriate.

Alienists employed moralist language (ideally suited to health) and mechanist language (ideally suited to illness), shifting with great ease between them. Yet sometimes they needed to be separated. It was the role of medical evidence to specify the moment at which the shift should take place. At some point the insane *became* non-responsible. 'If we are justified in considering every person accountable and amenable to punishment whose insanity can be clearly traced *to self-created causes*, where are we to draw the line?'[69] Most people accepted that the line could be drawn where there was an exaggerated character change without apparent 'reason'. 'When a man of uniformly mild character boldly and openly commits a deed of blood, – when a woman of previous purity gives way to lasciviousness . . . it is proper to consider how far unsoundness of mind may not be considered as the cause.'[70] Other clear breaks were associated with childbirth and menstruation. But alienists, as well as jurists, admitted that a sharp break was not always demonstrable and that moralist and mechanist discourse therefore overlapped in time.

The Bethlem case notes of John Taylor illustrate the dilemma caused by the continuity between bad habits and disease: 'This is a case where extreme perverseness and sulkiness amount to actual disease though these bad qualities are to some extent under his command and if his mind had been properly tutored, they would probably have become quite subservient.'[71] The same dilemma is evident in Bucknill and Tuke's textbook: first, they point out continuity between indulgence and a complete lack of control; second, they assert discontinuity, meaning that disease is a specifically medical object.

> It may be, that emotions and propensities which have acquired strength, by constant indulgence, become at length as irresistible, when the moment of temptation arrives, as those which are the result of mental disease. This, however, is a question more for the moralist than for the physician. The role of the physician is, to point out to the

magistrate that which is disease and that which is not.[72]

This was good advice to alienists. Yet it was advice doubly confounded in practice, by the temporal continuity of a person's life and by the alienists' persistent moral construction of disease.

These problems led alienists to call for the legal recognition of grada-tions of responsibility, to replace guilty and not guilty verdicts.

> In nature we find no such sharply defined classification . . . But nature herself must bend to the laws of man! and a dozen farmers and shopkeepers are compelled to divide the world of mind into two parts; and, on the most awful and momentous occasion, on a question of the life or death of a fellow-creature, to discern what the most scientific often fail to do, the exact position therein of a particular instance.[73]

With the partial exception of Scotland, however, neither parliamentary committees nor the judiciary was willing to countenance diminished responsibility in the nineteenth century. Jurists objected to the vague-ness of the concept, the difficulty of definition, the consequent misuse by juries, and the possible lessening of deterrence. Alienists responded by objecting to the abstractions which the law imposed on nature. 'The error which pervades the whole laws regarding idiocy and insanity is this, that they recognise them as something *absolute*.'[74]

The difficulty was made worse by the supposed inherited content of insanity. If 'insanity is, in a large proportion of cases, to be traced to hereditary predisposition', then a vast number of people existed who at least could be held only partially responsible.[75] Alienists weakened their own argument by exhorting people to rule their lives to minimise such hereditary predispositions. At the same time they hypothesised a break, in a past generation, when disease interrupted responsibility. No reformer could accept that a person should suffer for the sins of his fathers.

> He who of his own free will and accord 'puts an enemy into his mouth to steal away his brains,' is in a position with reference to any reason-able act he may then commit, entirely different to that of a man suffering from disease of brain, which he has like Westron inherited from his parents, or which has been imposed upon him against his free will and accord by accident or circumstance.[76]

Alienists claimed that hereditarian evidence was good evidence for exculpatory insanity. Courts, however, gave it a mixed reception, since there was no adequate way of proving that insanity in a particular relative was connected with possible insanity in a particular defendant. In addition, perhaps, jurists were suspicious of evidence which seemed to pre-empt a legal decision about responsibility. Late nineteenth-century criminological theory, which developed a biology of the criminal type, implied just such a pre-emption.

The problem of the temporal dimension of responsibility was all too familiar to the courts: they were filled with cases of crime committed under the influence of drink. Alienists compared drink and insanity in order to understand the latter. Jurists also made this comparison but with different implications for the insanity defence. The law generally maintained that drunkenness was no excuse for crime since the state was self-willed. Blackstone referred to 'artificial, voluntarily contracted madness, by *drunkenness* or intoxication, which, depriving men of their reason, puts them in a temporary phrenzy; our law looks upon this as an aggravation of the offence, rather than as an excuse for any criminal misbehaviour'.[77]

This point was used in some nineteenth-century trials so that the full rigour of the law would apply to drunken acts. Other cases, however, set more humane precedents, reasoning that crimes might be done when drunk which would not be contemplated when sober. Thus drunks, like the insane, had an unclear position in relation to their criminal responsibility.[78]

Mr Justice Park (Carroll 1835) denied the relevance of drunkenness in showing whether a murder was done with premeditation or in a sudden fury. In another similar case (Reeves 1844) the accused was found guilty even though he had formed no conception to kill when sober. These decisions were opposed to the more liberal position set out in Thomas's case in 1837. And in Meakin's case (1836) Alderson stated that though drunkenness was no excuse, it was nevertheless possible for a man to be so drunk that the jury might less strongly infer malicious intent. Nevertheless, 'if a man chooses to get drunk, it is his own voluntary act: it is very different from a madness which is not caused by any act of the person'.[79] The possibility that the accused was incapable of forming an intent was further developed in Cruse's, Monkhouse's and Moore's cases, establishing precedents in which a defendant's earlier responsibility for his or her future condition was to a degree excluded. In the case of Moore, who attempted suicide while drunk, Lord Chief Justice Jervis gave his opinion that, 'if the prisoner was so drunk as not to know what she was about, how can you say that she intended to destroy herself?'[80] This effectively made Moore irresponsible in the same way that the Rules made people who did not know the nature of their deeds irresponsible. In cases like Patteson (1840) or Price (1846), who killed under the illusion of being attacked, drunkenness was allowed to alter the verdict. Price was acquitted after killing a friend who, for a practical joke, pretended to rob him. Patteson, however, was found guilty of manslaughter. It was held that he would hardly have suffered the illusion had he been sober.

Case notes for some defendants acquitted on the ground of insanity and sent to Bethlem record a history of intemperance rather than insanity (for example, Bloomfield and Simmons). This suggests that all parties involved associated insanity and drunkenness. Association became virtual identity when crime was committed during a fit of *delirium tremens*. The medical definition of *delirium tremens* as a disease prevailed in courts; judges countenanced the special verdict in such cases. Thus Thomas Clark was found insane at Leicester in 1856 for shooting a man without provocation, and both Simpson and Watson were acquitted of murder in 1845. Taylor later thought that the medical evidence of *delirium tremens* was insufficient to warrant Watson's verdict: the court had been too liberal.[81]

That courts were willing to find a lack of guilt in such cases indicated that they accepted a relationship between present disease and present non-responsibility. Yet few people doubted that this disease grew from a long history of indulgence involving a decreasing quantity of volition and an increasing quantity of habit. At some indefinable stage habit turned into structural change or disease, and at the same time responsibility changed into non-responsibility. It was up to the jury to decide whether this had occurred in each particular case, but medical evidence seems to have been valued. Perhaps this was because the symptoms of *delirium tremens*, unlike those of insanity, could be clearly described; because such symptoms accorded with the well-known and very visible effects of prolonged drunkenness.

The problem of distinguishing drunkenness from the disease to which it leads provoked Stephen (by then a judge) to try to broaden the meaning of the Rules. He argued (Davis 1881) that a man diseased by drink should be treated as mad in law, and he used the example of drunken movements to suggest that a man who cannot control himself cannot 'know' the nature of his deeds.[82] Later judges rejected this since it might imply that impulsive conduct created a state of mind where knowledge was impossible. This interpretation could lead to acquittals for any drunk or insane person.[83]

The most sensational case linking drunkenness and insanity concerned Captain George Johnston, master of *The Tory*, tried in 1846 for murdering a crewman and wounding several others. The crew had in effect mutinied against his drunken and brutal running of the ship, though Johnston always maintained it was the crew who were drunk and brutal. Though no medical evidence was given, the defence plea of insanity was not rebutted by the Crown and an acquittal followed. Johnston later became a key example in Dr Mayo's attack on the spread of the insanity verdict. After visiting Bethlem, Mayo claimed that Johnston was depraved and required punishment, since only punishment could act as a deterrent to others. While he thought Johnston should have been hanged, his general position was utilitarian rather than vindictive (in intention, if not in result). 'I am far from affirming that all these unhappy persons deserve death ... But in these cases there is a sad expenditure of unfruitful suffering; for the confinement being entirely and sedulously deprived of the character of a punishment, operates unpreventively.'[84] Johnston, however, certainly saw his confinement as punishment: he published his own account of the events and he carried on a correspondence with Dr Winslow to try to obtain his release.[85] Just how much Johnston confused the boundary of insanity and depravity is illustrated by an exasperated remark in his case notes: 'At times his irritability amounts to disease.' [86] Was it depravity or disease that caused him to attack his fellow inmate Edward Oxford with a loaded chamber pot ?

There was a comparable case in 1856 when Thomas Corrigan stabbed his wife to death during one of his habitual drinking bouts. The jury decided he was responsible for his drunken condition and hence for the murder. *The Times* used this conviction to argue for the responsibility of another murderer, Charles Westron, at whose trial medical evidence of insanity led the jury to convict but recommend mercy.[87] An alienist objected to the comparison, and claimed that the courts had been right to distinguish between Corrigan – the 'outrage of a brutal drunkard' – and Westron's mental disease.[88] A third view came from the abolitionists who submitted evidence to the Home Secretary in mitigation, arguing that Corrigan was diseased by *delirium tremens* and therefore irresponsibly insane. Drink and insanity thus provided variables for expressing different group interests. The abolitionists claimed final victory in this case: Corrigan's sentence was commuted to transportation, he was joined by his children in Australia, and he became a Christian missionary against drink.[89]

The difficulty of deciding responsibility for crimes influenced by drink occasioned a Scottish verdict which was cited for its recognition of degrees of responsibility. Alexander Dingwall, a notoriously violent and drunken laird, was tried at Aberdeen in 1867 for the murder of his wife, who had stayed loyally with him over a long period of hardship. The murder was committed when Dingwall was drunk, and there was in addition medical evidence for a long history of both epilepsy and alcoholism. Lord Deas suggested a course, which the jury eagerly accepted, namely, to translate a conviction of murder into one for culpable homicide. Dingwall received ten years penal servitude. Deas gave his reasons for allowing extenuating circumstances:

> The prisoner appeared not only to have been peculiar in his mental constitution, but to have had his mind weakened by successive attacks of disease. It seemed highly probable that he had had a stroke of the sun in India, and that his subsequent fits were of an epileptic nature. There could be no doubt that he had had repeated attacks of *delirium tremens*, and if weakness of mind could be an element in any case in the question between murder and culpable homicide, it seemed difficult to exclude that element here.[90]

He indicated the convenience of a flexible response to depravity and insanity; it was used on several more occasions in Scotland.[91] Such flexibility was not available in England, with its statutory definition of murder and its Rules for deciding criminal responsibility, but the same practical effect was achieved through the Home Secretary's mercy.

Drugs had similar physical and legal consequences as drink, but such cases were rare. A woman named Weaver was tried at Chelmsford in 1861 for strangling her child. The defence was that she was half-stupified or even unconscious owing to an excess of laudanum. The jury nevertheless found her guilty, since people taking drugs were legally responsible unless there was actual disease of the brain. The problem was better known in the Indian administration where horrific tales were told about drugs and bizarre murders.[92]

Cases of people 'insane with drink' illustrated the difficulty of being coherent about individual responsibility. The elements of choice, time, circumstance, and inheritance could be weighted differently, and there was a great deal of variation in practice. The law was adept at arbitrating such weightings, though inconsistencies did upset some jurists' view of justice. Alienists claimed that inconsistency represented ignorance of nature, but because they too maintained a moralistic conceptual world, 'nature' never fulfilled the objective role they imputed to it.

Medical evidence for criminal lunacy existed in a very complex set of meanings, expressed both as technical legal rules and as general moral precepts. All questions centred on the issue of individual responsibility. Juridical views, unlike medicine's, were entrenched in powerful institutions. The criminal law embodied an idealist theory of action and a retributive theory of punishment which had both its philosophical and popular dimensions. Legal rules and procedures forced alienists to make statements isolated from the discourse which supported them. Even if medico-psychologists had understood legal matters (which they did not) they would not have gained greater acceptance. Criminal law still meant direct social control; only slowly did it adjust to indirect control, whether through penal or medical thought.

The history of the insanity defence is not just about technical controversy but about the nature of law itself. Jurisprudence took the view that a certain mental state was necessary for guilt. Alienists eschewed this language for one modelled on physical disease and scientific naturalism. It was therefore impossible that a mutually acceptable form of words for dividing criminality and insanity could have been devised. Lawyers and alienists did not mean the same thing by a 'fact' (though their 'facts' often coincided in practice). The law was of necessity a series of open compromises; the Rules provided a verbal umbrella under which such compromises were possible. Each trial was special, no consensus on verdicts was reached, and controversy remained the insanity plea's hallmark.

Dr W. C. Sullivan, the Medical Superintendent of Broadmoor in the 1920s, prefaced a criticism of the Rules by acknowledging that 'in practice

... the legal doctrine of criminal responsibility has been innocuous : it has not produced its logical consequences, because it has never been fully applied'.[93] The Rules' elasticity was complemented by the Home Secretary's power to commute capital sentences. When the Rules were originally formulated, however, they appeared to many alienists both ignorant and inflexible, and several judicial pronouncements justified this view. Later on, when alienists saw that a serious miscarriage of justice (i.e. hanging a lunatic) was unlikely, their anger lessened. Yet they still looked forward to a time when their discourse would achieve formal recognition. Jurists insisted that this would be a reprehensible political change rather than a beneficent scientific advance.

CHAPTER FIVE

MEDICAL INSANITY AND
THE INSANITY PLEA

1 *Raving Lunatics and Delusion*

The concept of a discourse is an abstraction; its ideal form cannot be found in the historical record. Medical and legal discourse can only be seen in elements and in the relationships between them. Trials of individual crimes, bringing so many elements together, reveal much of this. Further, since medico-legal matters were not subject to an agreed set of rules, each trial was a debate in itself. There is therefore need to deal with particulars. These details are easily described, but their meaning is obscure without previously having considered the structure – theoretical and practical – of law and medicine. Actors in criminal trials drew upon pieces of this structure as the occasion demanded and as opportunity allowed. With so many such elements present, all aspects of the trial were highly context-dependent.

Nevertheless, trials can be grouped to highlight specific medical and legal interactions. This chapter describes three types of lunatic – deluded, impelled, and morally incapacitated – which featured in defence strategy.

A person's career following arrest was extremely variable. Locality, social class, friends and relatives, police efficiency, prison facilities, nature of the crime, magistrates' predilections, all played a part which was sometimes decisive. The suggestion of insanity could appear at any stage between arrest and execution of sentence. When a person showed extremely abnormal conduct (the 'raving madman' was his most popular image) there was of course greater likelihood of insanity being raised early on. The ancient tradition of excusing criminals exhibiting extreme forms of raving madness, delusion or idiocy coincided with nineteenth-century medical views. Given reasonably common agreement about a humane reaction to such people, a finding of insanity supplied an obvious need. If 'only organisms to which actions, motives, rights and duties are attributed constitute part of the social system', then extreme abnormality made people so 'non-human' that legal sanctions were irrelevant.[1]

Following the development of institutional solutions to social problems, most raving lunatics were in no position to commit public crimes because they were already locked away. When such people committed murder, it was likely to occur inside an institution, and their presence within the institution was *prima facie* evidence for a lack of responsibility.

Certification had already defined them as irresponsible, by virtue of substituting collective responsibility for their own. Since they were outside society, they were not culpable.

Laycock believed that no asylum inmate had ever hanged for murder, though he was confident that hanging would have followed if the same individuals had not already been inmates. This he considered proof of the arbitrariness of the M'Naghten Rules.[2] James Hadfield, who had precipitated the 1800 Criminal Lunatics Act, killed another man while in Bethlem but was not sent for trial. Henry Hills, an inmate of the Kent Lunatic Asylum, killed a fellow inmate; the inquest found him insane and there was no trial. Thomas Wheeler was a patient at Bethlem – in the hospital not the criminal wing – until his mother insisted, against the hospital's advice, that he be allowed home. He subsequently killed his mother. But when sent for trial at the Old Bailey, he was found unfit to plead and was returned to Bethlem, this time to the criminal wing. Farmer was acquitted in 1837 for killing a keeper in an asylum even though he had openly stated his revengeful motive.

These decisions were made in the light of the killer's institutional position and were probably supported by medical statements from those administering it. In these cases, alienists were fulfilling their social role rather than raising new and controversial suggestions about lunacy. Yet even here the implications were disturbing.

> Already a notion prevails among reasoning lunatics, that they may commit any act of violence – even murder – in an asylum, without incurring the least risk of punishment. They argue, that the medical certificates of their insanity exempt them from all responsibility, and although capable of distinguishing right from wrong, many, flattering themselves that they are not amenable to the laws of their country, will foster the most malignant feelings.[3]

Society was caught in a trap of its own making; having signed away responsibility through certification, it had simultaneously sanctioned violence which could not be punished.

There was a certain comedy in this contradiction. Jonathan Martin, the famous incendiarist of York Minster, was so accepted as insanely deluded (he had set fire to the Minster on instructions from God) that an inmate in a madhouse was reputed to have said: 'Oh, they cannot punish him; he is one of us.' This is on a par with 'a madman who tried desperately to kill his keeper, and on being overpowered cried out, "I will murder you yet; and they can't hang me for it, I am mad!"'[4] These anecdotes (whether authentic or not) reflected ambivalence towards lunatics who were both deluded and cunning – the latter a hallmark of intelligence. Alienists (and asylum inmates) were familiar with this conjunction but it upset a standard picture of the raving lunatic.

Cases of people detained for crimes but found insane at an early stage were not systematically recorded. It is likely that this was a common procedure for lesser crimes (as is testified by the overall number of criminal lunatics compared with those considered dangerous). But it also occurred in murder cases, when special circumstances raised the question of insanity and commonsense criteria supported it. A dramatic example was the young artist Richard Dadd, who killed his father in 1843. He was certified insane (by Home Office procedure under the 1840 Act) without being sent for trial, a response reflecting the facility with which his educated friends and relatives supplied evidence of earlier delusions and character change. This consensus revealed administrative pliancy, in spite of the apparent rigidity of the recently formulated Rules, which stated that ignorance of the nature of the act was necessary for exculpation. Dadd, however, was so conscious of the nature of his deed that he prepared a passport, lured his father to a chosen murder site, and then escaped to France.

The judiciary was not happy with a law which allowed certification by local justices and doctors, or by the Home Office, without the issue coming to court. Mr Justice Patterson was irritated when Dwerryhouse, who was accused of murder in 1847, was transferred to an asylum before the trial. The prosecution was so upset in Peacock's case (1870) that the accused was forced to attend trial under a writ of *habeas corpus*, only then to be found unfit to plead.

Insanity could be assessed at a later stage when there was a question of the prisoner's fitness to plead. Judges raised this question if the accused might not be able to follow the proceedings or understand his or her rights. This occurred when the accused was an idiot, deaf and dumb, or showed unmistakable 'weakness of mind'. Courts were perhaps rather narrow in interpreting these categories. Alienists certainly thought so in the cases of James Potter and George Broomfield in 1865; they found raving madness where a court had found not only fitness to plead but guilt. Furthermore, the medical view prevailed after conviction. Potter's career is understandable in view of his virtually non-existent defence, which showed that there was a general lack of interest in his crime.

'Idiocy' had for a long time been part of common vocabulary. A category of 'imbecility' or 'fatuity' was also well established in medical nosology.[5] Nevertheless, separate legislation for idiots was not passed until the end of the century; until then the insanity plea was used to excuse such people.[6]

Alienists were shocked by decisions which found idiots responsible. Dr Prichard of Northampton organised petitions to the Home Secretary, describing Isaac Pinnock as a locally well-known idiot, after he had been convicted. As he had no money, he had not had a proper defence and his crime attracted little attention. Abolitionists used cases like this to demonstrate how a hanging might occur simply because a defendant was poor. Higginson and 'daft' John Barclay were executed in 1843, though both were described as being of weak mind. The prison surgeon's evidence of Higginson's imbecility was overridden by evidence that he had known what he was doing. Barclay's jury recommended him to mercy but it was ignored for the same reason. In one medical man's opinion he was obviously an imbecile. Both these cases occurred shortly after M'Naghten's and they possibly reflect efforts by the judiciary and the Home Secretary to tighten procedure and avoid further criticism.

One distinct group, often described as 'idiots', consisted of those convicted of bestiality, a crime which, in theory but not in practice, remained capital until 1861. We do not know whether those accused of bestiality were abnormally incapacitated in intellect, or whether it was a poor rural background, not to mention the nature of the crime itself, which led to their being defined idiotic. Several lived in Bethlem's criminal wing, though it is not always clear whether they had been found unfit to plead or acquitted on the ground of insanity. It was during a 1836 case of bestiality involving Pritchard, a deaf mute, that Baron Alderson deemed it was necessary to decide first whether his muteness proceeded from malice or from a 'visitation from God'. If the latter, it was then necessary to decide whether the accused had sufficient understanding to plead. (The jury found him unfit.) Only subsequently could the third question, of possible insanity, have been raised.

Unfitness to plead was not restricted to idiots or the deaf and dumb; it could also be found where the accused exhibited delusions which seemed to preclude a capacity to understand the proceedings. In 1853 David Davies fired into a group of people outside his house resulting in the death of one woman. The incident was preceded by a history displaying delusions of self-importance and it was these delusions which apparently provoked the mob into which he fired. Mr Justice Vaughan Williams examined the gaoler and medical witnesses privately to determine fitness to plead, since the prosecution argued that Davies' insanity was feigned. Agreement was not reached. The issue was then put to a jury, which found the accused unfit.

Pre-trial certification and unfitness to plead did not filter out all the more obvious cases. Many judges preferred that the issue of insanity should be left to the jury even if the outcome was predictable. The defence gave no medical evidence in Shaffer Wood's trial (1865) but the jury found him to be clearly of 'weak mind' and therefore insane. Juries decided that some defendants manifestly came within the scope of the Rules. William Stalker in 1847, for example, showed an unambiguous ignorance of the difference between right and wrong.

The law was imprecise about the role of delusions in finding a lack of responsibility. Delusions were good public evidence for madness, but the delusion had to be of a certain quality to satisfy the law. Jurists regarded

Offord's case (1831) as a fairly liberal precedent. Offord was acquitted for shooting a man while believing that the inhabitants of his village, Hadleigh in Suffolk, were in conspiracy against him. Chief Baron Lord Lyndhurst's statement of the law was regarded as important authority for the right-wrong test: the jury must be satisfied that 'he did not know, when he committed the act, what the effect of it, if fatal, would be, with reference to the crime of murder. The question was, did he know that he was committing an offence against the laws of God and nature ?'[7] In the case of John Campbell, who killed a servant while serving in Madras, the defence successfully argued that delusions of persecution meant that, at the time of the killing, Campbell believed his life to be in danger and therefore justifiably acted in self-defence.[8]

The cases of Hadfield and M'Naghten, both of whom exhibited delusions, were much less clear cut. It was by no means apparent that the delusions from which they suffered actually prevented them from knowing the illegality and immorality of their crimes. Indeed, Hadfield fired at George III at the Drury Lane theatre precisely because he did know the nature of the deed: he believed that he 'must be destroyed, but ought not to destroy himself'.[9] His acquittal was due to three special factors. First, he had a right to counsel, and this counsel (later Lord Erskine) took the opportunity to give a brilliant performance; second, he had severe head injuries from military service (jurors were invited to look at the wound); third, a battery of witnesses described his delusions, which the judges apparently accepted as evidence for exculpatory insanity without examining too closely Hadfield's preparation for the shooting and his later coherence under cross-examination.

Similar elements of prepared pistols and a long history of delusions represented the opposite poles of intention and insanity in M'Naghten's case. M'Naghten was reported to have stated on arrest:

> The Tories in my native city compelled me to do this. They follow and persecute me wherever I go, and have entirely destroyed my peace of mind. They followed me to France, into Scotland, and all over England; in fact, they follow me wherever I go . . . They do everything in their power to harass and persecute me; in fact, they wish to murder me. It can be proved by evidence; that's all I have to say.[10]

His counsel, Alexander Cockburn, supported this general picture with many witnesses (including the Lord Provost of Glasgow, to whom M'Naghten had complained). Again it was accepted, without too close a legalistic examination, that this proved exculpatory insanity.

Delusions did not ensure an acquittal, since 'delusion' covered many psychological states including everyday ones like dreaming and reverie. It might be more accurate to say that phenomena like dreaming were seen as essentially morbid (though so normal as to be innocuous) because they involved the suspension of the controlling will. Reverie, dreaming, sleep-walking and insanity formed a continuous sequence in which reason progressively failed. Insanity appeared when the will became unable to redirect the reason.[11] Therefore, delusion '*per se*, is no test of insanity at all'.[12] The question from the medical viewpoint was whether a person could still perceive the existence of delusion. 'Physicians discuss the characters of a delusion, not so much with the object of determining whether the individual be really labouring under a delusion or not, but as a means of further studying and gauging the integrity of his mental faculties. They seek to determine *how the individual in his judgment and volition deals with his delusion.*'[13] When the delusion was of a certain character, and when there was evidence of repeated inability to control it, legal and medical viewpoints coincided. The Rules may be seen as formalising this area of agreement.

Evidence for delusions did on occasion encourage judges to make very liberal interpretations of law. In Milne's trial at Edinburgh (1863), the Lord Justice-Clerk stated that, 'if you are once satisfied that this man was under the influence of insane delusions at the time this act was committed, you have no occasion to inquire farther, whether he knew what was right from what was wrong ... if he was in point of fact at the time under the influence of insane delusions, the law at once presumes from that that he cannot appreciate what he is doing.'[14] This interpretation was acceptable to alienists since it presupposed the integrated character of mental incapacities rather than pursuing a legalistic relation between a specific mental state and a specific deed.[15] Alexander Milne, an 'artist in hair', stabbed to death a jeweller who had been working for him. He stated that 'the fellow has been poisoning my wife and my children. I have caught him in bed with my wife. I am suffering from poison too'.[16] Friends and medical witnesses attested to his delusions of persecution, though Milne explained his crime as an accident. The prosecution produced a third view, attributing it to the 'shattered nerves of a drunkard', and claiming he was therefore accountable.[17] In spite of the judge's liberality, the jury was divided. It returned a majority verdict of guilty by nine to six but recommended mercy on the ground of its divided opinion. The sentence was subsequently commuted. This majority verdict (peculiar to Scotland) suggested that the area of consensus was small, even when there was every legal facility for finding a lack of responsibility.

The presence of delusion still left the court with a substantial decision. Even when there was cognitive disorder of reason which jurists and alienists both accepted as a possible excusing condition, the problem of assigning responsibility recurred in each case. Robert Handcock was a respected Devon village craftsman who murdered his wife believing she had committed adultery with a neighbour. A carefully organised defence produced evidence that this belief was indeed a delusion, and that it had

grown over the last sixteen months into a condition which contrasted with
his earlier character. His medical practitioner also testified that he
suffered from delusion. On the other hand, the prosecution showed that
the murder took place when his wife refused to allow him into bed with
her and that she had often been angry and irritated; this suggested that he
might have been rationally motivated. The defence also secured the
interest of Dr Bucknill, the local insanity specialist, who described Handcock's symptoms as monomania: 'Delusion is a symptom of insanity, and
monomania means that a person is entirely mad upon one point. On that
subject he would be unable to distinguish between right and wrong.'[18]
Handcock was found insane through this combination of medical evidence, character change, evidence for his wife's faithfulness, and the judge's
stance. Bucknill wrote up the case to support monomania as a category
which might lead to acquittal. But in practice, neither alienists nor
lawyers were able to generalise successfully from any one case to statements about what should or would be done in others.

Character change – evidence of a respectable working man losing his
reason – was important in arousing the sympathy of the jury. Joseph
Baines was a Lincolnshire tailor who beat his father-in-law's second wife
to death in the middle of the street. Before this he had changed from being
friendly and cheerful to being depressed about his family's prospects. He
was found insane and sent to Bethlem where he recovered and was
released ('pardoned') after eight years. In an unusual case tried at Edinburgh, Dr George Smith was acquitted of wilful fire raising. When
fantasies about emigrating to America with a farmer's wife were frustrated, this once sober practitioner set fire to the farmer's stacks. Medical
evidence argued for insanity and the jury agreed in spite of the revengeful
nature of his motives.

Another medical practitioner, Dr Pearce, was tried for attempting to
murder his wife. With a curious reversal of roles, Dr Pearce persuaded
Mr Justice Bosanquet to call witnesses to prove sanity in opposition to his
own counsel's plea of insanity. The judge also allowed Dr Pearce to
suggest questions which the court might ask to contradict insanity. But
witnesses and jury agreed that Dr Pearce was deluded and he was sent to
Bethlem. Clearly there were commonly agreed criteria for labelling some
criminal lunatics.

2   *Impulsive Insanity*

If delusion did not of itself constitute exculpatory insanity, it was important evidence for it. Witnesses to the delusion could be cross-examined,
everyone understood what it was to have a delusion, and there was an
affinity between the criteria of delusion and the right-wrong or M'Naghten
test. The other form of evidence that satisfied these conditions was
marked character change. But was such evidence the only kind which the

law should acknowledge? Dr Mayo shocked alienists by arguing that it was, claiming that all truly insane criminals exhibited some delusion: a 'more profound analysis of the patient's history, in cases in which the crime is at variance with his normal character, would detect a specific insane delusion, or a continuously morbid state of the imagination'.[19] Insanity specialists did not accept this; it was completely at odds with the two major developments in nineteenth-century psychological medicine: the description of emotional and volitional lunatic types, and the explanation of insanity in physical terms. Scientific progress, they claimed, had discovered two broad classes – impulsive and moral insanity – of which the law was ignorant. Clinical evidence demonstrated that emotional and volitional disorders were the dominant symptoms in lunacy, while physicalism meant that conduct influenced by insanity could not be self-controlled. It was on this basis that alienists argued for the expansion of evidence for exculpatory insanity. And defence counsel, in specific cases of extreme need, pressed these arguments as hard as possible.

Impulsive insanity and moral insanity were rarely thought to exist in a pure form; rather, they were two overlapping classes. In the former, the dominant feature was uncontrollable, motiveless, sharp and spasmodic violence; in the latter, it was disordered emotion leading to general violence and aggressiveness.

When alienists criticised the Rules they often had in mind rare occasions when someone performed a complicated sequence of 'purposeful' movements without exercising any conscious control. Such a condition would now be described as automatism. Victorian alienists were less precise, referring to 'automatic', 'instinctive', or 'impulsive' acts, which they interpreted in the light of contemporary reflex action theories. Such automatic movements vindicated mental physiologists' programme to connect human nature with animal nature.

> Modern physiology teaches that there is a *reflex action* of the cerebrum, as well as of the spinal cord; and thus satisfactorily explains the existence of the automatic or instinctive acts. To such cases Dr. Carpenter alludes when he says, 'So far as the directing influence of the will over the current of thought is suspended, the individual becomes a thinking automaton, destitute of the power to withdraw his attention from any idea or feeling by which his mind may be possessed, and is as irresistibly impelled, therefore, to act in accordance with this, as the lower animals are to act in accordance with their instincts.'[20]

Complex activities with an automatistic element included sleepwalking, hypnotic trances, spiritualist seances, hysterical phobias, acquired skills, and obsessional preoccupations. But it was unusual for any of these to result in criminal proceedings, though some examples are recorded. More often alienists identified an element of automatism mingled with other characteristics.

Walker emphasises a case reported by Bucknill and Tuke in 1862. Esther Griggs threw one of her children through a closed window, believing the house to be on fire. A passing policeman stated that she had had a nightmare which caused her to try to save her children. Though arrested, she never faced trial as the grand jury did not find a true bill against her, presumably on the ground that she had behaved as an automaton. Her movements illustrated what the physiologist Carpenter meant by an 'ideo-motor' action or Laycock by a 'reflex action of the brain'. 'In physiology it is perfectly well known that an idea may cause action quite independently of volition, and a class of movements are described as *ideomotor* in the text-books of that science. It is in strict correspondence, then, with physiological fact, that in cerebral pathology a variety of disease is recognised in which morbid idea causes morbid action.'[21] Mental physiologists argued that a single idea had acted as a stimulus in Esther Griggs's brain, making her motor system operate without reference to external reality. The grand jury's decision was probably not affected by medical psychology, but Bucknill and Tuke later utilised this case to illustrate how medical psychology could describe conditions recognised by laymen. Such cases were useful for expanding the area in which automatism might be accepted.

There were few cases which claimed that a person had been in a completely automatistic condition. Sleep-walking was perhaps the most common condition and came in for a great deal of discussion, but it rarely resulted in violence.[22] It was used, however, in the case of Sarah Minchin, a young domestic who stabbed one of her employer's children during the night. Her defence was not believed and, though no satisfactory motive was put forward, she was found guilty of murder.

Only one case of sleep-walking from this period reached the law reports, that of Fraser who in 1878 battered his baby to death by hitting its head against the wall. The Scottish court had such difficulty in reaching a decision (the special insanity verdict not being available by statute) that it adjourned. The Lord Justice-Clerk suggested to the jury 'that you should return a verdict such as this – that the Jury find the panel killed his child, but that he was in a state in which he was unconscious of the act which he was committing by reason of the condition of somnambulism, and that he was not responsible.'[23] The court resolved the dilemma by the unique formula of Fraser undertaking always to sleep in a room by himself. This 'imprisoned' that isolatable part of Fraser which had caused the murder, namely his sleeping self. The court reached its decision on the evidence of a dramatic life history of sleep-walking accompanied by potential or actual violence. There was such a wealth of folklore about sleep-walking that the jury readily accepted evidence from lay witnesses. It heard medical evidence only at the judge's insistence. Medical witnesses were eager to add their authority and link this condition with insanity through the diagnostic label 'somnomania'.[24] This was an attempt to subsume lay evaluations under medical theory; the label explained nothing, but it did have social meaning.

Another class of automatic movements which greatly concerned medical men was associated with epileptic attacks. Epilepsy exemplified the medical position that there were uncontrollable movements which the law should recognise.[25] As Bucknill observed, 'the psychical phenomena of the epileptic are of a kind to set the metaphysicians at defiance'.[26] Physicians described epilepsy's barbaric history in the realm of spirit possession, superstition and ignorance, and they contrasted this with humanitarian medical progress. This paralleled the alienists' history of insanity. Contemporary clinicians like J.G.F.Baillarger, J.P.J.Falret and John Hughlings Jackson classified the various forms of epilepsy and related them to the histories of individual attacks. Clinical description clearly revealed automatism. Jackson related epileptic symptoms to Laycock's theories of reflex action and functional levels in the brain.[27] The inevitable conclusion was that during an attack an epileptic could not be considered responsible. 'All kinds of doings after epileptic fits, from slight vagaries up to homicidal actions . . . have one common character – *they are automatic*: they are done unconsciously, and the agent is irresponsible.'[28]

Even when medical descriptions of epilepsy were accepted, it was still debated whether a potential for epileptic attacks should lessen responsibility on all occasions; alienists argued that it should.[29] They went on to emphasise that, in their experience, insanity commonly associated with epilepsy; one kind of symptom therefore alerted them to the possible presence of the other.

> The presence of epilepsy in homicidal mania is a complication of extreme importance. In doubtful instances careful inquiry should be made whether epileptic seizures, however slight or transient, have been present. Some of the most dangerous homicidal lunatics, without delusion, are subject to attacks of epilepsy. They may be under the influence of destructive impulses only when a fit is threatened.[30]

In addition, theoretical neurophysiology, which referred to controlling and automatic levels in the nervous system, was applicable equally to epilepsy and insanity. Jackson himself commented on this relationship. It was perhaps a measure of the growing split between medical specialisms that Jackson's detailed neurological work had little or no impact on medico-legal literature. Nor did alienists add to Jackson's precise clinical delineations.

The courts resisted the view that a history of epilepsy in itself constituted an excusing condition. I have found few cases in which such a history helped the jury to reach an insanity verdict. Elizabeth Flew's epilepsy perhaps substituted for insanity in finding her not guilty of murdering her child; Bethlem notes recorded epilepsy but no symptoms of insanity. Frederick Treadaway (1877) had a fit in court and Dr Hughes Bennett, the superintendent of Hanwell Asylum in Middlesex, confirmed that it was genuine. The jury, however, chose not to link this with possible insanity at the time the crime was committed and he was found guilty. The defence case was that Treadaway had bought a revolver to shoot himself (he had attempted suicide on several previous occasions) but that a fit intervened and another person was shot. In Richards's case (1858), a medical witness argued that criminal violence had been caused by a fit, but the problem facing the jury was whether it had actually been done during the fit. Some alienists accepted epilepsy as *prima facie* evidence for a lack of responsibility in such cases, but juries stuck to the specific deed.

The linkage between epilepsy and insanity was an important part of nineteenth-century medical psychology. Fits of an epileptic nature were extremely common in asylums; alienists assumed an organic connection between these fits and the symptoms of insanity, though they could not specify any details of such a connection. 'The existence of epilepsy would, in our judgment, go far to prove that acts of violence were the result of cerebral disease.' [31] In this period, educated laymen agreed that epilepsy was the product of disease in the nervous system, and few people, face to face with an epileptic fit would have failed to see that it exemplified an incapacity to exercise control. For alienists, epilepsy led to a strategically useful argument about exculpatory insanity which featured a lack of control rather than disorder of reason.

Maudsley expressed the link between epilepsy and insanity most forcibly, in his degeneration theory of nervous disorder. He argued that whenever a retrogressive hereditarian element was present (as was claimed in Treadaway's case), responsibility was necessarily reduced. He used the term 'epileptic mania' to describe people like Bisgrove, who was found guilty of murder but later certified insane and transferred to Broadmoor. Maudsley claimed that if Bisgrove's poverty had not precluded a proper defence, his epileptic history would have been brought out at the trial and an insanity verdict would more likely have followed.

> Immediately after the fits he was dangerous, being prone to seize upon anything which might be at hand, and to attack blindly those who were near him ... At the trial, where, like other poor men who have not means to pay the heavy price which justice costs, he was practically undefended, not a word was said of his epilepsy, nor of his weak intellect, nor of his history up to the events of the night of the murder. [32]

It was only because a local clergyman was struck by the motivelessness of Bisgrove's crime that attention was later drawn to epileptic history.

The key link between insanity and epilepsy seems to have been ignored in another case. Thomas Donelly was accused of assault, with intent to rape, at Glasgow in 1862. Medical witnesses argued that epilepsy had led to insanity and that other evidence of insanity was shown by his delusions of persecution. Donelly described his own crime: 'On going into the house I found a woman there. I thought that I was under the influence of the magistrates, and that I would lose my life if I had not connexion with the woman. I had felt my head ringing, and the sound of music I thought I heard; but I was not under one of the fits I am subject to.'[33] The jury's insanity verdict probably owed more to these delusions than to the medical view that epilepsy led to a lack of control.

That epileptic automatism rarely featured in criminal trials reflects the fact that those subject to violent fits were probably institutionalised already.[34] Alienists and their critics lived, literally, in different worlds. What was an obvious empirical reality to insanity specialists was unknown, and therefore assumed fictitious by others. The institutional response to insanity greatly increased the divergence of views about abnormality. Severe epileptic fits were common only *in* asylums.

Bethlem records suggest that William Godfrey was found insane on the ground that an epileptic fit had led to an assault. But the only well-known case from this period came from New York. Montgomery's defence was post-epileptic automatism; it was unsuccessful, but it stimulated a review of the law's attitude towards epilepsy and became the starting point for an important summary of existing medical theory.[35]

Examples of extreme automatism graded into movements with some automatistic element. It was this continuity which justified Laycock's and Carpenter's argument that reflex theory could be used to understand complex 'purposive' movements, even when accompanied by consciousness. This continuity also underlay the alienists' argument that the law should expand the conditions recognised as exculpatory. Conversely, however, it also supported their opponents' logic; it was reasonable to fear the dissolution of all responsibility if one accepted a continuous gradation from automatistic movement to conscious conduct. Evidence for uncontrollable movements was easily represented as a first step towards social disintegration.

Some movements, however, were by common agreement uncontrollable. Byron was acquitted of manslaughter in 1863 because he clearly had not knowingly done the deed for which he stood accused. While asleep following a drinking bout he had struck out with his booted foot, hitting his host in the abdomen. The latter subsequently died. This was an unfortunate conjunction of circumstances rather than an automatistic condition. But it graded into Milligan's case, when the defence for manslaughter was that the accused killed while still unconscious from sleep.

A pedlar in the habit of walking about the country armed with a sword-stick, while lying asleep on the highroad, was roused by a man accidentally passing, who seized and shook him by the shoulders. The pedlar suddenly awoke, drew his sword and stabbed the man, who soon afterwards died. The pedlar was tried for manslaughter. His irresponsibility was strongly urged by his counsel, on the ground that he could not have been conscious of an act thus perpetrated while in a half-waking state . . . It was not unlikely that an idea had arisen in the prisoner's mind that he had been attacked by robbers, and therefore had stabbed the man in self-defence.[36]

The defence was not accepted. Milligan's story was not persuasive, since half-awake people should check before they do anything drastic and he was the only witness to his own automatism. As Esther Griggs's case showed, however, where independent evidence corroborated a story of automatism, the idea was not completely foreign to laymen.

The real conflict between man-the-machine and man-the-agent surfaced when alienists attributed an obviously criminal deed to 'uncontrollable' or 'irresistible' impulse. Esquirol provided the classic description of impulsive insanity. (As in other descriptions, the physicalist concept of lesion was imposed on the mentalist concept of will.)

In a third class of cases [of monomania], a lesion of the will exists. The patient is drawn away from his accustomed course, to the commission of acts, to which neither reason nor sentiment, determine, which conscience rebukes, and which the will has no longer the power to restrain. The actions are involuntary, instinctive, irresistible. This is *monomania without delirium*, or, *instinctive monomania*.[37]

The rules made no reference to any such morbid state, but this did not mean that the medical category was inevitably dismissed in practice. No simple generalisation covers every verdict. Though cited, the Rules were sometimes waived; on the other hand, some murderers for whom a strong case for non-responsibility had been made went to the gallows. Each case was exciting and potentially divisive.

M'Naghten's trial is a good illustration of the problem. Cockburn, the eloquent defence counsel, blurred a defence of irresistible impulse with the more acceptable plea that disordered reason had led to ignorance.

The mistake existing in ancient times, which the light of modern science has dispelled, lay in supposing that in order that a man should be mad – incapable of judging between right and wrong, or of exercising that self-control and dominion, without which the knowledge of right and wrong would become vague and useless – it was necessary that he should exhibit those symptoms which would amount to total prostration of the intellect; whereas, modern science has incontrovertibly established that any one of these intellectual and moral functions of the mind may be subject to separate disease, and thereby man may be rendered the victim of the most fearful delusions, the slave of uncontrollable impulses impelling or rather compelling him to the commission of acts such as that which has given rise to the case now under your consideration.[38]

Cockburn's justification for saying that 'science has incontrovertibly established' the reality of uncontrollable impulse lay in statements such as Esquirol's. He brandished a scientific discourse in which facts 'proved' a lack of accountability. As part of this proof, he quoted from the American alienist Isaac Ray (one of the strongest believers in the factual reality of uncontrollable impulses) who had written: 'That the insane mind is not entirely deprived of this power of moral discernment, but on many subjects is perfectly rational and displays the exercise of a sound and well balanced mind is one of those facts now so well established that to question it would only betray the height of ignorance and presumption.'[39] Ray had also complained about legal prejudice against science: 'Innovations have been too much regarded rather as the offspring of new-fangled theories than of the steady advancement of medical science.'[40]

Cockburn, of course, drew on Ray in order to achieve success in a particular case. He used references to medical science to manipulate the court into a deference towards expertise. 'You should listen with patient attention to the evidence of men of skill and science ... I feel that I may appeal to the many medical gentlemen I see around me, whether the knowledge and pathology of this disease has not within a few recent years first acquired the character of a science?'[41] Nine medical men gave evidence for M'Naghten, all emphasising that his delusions of persecution meant that 'his moral liberty was destroyed'.[42] The Crown presented no medical evidence to rebut this, even though M'Naghten had obtained firearms, had watched his victim for several days, and had waited till his victim's back was turned. Dr Winslow, one of the two medical witnesses who had not personally examined M'Naghten (though they had been in court throughout the trial), later argued that the law should adopt a simple test for responsibility: had the accused '*lost all power of control over his actions*'?[43] The success of M'Naghten's defence, the role which medical texts and witnesses played, fears that insanity and a lack of responsibility had become confused, and the possibility that the law had recognised irresistible impulse, all contributed to the taking stock which the trial provoked.

The M'Naghten verdict (and a few others like Oxford, Brixey or Touchet), when the law could be interpreted as unduly liberal towards medical categories, did not set a precedent. Such verdicts sometimes had the reverse effect, making judges feel it was incumbent on them to reject medical opinion (especially the concept of irresistible impulse) as excusing crime. Shortly after M'Naghten's trial a man called Laurence, apparently wishing to be hanged, committed an otherwise motiveless murder. He was found guilty and his wish fulfilled. Offended medical men stated that Laurence's deed had been insanely 'impulsive': 'The

differences between the case and that of *M'Naghten* were, that there was
in *Laurence* less evidence of deliberation, with stronger evidence of
sudden impulse; but there was not sufficient interest about the deceased,
the prisoner, or his crime, to attract any great public attention!'[44] The
contrast between M'Naghten's and Laurence's verdicts demonstrates
the importance of individual circumstances – in this case the victim's
social position.

Mr Baron Parke attacked liberal interpretations of the law in his
address to the jury in Barton's trial in 1848. He argued that the only safe
course, if the law were not to let crime go unpunished, lay with the right-
wrong test.

> This mode of dealing with the defence of insanity had not, he was
> aware, the concurrence of medical men; but he must, nevertheless,
> express his decided concurrence with Mr. Baron Rolfe's views of
> such cases, that learned judge having expressed his opinion to be
> that the excuse of an irresistible impulse, co-existing with the full
> possession of reasoning powers, might be urged in justification of
> every crime known to the law – for every man might be said, and
> truly, not to commit any crime except under the influence of some
> irresistible impulse. Something more than this was necessary to
> justify an acquittal on the ground of insanity, and it would be there-
> fore for the jury to say whether . . . the impulse under which the
> prisoner had committed this deed was one which altogether deprived
> him of the knowledge that he was doing wrong.[45]

Barton had killed his wife and child with a razor and then attempted
suicide; he was tormented by the threat of starvation following financial
ruin. The jury agreed with the judge that he was responsible, thus placing
the event within the collective social sphere, where misfortune was
judged, rather than the individual medical sphere, where misfortune
was treated. This verdict on an adult man's reaction to poverty contrasted
with the insanity verdicts for destitute women who murdered their babies.

The judge who rejected medical views most forcibly was Mr Baron
Bramwell, because he considered them to be subversive of justice and
society. One of his most cited pronouncements came in Haynes's case in
1859. Henry Benjamin Haynes, a soldier, was accused of the murder of
Mary MacGowan, a prostitute at Aldershot. He and the woman were on
friendly terms and he seemed to have no motive for cutting her throat.
Defence witnesses testified that he had been disturbed since returning
from Canada where he had deserted a pregnant girl. Haynes rambled
when interviewed and said incoherently that he meant to murder the
Canadian girl, and not MacGowan. Bramwell directed the jury within the
terms of the Rules: 'Did the woman die by the hand of the prisoner? If so,
he was guilty, unless he did not know the nature of the act, or did not
know that it was wrong. These were the only two matters for their

consideration.'[46]

Bramwell made his significant remarks when the jury returned after two hours for clarification because they had doubts about the prisoner's state of mind. One juror had the temerity to suggest that the prisoner might have suffered from an uncontrollable impulse. Bramwell replied sharply:

> That did not make the offence the less murder. Malice was implied when there was a deliberate cruel act committed, however sudden it might be. It was no matter how sudden the impulse – whether it was the result of long previous deliberation, or whether it was the impulse of an instant – it would be as much murder in one case as in the other. No jury could properly acquit on the ground of insanity, if they believed the accused was conscious of the act he was committing, and that he knew that act was contrary to law. If they gave a verdict contrary to this, the result would be to increase the number of cases of uncontrollable impulse.[47]

Bramwell was not content just to administer the Rules. Elsewhere he argued that if it looked like a case of uncontrollable impulse, then the need for punishment was even greater: the stronger the punishment the stronger the deterrence. 'I would control it by the fear of hanging, mad or not mad.'[48] This was a strongly held view which he repeated on more than one occasion.[49] It was logical enough, given his utilitarian philosophy of punishment and his assumption that the pleasure-pain principle explained all human behaviour. As he intended, his sentiments were utterly opposed to those of alienists and liberal reformers. He enforced a strictly legal discourse which left no opening for the medical way of thought. However, in as far as medical thought shared certain general humanitarian values, alienism acquired some credence when the Home Secretary commuted Haynes's capital sentence.

Alienists considered Bramwell's opinion prejudiced and vindictive. Ray's stricture that the law committed 'the metaphysical error of always looking on right and wrong in the abstract – as things having a positive and independent existence' was appropriate.[50] The Association of Asylum Officers took Haynes's case as an opportunity to propose that 'a committee of the Association be formed, to put itself into communication with the Legislature, with a view of exposing the present defects of the law'.[51] Nothing came of this, perhaps because alienists themselves disagreed about what new legal rules were needed or how far capital punishment should be opposed. But there was a vague sense at the Association meeting that its humanitarian image required it to go on record against Bramwell's penal attitude.[52]

Such gestures indicate the extent to which criticism of the law for ignoring scientific facts was bound up with considerations of individual and professional standing and with the conflation of medicine and humanitarianism. The phrase 'irresistible impulse' evoked this cluster of emotions and values; alienists saw its acceptance or rejection as a measure of their achievement.

The greatest insult and setback to medical evidence came from the Lord Chancellor, Lord Westbury, in 1862. Westbury was introducing a bill in the House of Lords following an extremely expensive and long drawn-out lunacy inquiry into the state of mind of William Frederick Windham. Windham, the heir to a large estate, lavished money on a 'woman of easy virtue' who was also his wife. His relatives tried to have him certified by inquiry in order to preserve the rapidly diminishing property. This was an attempt to solve human problems by exploiting medical discourse. Windham was in fact found sane after thirty-four days and a hundred and forty witnesses. Westbury deprecated the role of medical evidence in the case and took the opportunity to attack the relevance of the alienist expertise.

> It is a radical error to deal with these cases as if the subject were to be inquired into physiologically, and not like every other question. If the inquiry were whether the brain is in a state of disease, then it might be right to prosecute the matter as a question of physical science . . . But a jury should only receive evidence by which ordinary men can arrive at the fact of the state of mind as they would arrive at any other alleged fact – such evidence as every man can understand . . . But when the subject is one upon which a man of ordinary understanding is competent to judge you do not open the door for the reception of scientific evidence.[53]

Alienists were angered and embarrassed, particularly as they had given conflicting and well-paid evidence in the inquiry; as Westbury sarcastically remarked, 'between these learned doctors, who is to determine?'[54] Laycock responded to the attack, in a lecture published from his Edinburgh course on medical psychology. His statement explained why so much was at stake in the reception of 'scientific facts' in court.

> Medicine says a man may be insane and irresponsible, and yet know right and wrong; law says a knowledge of right and wrong is the test of both soundness of mind and responsibility to the law. Medicine says, restrain and cure the insane and imbecile offender against the law; law says, hang, imprison, whip, hunger him, and treats medical art with contempt . . . For with such direct antagonism to medical doctrines and practice on the side of the law, the existing prejudices in the mind of the public, and which have been exhibited in very high quarters, will be more deeply rooted; so that we shall have greater difficulties to encounter in treating the insane, in bearing witness to their infirmities in courts of law, and in enlightening the public on a subject which most deeply concerns it.[55]

This was the fighting language characteristic of the Victorian reformer:

facts, progress and humanity against prejudice, entrenched interests and barbarism. Alienists derived a great deal of much needed confidence and solidarity from linking their humanitarian sentiments to scientific objectivity. That the Lord Chancellor should attack this called into question every aspect of lunacy reform.

There was good evidence for delusion in Haynes, M'Naghten and Laurence. But the legal question was whether the delusion created an inability to know the nature of the crime. Among these three perhaps the one who best fulfilled this condition was Laurence, and he was hanged. The Rules were no more rigorous a test than any other rule of thumb. Alienists objected to the Rules because they were unjust in practice and because a 'rule of thumb' was incommensurable with 'science'. Further, clinical evidence negated the idea that one part of the mind, the rational faculty, could be disordered in isolation. Alienists tried to base their judgements about insanity on the relation between rational, emotional and volitional faculties, and especially on the degree to which delusions could be controlled. This contrasted with the legal view which appeared to judge lack of responsibility in relation to delusions alone. However, in actual trials (such as M'Naghten's or Handcock's), it was sometimes accepted that it was not so much the delusion itself but the inability to control it which led to a lack of accountability.

Medico-psychologists wanted the law to recognise formally that inability to exercise control was an excusing condition. It seemed to them that a failure to do this was a gross presumption against the facts. However, it was not so much 'facts' but the logic of medical discourse – complementary relationships between physicalism, determinism and delegation of responsibility – which opposed the law. In this discourse, inability to exercise control carried more meaning than any other psychological possibility: reflex action theory was the abstract pole, and clinical descriptions of relations between mental faculties, the concrete one. A definition of exculpatory insanity in terms of the diseased will would have been their natural practical complement.

The very idea of irresistible impulse, let alone its use in court, brought alienists into disrepute because it appeared to endanger the rationale of justice and punishment. Jurists could not see how to maintain a distinction between an irresistible and an unresisted impulse. Empirical evidence for such a distinction existed only in the accused's subjective experience. They therefore feared that 'irresistible' would become a euphemism for 'unresisted'. Bramwell in 1856 laid down a stock legal response: 'Supposing a man had been standing by him [the accused] with a loaded pistol in his hand when he was going to poison his wife, do you think that he would have done it then?'[56] Humanitarians discerned an intolerably harsh sentiment underlying the question. While conceding that conclusive evidence was impossible – 'God only knows the heart;

Omniscience alone can estimate accurately the degree of irresponsibility produced by cerebral disease' – Bucknill believed that we must work with a rough notion of irresponsibility: 'If complete freedom were necessary to establish responsibility, who could be found in the possession of it ?'[57] Bramwell argued that this soft humanitarianism had no place in the law; indeed, he claimed that the law could cure lunatics more easily than alienists could: 'You would try one or two floggings first ? – Yes; I would first see what the medical opinion was worth, because medical men talk a very great deal of nonsense.'[58]

The most incisive medical response to this self-righteousness was to argue the injustice of judging a lunatic by the standards of healthy consciousness. Maudsley understood that the only answer to Bramwell's question was to reject his discourse.

> The fact that a person so afflicted can, and sometimes does, resist the diseased idea or impulse, causes many to think, and some to argue, that it might always be successfully resisted . . . It is impossible, however, that true conceptions of mental disease can be acquired until men cease to regard its phenomena entirely from a psychological point of view, and consent to study them by aid of the established principles of physiology and pathology. The despair of any one writing upon mental diseases at present is, that he cannot convey just and adequate ideas of them by any care or labour of expression so long as men will judge them by the revelations of sane self-consciousness.[59]

There was no logical answer to Bramwell as long as legal discourse prevailed. Alienists campaigned for a new human science discourse; this could not be superior to the legal one on empirical grounds but only on the grounds of the values it covertly expressed. Bucknill saw the point: medical psychology aimed at replacing the mentalist language of 'uncontrollable' with the physicalist language of 'disease': 'The real question is, not whether the emotions occasioning the overt act are beyond the power of the individual to control, but whether they are the result of disease. If the objectionable terms, *impulse* and *uncontrollable*, are disused, the simple and intelligible question of the existence or nonexistence of disease will take its rightful and prominent place.'[60] This was not just a matter of words, but a major philosophical claim about the meaning and value of human nature.

Alienists used 'irresistible impulse' as a physiological term. In court it became a legal term and inevitably sounded like dangerous nonsense. Further, the prosecution sometimes showed that it was nonsense, even in a medical context. Defence counsel in Mrs Jackson's case argued that she had attempted to murder her son-in-law during her sleep. The prosecution was able to demonstrate that she possessed malice and had prepared for the murder attempt by sharpening a kitchen knife.

The idea of irresistible impulse was denigrated in several trials. It was put forward for Alnutt, a twelve-year-old boy who poisoned his grandfather. As well as suggesting that it was implausible to poison impulsively, Baron Rolfe directed the jury to scrutinise such a defence because an uncontrollable impulse was not perhaps distinct from a 'non-resisted impulse'.[61] John Smith was hanged following Lord Denman's direction to the jury to ignore the defence: 'To say a man was irresponsible without positive proof of any act to show that he was labouring under some delusion, seemed to him to be a presumption of knowledge which none but the great Creator himself could possess.'[62] Denman understood that evidence in law should be witnessed; delusions might fulfil this criterion but a state of irresistibility certainly did not. Dr Winslow criticised Denman, though of course he had no more privileged access to Smith's subjective state. Rather, he identified Smith as a member of a class defined by symptoms of uncontrollable conduct. Deductively, then, Smith's defence may have been genuine; Denman was attacked for ignoring 'this great psychological truth': that there could exist 'an overwhelming and uncontrollable desire to take away human life'. Thus he had sent a possible lunatic to the gallows.[63] Such 'truth' was not part of the jurist's discourse; his domain was evidence about the specific case. Stephen provided the legal emphasis when he stated that 'there *may have been* many instances of irresistible impulses of this kind, though I fear there is a disposition to confound them with unresisted impulses'.[64]

The judiciary considered medical theory pretentious and showed little sympathy with medical men who tried to explain the grounds on which they based their opinions. It is important to understand that this was a structural feature and not just due to particular judges or particular alienists in court. Only medical theory could render a particular medical opinion intelligible. Theory summarised and explained the clinical experience that created categories like 'homicidal mania', 'suicidal mania', 'erotomania', and 'pyromania'. When alienists used these labels in court they were trapped in circularity, appearing to explain nothing.

Nevertheless, there were occasions when the defence of irresistible impulse succeeded, though it has to be questioned whether the jury's verdict depended on special circumstances rather than on the persuasiveness of medical argument.[65]

Denman again attacked the notion of irresistible impulse when Martha Prior was tried for the murder of her baby at Chelmsford. He nevertheless conceded that the jury would act on the medical testimony ('that she committed the act under an uncontrollable impulse acting upon a mind previously diseased') in order to acquit the young mother.[66] He expressed the problem in the following way:

The judgment of the medical gentleman *had been very rashly formed*. How could one person dive into the mind of another, and express an opinion with regard to its being in an unsound state, when there was no evidence of any alteration of conduct, or any circumstances in the case to show alienation of mind ? . . . He could not help thinking that such opinions were too often given by scientific men upon too slight foundation for the safety of the public; but as he felt in this instance there *was no doubt that the jury would act upon the testimony of the medical gentleman* who had been examined, it would be useless to proceed any further with the inquiry.[67]

This discord also brought out the discrepancy between the law's formal rigour and its practical flexibility.

The medical practitioner James Pownall was acquitted of murder at Gloucester in 1859 in spite of appearing perfectly rational. Indeed, he had been rational enough to be released from Northwoods Asylum in spite of a history of infrequent homicidal attacks in the middle of long rational periods. His institutional background and the suddenness and motivelessness of the murder led to his acquittal. Medical witnesses gave no evidence for insanity apart from the impulsive murderous attacks themselves, though concealed delusions were suspected. 'It was a disease which came on quickly and lasted but a short time . . . was unattended with premonitory symptoms. It lasted till the impulsive feeling was gratified, and some act was committed by the patient by which he was, so to speak, morbidly satisfied, and directly the patient was so satisfied mental health was restored.'[68] The jury found this evidence for 'homicidal mania' sufficient. Richard Dadd was another case of homicidal mania, but here there was extensive evidence of a serious character change rather than irresistible impulse which was the deciding factor.

The same conditions appertained to French (who killed a stranger sleeping in the same room with her) and to William Frost (who killed his four children under a delusion of sin, which would be expiated by the murders). The judge directed the jury to accept the clear evidence of insanity in French's case. In Frost's case, Mr Justice Williams gave a direction which went beyond the Rules: 'It was not merely for them to consider whether he knew right from wrong, but whether he was, at the time he committed the offence, deranged or not.'[69] There was good evidence of Frost's derangement; after the murders, he had exclaimed, 'Glory be to God: my sins are now pardoned, and I am sure of heaven!'[70] Alienists reacted favourably to Williams's opinion. Dr Wood, the Medical Officer at Bethlem, also referred to it when criticising the Rules: 'The judge doubtless felt that the law, as expounded by the whole body of judges, could not be properly applied in such a case as this.'[71] But this case still illustrated the power of judicial discretion rather than any acknowledgement of medical discourse.

Mr Baron Rolfe, in Layton's trial in 1849, summed up a case in which lack of motive strongly suggested insanity: 'Perhaps it would be going too far to say that a party was responsible in every case where he had a glimmering knowledge of what was right and wrong.'[72] Layton had shot and knifed his wife in circumstances where he was easily detected. The judge, however, was perhaps unduly generous in stretching the Rules; Bethlem case notes record that Layton 'glorified in his crime saying when told she was dead that it was a d—— good thing too and that he would dance to the gallows'.[73]

Three other cases may be cited in which medical evidence for homicidal mania was perhaps important to the verdict. Dr Caleb Williams and Mr John Kitching from The Retreat gave evidence in 1856 when James Hill was tried for cutting off his nephew's head. The defence was that 'on that unhappy day . . . he was entirely bereft of his reason . . . he was afflicted with that kind of disease which medical men call homicidal madness'.[74] Williams and Kitching argued that Hill showed the classic symptoms of homicidal mania: the absence of motive, the solitary and sudden nature of the crime, and his indifference to what had been done. They recognised, however, that what the court needed was evidence of Hill's unawareness of the nature of the crime. Kitching therefore expressed their belief in Hill's irresistible impulse in the following way:

> I would say that in such a case I should think it quite possible, and very probable, that the man would know the act he was doing was wrong; that he would have condemned it as wrong if any one else had done it, and that he would acknowledge at any other time that it was wrong in himself, but that at the time he was committing it, his general knowledge of what was right and wrong, and his knowledge in particular of the act which he was about to commit being wrong, would be quite overpowered by the insane impulse to do it.[75]

Mr Justice Willes respected this medical opinion but he was in a quandary to know how to reconcile it with the law. On the one hand, he summed up by saying, 'Gentlemen, such a thing as a person not being able to control himself in the doing of an act which he knows to be wrong, is a phrase that is not known to the law of this country.'[76] On the other hand, he made the obscure statement that, 'nor . . . was it sufficient for a man to set up an irresistible impulse to the commission of crime, not resulting from a disease of the mind', implying perhaps that, if disease were independently demonstrated, then the defence of irresistible impulse might be countenanced.[77] He finally compromised by inferring that, as the question was the consciousness of right and wrong at the *moment* of the deed, consciousness might have been swept aside by the actual impulse. Later judges also utilised this. Both the jurist Stephen and the forensic expert Taylor considered the legal fiction of a person being 'insanely conscious' while committing a crime was a useful device for mitigating the law's severity.[78] Hill was acquitted and arrived at Bethlem three years later with a violent reputation not born out by subsequent conduct. According to Hill himself, the murder was caused by intemperance rather than insanity, though it looked very much as if the medical opinion about his insanity had been influential.

Dr Hood from Bethlem successfully argued that disease had led to uncontrollable conduct in Mrs Vyse's case in 1862. The accused was a respectable woman who had killed her two children with strychnine. That she had obtained the poison under false pretences was good *prima facie* evidence of forethought. However, she was 'strangely erratic and excited' at the time of the killing. No motive was discernible; on this occasion this was accepted as good supporting evidence for insanity. After careful inquiry, Hood demonstrated a correlation between her business anxiety, the strain of suckling a child, and the subjective experience which she spoke of as 'perspiring of the brain' (an irritation inside the head).[79] When there was a lack of motive and excessive abnormality in the deed itself, medical and lay classifications could coincide, as they did in this case.

The judge himself stopped James Kelley's trial in 1865 after the defence produced medical evidence (which was not rebutted by the prosecution), even though Kelley probably could tell right from wrong. A medical reporter believed that Kelley's own account realistically described the subjective experience of a homicidal impulse. ' "Something came over me. I seized my poor wife by the head, and knocked it against the flags again and again;" such is the articulate expression, as far as it can be articulately expressed, of that mental convulsion which in such cases utters itself in homicide.'[80] It is not clear what other evidence supported this account, so it is impossible to decide whether medical evidence provided the reasoning, or merely the wording, of the insanity verdict.

These cases demonstrate the inconsistency of the courts. The Rules set out a formal test for deciding responsibility (not insanity) but other variables often swept this aside in practice. The Rules vindicated judges who were antagonistic to the medical viewpoint, whether in general or in specific instances. Where judges were not so antagonistic, the Rules were ignored, stretched and compromised. Taylor concluded a review by recognising the *individual* character of each case, while advancing a general *theoretical* definition of irresponsibility as an inability to exercise control.

> There are no certain legal or medical rules, whereby homicidal mania may be detected. Each case must be determined by the circumstances attending it: and the true test for irresponsibility appears to be, *if it could be practically applied*, whether the individual, at the time of the commission of the crime, had or had not a sufficient power of control to govern his actions.[81]

It was the unpredictability of the defence rather than the law's severity which later worried him most. 'The great defect in the English law is . . . the *uncertainty of its application*. The cases referred to show that an acquittal on the plea of insanity is on some occasions a mere matter of accident.'[82]

Inconsistency had certain strengths; in particular, justice could be tailored to individual circumstance. 'Fortunately for humanity, the practice of the law does not always accord with the theory.'[83] Helped by the Home Secretary's powers, justice was tempered with mercy. Judges had the satisfaction of enforcing a deterrent law in public while knowing that their remarks to the Home Secretary could mitigate the effects in private. From this viewpoint, mitigation because of insanity was not a matter of chance. However, juries remained unpredictable, and many jurists accepted that this was as it should be.

> Probably, therefore, what really happens is that, consciously or unconsciously, the jury give their verdict according to their opinion upon a much more general question – namely, whether, under all the circumstances, the prisoner ought to be punished: and, where their decisions are not distorted by a special dislike of the punishment provided for the offence (as sometimes occurs in capital cases), the result is perhaps as good as any to which, in the present state of science, it is possible to attain . . . And at any rate the decision of a jury has this negative advantage; that, if unsatisfactory, it forms no precedent; on the contrary, the public condemnation which follows it, serves as a guide and warning, for some time at least, against similar errors.[84]

Nevertheless, jurists as well as medical men also complained about legal inconsistency. Alienists claimed that it could be eliminated by scientific truth, professional expertise and humanitarian values. They therefore fought courtroom battles to establish new precedents, even scorning the judiciary for its inability to reach a stable position: 'We, in our turn, might make merry did it not happen that the difference of opinion among chief-justices, sometimes involves the hanging of a man, and, therefore, is no joking matter.'[85] The judiciary was also worried, because of its duty to administer the sanctions which sustained society and to serve as the mouthpiece for wronged public opinion. Flexibility was tantamount to weakness and, because the social order was at stake, weakness could not be countenanced.

3 Moral Insanity

Alienists rarely supposed that an uncontrollable impulse could exist in isolation from other physical or mental disorder; they had strong views about the unity of the mind and the integration of the brain. In most cases, uncontrollable conduct was considered merely a symptom of emotional or volitional insanity and not the disease itself. This brought medical nosology, and particularly the class of moral insanities, into the courtroom. Defence arguments for irresistible impulse merged into claims about the defendant's general emotional and volitional morbidity. 'A case of sudden and irresistible impulse may, and generally does, afford an illustration of moral insanity.'[86]

'Moral insanity' was a generic term for emotional and volitional disorder. It probably confused more than it clarified: it was 'a disorder, which, more than any other, has puzzled the psychologist, perplexed the advocate, and disconcerted the divine'.[87] Dr Prichard acknowledged that 'in fact, the varieties of moral insanity are perhaps as numerous as the modifications of feeling or passion in the human mind'.[88] It was a catch phrase which led too easily to a cluster of related ideas being disguised as a fixed object, which moral insanity never was. It does not translate into the modern term 'psychopathy'.[89]

The term was confusing for two further reasons. First, it existed as a description of extreme moral perversity before and after Prichard gave it a medical meaning. The Scottish moralist Dr John Abercrombie wrote: 'In the language of common life, we sometimes speak of a moral insanity, in which a man rushes headlong through a course of vice and crime regardless of every moral restraint, of every social tie, and of all consequences, whether more immediate or future.' This loss of the power of the conscience 'is a point in the moral constitution of man which it does not belong to the physician to investigate. The fact is unquestionable; – the solution is to be sought for in the records of eternal truth.'[90] Non-specialists therefore meant something distinct from disease when they referred to 'moral insanity'. Lord Denman, during Oxford's trial in 1840, contrasted 'moral' insanity, which laymen could assess, with 'physical' insanity, which might require medical expertise.[91]

The second reason is that 'moral' could not logically or empirically be divorced from its ethical associations. Though Prichard's 'moral' insanity referred to the active powers of mind, these powers were inherently the agency of ethical decisions. Victorians recognised that to ascribe moral insanity to someone was to say something about the ethics of that person's conduct. Medical usage therefore blurred into a continuing lay usage.

Several doctors thought it would have been better if medicine had never adopted the term. Drs Hood and Mayo regretted that it incorporated ethical connotations into a disease description.[92] Winslow considered the phrase unfortunate because it mixed mental and physical languages and thereby denigrated the freedom of the will.[93] Conversely, Maudsley accepted the term precisely because he did hold that medical definitions contained meanings derived from socio-biological norms. While moral insanity was 'a perverted state of those mental faculties usually called the active and moral powers', it was also a diseased part of the social organism. 'As it is chiefly in the degeneration of the social sentiments that the symptoms of moral insanity declare themselves . . . the most typical forms of the disease can only be met with in those who have had some social cultivation.'[94]

Ethical judgements highly coloured the use of moral insanity in medico-legal cases. With moral lunatics (as with modern psychopaths) it was the crime itself which formed the principal evidence of disease. Some lunatics had symptoms evident to anyone, but the morally insane had symptoms hidden within their inner mental states. The visible outer signs were perceived as depravity. 'The outward acts of the individual are less convulsive in their manifestations, and answer more exactly to the morbid feelings and desires . . . Hence it is so difficult to induce the public to entertain the idea that moral insanity is anything more than wilful and witting vice.'[95] Alienists feared that the public conflated moral insanity with the immoral deeds which were often its outcome. They argued that moral insanity should be related to other disorders rather than to particular examples of vice.

> If moral insanity be only spoken of and recognized when vicious acts are threatened or committed, it is natural that the doctrine of moral insanity should be brought into disrepute, or altogether disregarded; and that a very erroneous idea should be attached to its area and limits. But if it can be shown that [melancholia] . . . may coexist with a sound condition of the purely intellectual part of our mental constitution . . . moral insanity, will not stand out in such prominent relief in its relation to vice, nor run so perilous a risk of being regarded as the mere apology for crime.[96]

It was difficult to get across this relatively subtle point under antagonistic cross-examination; it therefore sometimes looked as if medical witnesses accepted vice as the principal evidence of disease.

Medical views were stoutly resisted.

> 'Moral insanity' . . . a term which, since the publication of Dr. Prichard's book, has figured so remarkably, and, as we think, so dangerously in our courts of justice, paralyzing her arm, and securing impunity to those who have indulged their 'homicidal orgasm,' as it is the fashion to call a propensity to murder . . .
>
> It is therefore with no little satisfaction that we see men of mark . . . coming forward to stem the torrent which threatens to overwhelm the peace and happiness of society, and to give up the innocent and well regulated to the tender mercies of the cruel and violent.[97]

This anonymous journalist reflected and accentuated a feeling of social danger. The belief that the definition of lunacy was expanding, and that evil was therefore being excused, particularly affected responses to moral insanity.

Moral lunatics were of special interest for the crime-insanity boundary because here the elements of madness and badness coincided most nearly. Those whose job it was to draw the boundary had to be clear and persuasive about the criteria validating their particular description.

It was not uncommon to describe people persistently erratic or immoral in conduct as 'idiots' or 'imbeciles'. It is difficult in retrospect to know how many of these people would have come under the label 'mental defective' which separated congenital idiots from criminal lunatics after 1913. 'Weakness of mind' was another commonly used phrase. Almost anyone who pleaded insanity might have been described in this way. It did not refer specifically to intellectual incapacity; rather, it subsumed such incapacity under a general failure to conform with psychological normality. Individuals with a life history of general idiocy graded into those showing incompetence, perversity and delinquency. Somewhere this weakness passed into moral insanity.

> Delinquents of this description are, perhaps, not unable to distinguish between what is right and what is wrong; but their will is not governed by their understanding, and they want the power of restraining themselves from that which, when committed, they are afraid to reflect upon. Their will remains; but it springs from depraved sensations and emotions, or from passions inordinate and unrestrained, and is not under the direction of sound mental faculties.[98]

Juries were willing to find insanity without considering the Rules' precise meaning, if they perceived chronic weakness of mind which had existed long before the crime. William Campion was found insane at York in 1854 for stabbing a man without motive; he hanged himself in Bethlem. William Thomas was found insane at Chester the previous year for murdering his mother, even though he had attempted concealment by digging a grave. It was stated at Bethlem that he showed no symptom of insanity, except perhaps that of talking to himself. In such cases, the available evidence suggests that some alienists would have labelled the defendants morally insane, though it is not clear how the verdicts were reached.

It was accepted that emotional shocks might contribute to outbursts of limited violence. Both medical and legal discourse used the language of psychological faculties to describe such events. This sometimes created sufficient overlap to permit agreement. Where the shock or distress was clearly not of the defendant's own making, juries showed understanding by finding insanity. In cases where the defence was successful, *visible* social factors were important. In unsuccessful cases, however, alienists often described *invisible* causes in the nervous system. Only when alienists were persuasive in translating visible social factors into invisible nervous causes might juries accept the insanity defence for medical rather than lay reasons.

The acquittal of Ann Martin for murdering her granddaughter at Derby created little stir; evidence showed that she had been seriously disturbed by her son's earlier suicide. George Smith, in a distressed state, shot his wife. The jury found him insane at Maidstone on evidence about his obsessive dread of reduced circumstances. Many of the cases in which destitute women murdered their children also came into this category. As Stanynought's and Frost's trials showed, fathers as well as mothers were found insane for murdering their children and spouses because of terror of poverty and its effect on their children. Unfortunately, there is not enough information to know whether these verdicts were easily reached and whether medical opinion was used.

The judiciary was unhappy with a practice which in effect found dread of poverty an excusing condition. Burton murdered his wife and child in 1848 to save them from poverty. At Burton's first trial (for his wife's death) Mr Baron Parke disagreed with medical evidence, describing moral insanity as 'a dangerous innovation coming in with the present century'.[99] The jury found Burton guilty but his capital sentence was commuted following pressure on the Home Secretary from local medical men. After nine months in gaol and several attempts at suicide, Burton stood trial again (for murdering his child). This time he was acquitted on the ground of insanity and sent to the Bedford Lunatic Asylum, where he soon died. Society could not countenance the subjective conclusions which Burton drew from his circumstances, but it was unable to achieve a coherent representation – in terms of immoral character or of insanity – about why his conclusions must be rejected. The discourses available allowed only for emotions that ought to be controlled or emotions that could not be controlled.

Medical evidence for moral insanity was commonly attacked in the nineteenth century. Critics argued that it was redescribing crime in unacceptable ways; alienists replied that they were for the first time describing objective reality. Critics said such evidence was wrong in particular cases and the general medical approach was socially unacceptable anyway. They focused on medical psychology's prescriptive content rather than on its descriptive achievement. Alienists responded that their descriptions validated their prescriptions.

The case of Thomas Rowe, accused of attempting to murder his former employer in 1843, demonstrated the overlap of moral vice and moral insanity. There was no evidence of inability to distinguish right from wrong; the principal evidence of insanity was the extremeness of the deed in relation to the motive. His employer, considering Rowe too old and incompetent to do his job, had dismissed him. Rowe felt this was unjust and, when his employer refused to reconsider, shot him with a prepared pistol. Nonetheless, he was found insane; one suspects there was an unwillingness to hang a pathetic old man.

Dr Mayo sharply attacked this verdict. He accused Rowe of criminal intent and the law of providing Rowe with a comfortable retirement within an institution. 'Rowe's transgression provides a pauper assassin with a comfortable livelihood.'[100] This particular outburst has to be placed in relation to Mayo's repeated rejection of medico-psychological efforts to reform the law. He was concerned lest deterrence be undermined by sentimentality disguised as expertise. He thought society should control all miscreants by threatening sanctions.

> We trust that we shall not at once be accused of inhumanity for confessing our opinion, that the tendency of the law to give impunity to the offences of such persons, is mischievous in its effects, both as regards society, and as the offenders are themselves concerned. We cannot indeed overlook the fact, that insane persons may be intimidated by example. We have seen it illustrated in numberless instances, and we wish to see it recognized in our legal proceedings.[101]

He believed that much more empirical knowledge was needed before alienists should draw conclusions from categories like moral insanity. 'Fully to meet this evil, a much more searching inquiry into the nature of both moral and intellectual unsoundness of mind is required than has hitherto been effected, or, if effected, recognised as such by the public. The idea at present conveyed to the public mind by moral unsoundness, in its relation to crime, has a very prejudicial effect.'[102] Mayo represented a conservative medical establishment opposed to the social newcomers associated with the public asylums. He himself claimed special ability in treating insanity in private practice, but he rationalised his expertise as experience, knowledge of human character (in the manner of the Scottish philosopher Dugald Stewart), and insight into education. His approach contrasted with that of the new mental physiologists, though in practice both used traditional therapies. They also shared a belief in the primary importance of disorder of the will and moral faculties, both in the early stages of insanity and in disorders of reason. But in his later writings Mayo did not express this in terms of events in the nervous system. Though he described a condition in which the moral faculty was absent, he called it 'brutality' rather than insanity. He argued that people in a state of 'brutality' must be held accountable because they can both know the law and be disciplined to obey it, even if they do not comprehend its morality.[103]

Alienists considered Mayo's remarks offensive, especially those about Martha Brixey, a domestic servant who murdered her employer's child. 'The Greenwich murderess is at present in Bethlem, where her case will afford very mischievous evidence to all such hysterical young females as may be cognizant of it, how comfortably life may to appearance be spent after the indulgence of splenetic cruelty, provided a human being is destroyed. There is not about her the smallest evidence of insanity.'[104] Mayo only echoed the newspapers' response to Brixey's insanity verdict, but it meant that a leading physician rejected a defence hinging on the physicalist argument which linked obstructed menstruation with irrational conduct. To alienists it was a reactionary rejection of the foundation of modern scientific medicine.

A similar conflict was evident in reactions to Dalmas, the Battersea Bridge murderer. He was found guilty, but insanity was later certified because medical men decided his crime could be explained in the physical terms of a head injury. Mayo, however, placed greater weight on Dalmas' attempt to conceal the crime and called for punishment. This embarrassed alienists, especially when Dalmas was subsequently declared sane and returned to prison with his capital sentence commuted to transportation for life.

It was insulting to alienists that a leader of the medical profession should make such statements. When Mayo went even further and referred to disease of mind rather than brain, he seemed to personify outdated legal metaphysics. The modern mental physiologist considered Mayo's statement that 'the immaterial element may be just as subject to its proper affections as the material one' dangerous nonsense.[105] Nevertheless, Mayo pointed out that the modern asylum movement relied on self-control; thus that the reformers also worked with the 'immaterial principle'.[106] This revealed one of the central inconsistencies in the medical discourse.

Predictably, Mayo thought that M'Naghten should have been found guilty and punished as an example to ill-regulated minds. He also said that 'the entire escape of Oxford was confessedly most mischievous'.[107] This view was shared by Mayo's colleague at the Royal College of Physicians, Sir Benjamin Collins Brodie: 'There are many dogs whose natural and original instinct leads them to run after and kill sheep; but a proper discipline teaches them that they are not to do so.'[108] Mayo and Brodie echoed the juridical view that the law necessarily treats people as moral citizens and not as objects of nature. In these terms, moral insanity was exactly what was meant by vice.

Several trials illustrate complete disagreement on this issue. Laycock was an expert witness at the trial of a Newcastle craftsman, George Clark, for the murder of a tax-collector. It was alleged that Clark killed the collector when the latter distrained upon Clark's tools for the non-payment of a dog tax. Laycock claimed that 'the history of his conduct previously and subsequently to the murder, and his conduct during the trial, abundantly proved that he was an aggressive melancholiac, labouring under notional insanity'.[109] Whether or not the court agreed with this description, it did not agree that this absolved him from responsibility. Clark was found guilty because he clearly possessed power of reason. The

verdict rejected Laycock's label of moral insanity: 'Daily experience
rightly read, as well as medical science and experience, abundantly shows
that a man or woman may be imbecile morally from cerebral disorder and
disease, and yet have good intellectual, nay, high logical powers.'[110]
Laycock was partially vindicated when several parties – 'in common with
all who value justice rather than expediency' – considered it too severe to
hang him when disease might have been intermingled with immorality.[111]
The judge wrote to the Home Secretary to express disquiet (though he
had conducted the trial strictly within the Rules). Local doctors, pressed
by Laycock, tried to have Clark certified but the justices refused. Finally
the Home Secretary commuted the sentence. This was the social process
of boundary-drawing, both indecisive and divisive.

Dr Daniel Hack Tuke illustrated just how little correspondence there
was between jury verdicts and expert opinion with four cases from
1863.[112] Two of these, Thomas Lidbetter and Henry Dommett, were
found insane in opposition to the Rules and against the opinions of gaol
surgeons who stated that the prisoners knew right from wrong. Two
others, Fooks and Preedy at Dorchester, were hanged even though, in
Tuke's opinion, more considerable evidence of disease was adduced. Both
of these involved vicious murders in cold blood, and the judges probably
felt that a strict reading of the Rules would be compatible with public
opinion. At Preedy's trial a local philanthropist, the Reverend Lord
Osborne, argued insanity without expert medical assistance. He even
suggested – such was the disrepute of medical witnesses paid by the
defence – that the insanity plea might have a better chance if argued by an
outsider. 'Seeing that in civil cases it is known that experts of great
eminence can be retained on both sides to prove the case of the plaintiff
or defendant, in the criminal courts all such evidence is viewed with such
suspicion that I have known it to be the wisest course not to call for any
medical opinion at all.'[113] He argued that Preedy, the natural son of a
wealthy man, had been dropped on his head when young and was subject
to epileptic paroxysms, in one of which he killed his warder. Local
opinion, however, considered his violence after the crime (he had to be
kept in irons) a sham. The verdict reflected a suspicion of depravity.

I have referred to depravity as if it were a systematic theory, which it
rarely was. But it was generally seen as something real and tangible in
character, and therefore a recognisable social enemy.

> There are in the world many bad men who are the natural enemies of
> inoffensive men, just as beasts of prey are the enemies of all men.

> My own experience is that there are in the world a considerable
> number of extremely wicked people, disposed, when opportunity
> offers, to get what they want by force or fraud, with complete
> indifference to the interests of others, and in ways which are incon-
> sistent with the existence of civilised society.[114]

Depravity was identified by an intuitive act of classification, without considering its elements in any detailed way. Put colloquially, people knew it when they saw it. This was a circular process, logically speaking, comparable with the alienists' identification of impulsive or moral insanity. But its circularity was not worrying because it was a fundamental part of social reality.

The consequences of the dichotomy between insanity and depravity were brought out by the Honourable Ross Touchet. This gentleman shot the proprietor of a shooting gallery (he died after the trial) in order to be hanged. Mr Justice Maule permitted evidence of hereditary insanity in a grandfather, though the prosecution claimed it was procedurally irrelevant.[115] Touchet was found insane. To Mayo he was yet another example of a weak-minded person who would acquire an ability to exercise control if punished. 'The honourable Mr. Tuchet, cool, indifferent, and self-possessed, enjoys [in Bethlem] the immunity from punishment, which a well-chosen counsel can at any time obtain for an eccentric culprit, when the punishment of death is manifestly too severe for the occasion, and yet nothing but the plea of insanity can avert it.'[116] There was good reason to state that hanging was too severe in this case: Laurence was hanged in the same year for an identically motivated murder; that Laurence succeeded in getting hanged was apparently the inspiration for Touchet's own deed!

There was a twist of language which influenced reactions to the insanity plea; ordinary people used the word 'insane' to describe bizarre or gross breaches of the moral order. If a crime was extreme enough, it sometimes acquired a medical label when there was little specifically medical beneath it. The consequences, however, brought the person into the medical orbit, and with time this prescription influenced the acceptability of medical description.

The jury in some cases of peculiar violence such as Martha Brixey's or Mrs Brough's comprehended the events with the term 'insanity'. 'The very bad man, to the common sense and sympathies of society appears a madman, and though his case eminently requires penal preventives, because fear of consequences is his only moral check, he is liable, from the very strangeness imparted by atrocity, to escape punishment.'[117] The term was a receptacle for crimes which were otherwise anomalous. One lawyer commented: 'That every murderer is presumably a madman is a comfortable doctrine which men are naturally much inclined to accept. To admit that a horrible crime has been deliberately committed by a human being, is indirectly to reflect on ourselves, especially if the criminal, as a refined and educated person, represents human nature at its best.'[118] This description of abhorrent conduct as madness was more plausible when no motive could be discerned. 'Motivelessness' created an important area of overlap in medical and lay discourses.

Alienists expected an interview to reveal whether there was criminal motive, deluded motive, or no motive at all. Both alienists and laymen used the absence of motive as evidence for insanity, since the crime was then performed literally without reason. Motivelessness was sometimes treated as an objective factual state, though it is more accurately considered a social construct. When describing the murderer James Hill, Dr Williams said: 'This entire perversion of the natural feelings, this abolition of our common humanity, and the absence of motive itself, when the healthy instincts are all in the other direction, are surely indications of an unsound mind, and as surely render the individual no longer responsible for his actions.'[119] Taylor, by contrast, was aware how difficult it was to establish a negative condition; he warned against accepting motivelessness as proof of insanity, since the human mind was infinitely varied.[120] All alienists nonetheless accepted that an apparent lack of motive for an unusual deed was a sign to search for further evidence of insanity. Where a crime was sufficiently bizarre or atrocious, laymen sometimes agreed that no sane motive could explain it (as in Touchet's and Vyse's) and that the accused was therefore by definition insane. On the other hand, laymen sometimes considered that a state of depravity was itself an adequate explanation (as in Burton at Maidstone). In law, atrocity was certainly no excuse: 'Nothing could be more contrary to law, than to infer insanity from the very malignity and atrocity of the crime.'[121] Alienists agreed, while claiming that evidence other than the atrocity might be found, though this evidence was not always very plausible to others.[122]

The question of motive was central to Stokes's trial in 1848. Michael Stokes was a soldier and well-known eccentric who suddenly walked across the barrack room to shoot a woman right in front of her husband. It was argued in his defence that there was no motive, and certainly no criminal motive, since the deed was perpetrated with no hope of concealment or escape. Mr Baron Rolfe rejected both irresistible impulse and motivelessness:

> But who enabled them to dive into the human heart, and see the real motive that prompted the commission of such deeds? It has been urged that no motive has been shown for the commission of this crime. It is true that there is no motive apparent, but a very inadequate one; but it is dangerous ground to take to say that a man must be insane because men fail to discern the motive for his act . . . it would be a most dangerous doctrine to lay down, that because a man committed a desperate offence, with the chance of instant death, and the certainty of future punishment before him, he was therefore insane – as if the perpetration of crimes was to be excused by their very atrocity.[123]

Alienists apparently did not comment on this case, though defence counsel had tried to use medical categories to emphasise the crime's impulsive and meaningless nature. Rolfe was more generous a year later, when Layton, who had killed his wife in public, was acquitted.

One particular anecdote was repeated on several occasions to demonstrate just how bizarre a motive might be.

> We once attended a young gentleman who had committed a frightful assault upon a child; cutting the calves of its legs through to the bone with a knife! He was in love with windmills, and being placed by his friends in a part of the country where none of these objects existed, he committed the assault in the hope of being removed in consequence therefrom, to some place where windmills did exist.[124]

Yet even this anecdote was construed in different ways: by alienists to show the extreme abnormality of the insane mind, and by jurists to show that even the insane have their motives!

The cases in which the defence plea was successful therefore tended to be ones where there was evidence of idiocy, delusion or character change; where the accused was dramatically shocked or distressed; or (sometimes) where the crime seemed to transcend the bounds of intelligibility. Only on some occasions did medical opinion appear decisive in support of these lay criteria. The terms impulsive and moral insanity in particular were rarely helpful to the defence strategy. Nevertheless, there was scope under the Rules for some people whom alienists called impulsively or morally insane to be acquitted.

One of the most striking aspects of these individual cases is the way different parties formulated different descriptions of the same event. Events had the names that they did by virtue of the discourses in which they were constructed.

CHAPTER SIX

DEPRAVITY AND MADNESS
IN CONTROVERSIAL TRIALS

Boundary-drawing in the public courtroom engendered controversy; verdicts were dramatic symbols for the contesting parties. The process leading to them involved an empirical search for the presence or absence of certain elements, whether legal states of mind or medical diseases. It should now be clear that the meaning of these facts cannot be discerned without reference to the alternative discourses in which they were embedded. Boundary-drawing involved a decision about which discourse should be dominant. Normally, this decision was not an active one, since the court's institutional standing made its discourse appear self-evident. The beginnings of an institutional basis for a medical discourse created the conditions for an attack on that self-evidence. In the resulting conflict, each side claimed to possess objectivity (either natural morality or nature) and superior values (either moral order or humanitarianism).

Analysis in these terms makes possible new understanding of medico-legal controversy. It should not go unnoticed, however, that at a more abstract interpretative level, both sides and both discourses had fewer differences than they had things in common. Statements about the objectivity of morality and nature sometimes came so close as to be indistinguishable. Further, though differing in their justifications, both sides supported the same social order. A comparison of Stephen's and Maudsley's political values shows that they shared several commitments: professional dominance by experts, the isolation of deviants in the interests of the majority, and unsentimental anti-democratic principles. Their differences derived from the slowly shifting balance of power between administrative groups. Philippe Riot, commenting on the case of Pierre Rivière, writes: 'We believe that these selections and interpretations are not only the expression of a certain level of medical knowledge or the effect of the operation of the judicial machinery, but mark the border where two types of discourse confront one another and, through them, two powers.'[1] For many people such differences were condensed into the opposed symbols of judicial hanging and medical incarceration.

The only well-known English case is M'Naghten's. Jacques Quen suggests the outcry over M'Naghten's verdict reflected a fear of violence associated with Chartist agitation.[2] Subsequent interest stems from its being the occasion which produced the Rules. But of course M'Naghten's case no more created medico-legal controversy than it resolved it. No one trial could be of decisive importance in a confrontation between two discourses.

The liberal interpretation of the law at Oxford's trial in 1840 contributed to the outcry over M'Naghten. Edward Oxford fired pistols at the Queen when she was out driving. Whether or not the pistols were loaded (and this was never determined), it was an extremely shocking offence. Oxford knew what he was doing: he described it in notebooks as the plot of an imaginary secret society, he planned the attack, he bought and practiced with the pistols. Chief Justice Denman, however, allowed extensive medical and non-medical evidence for insanity. Medical witnesses diagnosed hereditary moral insanity; Drs Hodgkin and Chowne described Oxford as having a 'lesion of the will'. Surprisingly, this was not queried.[3] Denman summed up in a way which possibly suggested that disease itself was an exculpatory factor:

> If some controlling disease was, in truth, the acting power within him which he could not resist, then he will not be responsible . . . The question is, whether the prisoner was labouring under that species of insanity which satisfies you that he was quite unaware of the nature, character, and consequences of the act he was committing, or, in other words, whether he was under the influence of a diseased mind, and was really unconscious at the time he was committing the act, that it was a crime.[4]

This was rather an ambivalent opinion, but jurists did not interpret it as a statement that disease was an exculpatory factor.[5] The lawyer W. C. Townsend reconciled the verdict with the law by arguing that even if Oxford was not properly insane (as he believed he was not), his intellect was less than that of a boy of fourteen; therefore he was properly acquitted.[6]

The Rules looked medically retrogressive against the background of Oxford's trial. Indeed, this was what the judiciary intended; they were embarrassed by the sentiment which the Queen herself expressed:

> The law may be perfect but how is it that whenever a case for its application arises it proves to be of no avail ? We have seen the trials of Oxford and MacNaughten conducted by the ablest lawyers of the day – and they *allow* and *advise* the Jury to pronounce the verdict of not guilty on account of insanity, whilst *everybody* is morally convinced that both malefactors were perfectly conscious and aware of what they did.[7]

Without sufficient disorder of reason to render the accused unaware of the nature of the crime, the deed corresponded exactly to what was meant by a bad act.

A liberal interpretation of the law was repudiated in another trial involving an attack on the Queen. In 1850, a former cavalry officer, Lieutenant Robert Pate, hit the Queen on the head with his walking stick;

he was found guilty of high misdemeanour and sentenced to seven years transportation. The defence argued that his earlier conduct showed he was mentally deranged, with John Conolly and Henry Monro (son of the visiting physician at Bethlem) giving expert medical testimony. Mr Baron Alderson, however, laid down that the Rules were tests of responsibility and not insanity and that evidence about Pate's earlier conduct only proved eccentricity. Further, he stated, evidence of delusion must precede the crime in order to establish exculpatory conditions. He also directly attacked the concept of irresistible impulse: 'The law did not acknowledge such an impulse if the person was aware that it was a wrong act he was about to commit, and he was answerable for the consequences. A man might say that he picked a pocket from some uncontrollable impulse, and in that case the law would have an uncontrollable impulse to punish him for it.'[8] Though there was common agreement that Pate was abnormal in both his intellectual and his active powers, that did not provide sufficient grounds to find insanity. The trial was a social judgement against reform, since the judicial opinion and the verdict were given in opposition to statements from leading alienists.

A similar antagonism was evident in the trial of Edwin Bates in the same year for attempting to extort money from the Prince Consort. Bates stated in his own defence that he was insane, but the sessional court declined to hear medical evidence, found him guilty and bound him over.

It did not help the acceptance of medical evidence when the crimes utilising it were extremely violent and physically revolting. Such crimes understandably provoked a revengeful attitude. Maudsley and his colleague Lockhart Robertson cited Burton's trial at Maidstone in 1863 as a case in which vengeance had overriden justice. They claimed that Burton illustrated 'a moral insanity in which the crime was *logically* traceable to disease'.[9] By contrast, Mr Justice Wightman expressed a gut reaction that Burton's crime was a repellent evil.

'The case was very simple, but very shocking.' The prisoner said that he had felt 'an impulse to kill some one;' that he had sharpened his knife for the purpose, and went out to find somebody on whom he should use it; that he followed a boy, who was the first person he saw, to a convenient place; there he knocked him down, stuck him in the neck and throat, knelt upon his belly, grasped him by the neck and squeezed till the blood came from his nose and mouth, then trampled upon his face and neck until he was dead. He then washed his hands, and went quietly to a job which he had obtained. He knew the boy whom he had murdered, and had no ill-feeling against him, 'only I had made up my mind to murder somebody;' he wished to be hanged. His counsel argued that this vehement desire to be hanged was the strongest proof of insanity; the counsel for the prosecution urged that the fact of the prisoner committing the murder to be hanged showed that he knew the consequences of his act, and that to say he was insane was to confound depravity with insanity. He was found guilty; and Mr. Justice Wightman, in passing sentence, informed him that he had been 'guilty of a more barbarous and inhuman murder than any which has come under my cognizance during a judicial experience of upwards of twenty years.' Indeed, the murder was so cruel, that in the tenderness of his heart the Judge 'could not trust himself to dwell upon its shocking details.' When sentence had been passed, the prisoner said, with a smile, 'Thank you, my lord,' and went 'down the dock, followed by an audible murmur and almost a cry of horror from a densely-crowded audience.' That cry was, perhaps, an unconscious testimony that the theory of moral depravity did not quite suffice to explain Burton's case. His hereditary antecedents, his previous history, the motive with which he committed the murder, the desperate way in which the act was done, his conduct immediately after the murder, the readiness with which he told all about it, and his behaviour during the trial and after the sentence, – all pointed, as definitely as circumstances could point, to insanity and not depravity.[10]

The insanity specialists were clear that it was disease, the court that it was depravity. The 'logical' connection which Maudsley and Robertson saw between the disease and the act consisted of evidence of Burton's habitual strange conduct and the insanity of his mother and brother. The conclusion that Burton was insane followed only if one accepted physical disease as his inheritance. They were advancing a way of seeing rather than deducing the crime's necessary relation to the disease.

The verdict indicated that the court did not accept their way of seeing. Wightman distinguished between a morbid mind and delusion: '[Burton] was supposed to desire to be hanged, and in order to attain the object committed murder. That might show a morbid state of mind, but not delusion.'[11] Alienists deplored this because it ignored the fact that a morbid state of mind indicated physical disease. But the judge's remarks made sense within the discourse of depravity, where a morbid mind had its own factual existence. Maudsley and Robertson attempted to explain Burton's outrage, not in terms of psychological elements, but in terms of physical ones. An inherited abnormal physical constitution supplied 'reasons' for conduct which everyday psychology found senseless. But their argument missed the central point of the gut reaction: that evil *was* a sufficient reason for the crime.

Maudsley argued that heredity explained another case of brutal and unpremeditated murder. A man known only as the Alton murderer made an entry in his diary which read: 'Killed a little girl; it was fine and hot.' While he was a known eccentric and subject to fits of depression, the principal defence evidence was 'it was proved that his father had had an attack of acute mania, and that another near relative was in confinement, suffering from homicidal mania'.[12] As at Burton's trial, the jury did not accept this. According to Maudsley, however, 'the course of the hereditary disease downwards to its desperate evolution was traceable'.[13] He reached this conclusion from two directions: from the specific evidence, and from his theory which defined such conduct as degenerate and treated degeneracy as a theory of inheritance. 'The hereditary predisposition to insanity implies an innate disposition in the individual to act out of harmony with his relations as a social being: the acquired irregularity of the parent has become the natural infirmity of the offspring.'[14]

Laycock appeared as an expert defence witness in a trial with similar characteristics at the High Court in Edinburgh in 1864. George Bryce was not recognisable as the same person in Laycock's and the *British Medical Journal*'s accounts.[15] Laycock described Bryce as a congenitally weak individual who had been cared for at home (a practice receiving greater encouragement under the Scottish management system). He claimed that Bryce's mental weakness was the product of a brain disease visible in facial asymmetry and in imperfect skull development. 'This wasting corresponded to some internal brain defect . . . the nature of which a careful examination of the brain after death might have revealed.'[16] He speculated that the crime (cutting a maid's throat) was followed by loss of memory 'such as is so characteristic of the homicidal delirium of epileptics'. He maintained that this was supported by Bryce's somnambulistic expression and statement that he did not remember what he had done.[17]

The *British Medical Journal* correspondent, on the other hand, described a passionate and depraved individual, over-indulgent with drink, who murdered a girl when she thwarted his advances, and who later admitted the justice of his conviction and the fraudulence of his memory loss.

> The public saw in the case of Bryce the ordinary chain of circumstances revealed in trials for murder. A man of degraded mind, given to vicious habits, of an uncontrollable temper, suspects, from certain circumstances, that he is the object of the ill-will of another person; and, after meditating over his crime for some time, he carries it into effect.[18]

The latter discourse prevailed at the trial; medical witnesses called by the prosecution rebutted Laycock's diagnosis. This damaged the medical viewpoint as a whole, since its claim to objective validity was in public disarray. In any case, the judge remarked that the jury was not faced by a medical question since it had to determine responsibility and not illness.

> The medical gentlemen have opportunities of observation which make their testimony frequently very important in reference to such matters; but the question is not a medical question; it is a question

of fact whether the insanity amounted to this, that he was doing a thing which he himself considered, and had grounds to believe, and respecting which his belief was a sincere one, that he was warranted in doing.[19]

This defined the question within legal discourse; the jury had to decide between depravity and exculpation ('insanity'). When the judge then stated that calling something a 'paroxysm of monomania' provided no grounds for an acquittal, he completed the dismissal of the medical discourse. Laycock was partly right in attributing the failure to apply scientific knowledge of insanity to 'the influence on public opinion of ancient, deeply-rooted, and barren systems of philosophy'.[20] Different philosophies of mind were indeed the counterparts of opposed social interests.

Whereas it was accepted as legitimate practice to identify depravity through a depraved act, insanity was expected to be identified through evidence of conduct or delusion apart from the act. Dominant social values do not require justification. The onus of proof, when a change is proposed, lies with the innovation. Insanity specialists hoped that this proof would emerge through life histories revealing the course of disease. Disagreement among medical witnesses, however, demonstrated the extreme difficulty of determining 'how far the criminal's will has been impaired or destroyed by disease'.[21] Thus the alienists' viewpoint prevailed only when other factors persuaded juries to entertain medical language in the first place.

The process of locating depravity, and the disturbing medical proposal to reclassify some examples of it as moral insanity, can be seen in three controversial trials involving murder of woman friend, fiancée or wife. When James Atkinson was tried at York in 1858 and the infamous George Victor Townley was tried at Derby in 1863, there were obvious grounds for accepting jealousy as the motive, and depravity as the means. Sheer depravity seemed equally obvious in William Dove's slow poisoning of his wife in 1856. Yet the insanity plea was argued in all three cases and in Atkinson's, successfully. Alienists disagreed among themselves in all three cases, while critics described the insanity defence as a means of escape for murderers. Medical expertise was perceived as biased, evaluative and inconsistent – precisely those qualities which its scientific grounding was supposed to have eliminated.

Atkinson was a twenty-four-year-old mill overseer who killed a woman after she had aroused his jealousy. At the opening of his trial he refused to plead or showed insufficient comprehension to plead. The court decided he was 'mute of malice' and recorded a plea on his behalf. The prosecution case was straightforward; it emphasised the role a motive of jealousy might play in a habitually self-indulgent person. The defence called four medical witnesses, Dr Williams and Mr John Kitching from The

Retreat (both played a successful part in establishing homicidal mania in
Hill's earlier case), Dr North, and the ardent campaigner, Dr Winslow.
Counsel used their evidence to try to establish that Atkinson was a 'moral
imbecile': violent, anti-social and unreformable from early childhood,
peculiar in behaviour at the time of the crime, genuinely stupid at the
time of the trial, and probably influenced by deleterious hereditary
factors. Frustrated by this battery of assertion when depravity seemed
perfectly obvious, the prosecution called the doctors 'hired advocates',
attacking in one loaded phrase the whole basis of their evidence in science.
Nevertheless, the jury reached an insanity verdict, for which critics
found the alienists responsible.

This trial had repercussions that were deeply regretted by other
alienists because the specialism as a whole was discredited. Atkinson was
sent to Bethlem where Dr Hood wrote in his case notes, 'It is quite
impossible to understand the medical evidence given at his trial, in
favour of his being of unsound mind.' [22] The key issue was whether selfish
wilfulness could be translated into Kitching's statement that 'his animal
instincts have greatly developed and are beyond his control' or Williams's
that 'during a sudden outburst of passion . . . he would have no power to
appreciate the nature and quality of an act'.[23] Hood had occasion in 1860
to write to the Chairman of the Commissioners in Lunacy setting out the
number of patients committed to Bethlem. With Atkinson one of the
cases in point, he stated that several of the criminal patients showed no
sign of insanity. This statement confirmed the view that the insanity
defence was an 'escape' for criminals and therefore a danger to society.

> These words we heard quoted in the House of Commons by a dis-
> tinguished member, and quoted amidst approbation, as convincing
> evidence of the absurdity of medical theories with regard to insanity,
> and as constituting a fatal objection to the establishment of a medical
> commission for the purpose of ascertaining the state of a prisoner's
> mind, when insanity was pleaded.[24]

Medical statements at Atkinson's trial were difficult to substantiate.
Letters written by him were produced at the trial to show that he was
capable of both intelligence and moral feeling and that his insanity was
feigned. The defence argued that they were actually written by a
Wesleyan minister. Nevertheless, they were later published in the
Journal of Mental Science, perhaps reflecting disagreement within the
specialism.[25]

Though the insanity defence was successful in the one case, it reinforced opposition in general. It particularly damaged the proposal to
establish a specialist panel of alienists as an instrument of the court.
Alienists not involved with the trial tried to dissociate themselves from it.
'We protest most earnestly against its being supposed that the medical
profession, or the medico-psychological speciality, is entirely incapable

of rising from the narrow view of the individual as a subject of medical science to the larger view of him as an element in a social system, – of the man as a citizen, and of the relations of his crime to society.'[26] These issues were exacerbated by Townley's more famous case. Both trials produced disagreement, not just between alienists and the wider medical profession but between alienists themselves. They revealed different strategies for establishing the same goal. Medico-psychologists such as Laycock, Conolly and Winslow believed in a direct confrontation, arguing for insanity even in those cases least likely to gain public sympathy. Possibly this strategy accompanied strongly held evangelical or moral reformist attitudes towards social problems in general. But the majority of alienists, including Hood, Bucknill and Maudsley, worked tangentially – through the influence of the Commissioners in Lunacy and through acceptance by established general medical bodies. They were embarrassed by the public excesses of their more over-enthusiastic colleagues.

It is possible that the insanity specialism had existed long enough by the 1860s for these disputes to be a help rather than a hindrance in furthering professional goals: they led to the discrediting and isolation of the more uncompromising reformers. The dominant group identifying itself with existing reform procedures was then better able to establish itself. The Commissioners in Lunacy and the Medical Superintendent of Broadmoor secured a position of influence within the civil service for this latter group, while Maudsley achieved his own pre-eminence at London University and the Royal College of Physicians.

Townley's trial exposed these differences, as well as the weaknesses of knowledge and practice within the specialism, and it did so in a way which aroused parliamentary interest. When Townley's fiancée, Miss Goodwin, asked to be released from a three-year engagement in order to marry another man, he persuaded her to meet him for a final time and then stabbed her to death. He did nothing to hide the crime, saying: 'She has deceived me; and the woman that deceives me must die. I told her I would kill her. She knew my temper ... I am far happier now I have done it than I was before, and I trust she is.'[27] Townley's defence was that by the 'mysterious dispensation of Providence he had been deprived of his reason', in spite of his manifest motive.[28] This defence rested on two supports: the presence of insanity in his family suggesting an inherited disposition which linked with his own excitability and excess of temper; and Winslow's evidence that he was morally insane. Mr Baron Martin directed the jury in terms of the Rules and they returned a guilty verdict within five minutes. There was a general presumption that, in a specially abhorrent case, justice had been done.

Though the judge believed the conviction correct, he wrote to Sir George Grey, the Home Secretary, that medical opinion considered Townley 'absolutely insane' at the time of the trial (three months after the murder). Grey then asked the Commissioners in Lunacy to inquire into Townley's condition. The Commissioners found him both justly convicted and insane.

> 'We think that, applying the law as laid down by Mr. Baron Martin to this case, the prisoner, George Victor Townley, was justly convicted.'

> Having thus answered Sir George Grey's inquiry, they proceeded to say that, 'in view of the extravagant opinions deliberately professed by him, of his extraordinarily perverted moral sense, and of the hereditary taint alleged and apparently proved to have existed in the family of the prisoner's grandmother, we cannot consider him to be of sound mind.'

They believed that Townley had taken 'a disordered and morbid view of an actual occurrence' (rejection by his fiancée and her relatives) which did not, however, exonerate him from responsibility.[29] Meanwhile, Grey received a certificate of Townley's insanity signed by two justices and two medical men, which led him (under the 1840 Insane Prisoners Act) to respite Townley's sentence and to remove him to Bethlem. This was not popular. 'Immediately there arose a great outcry throughout the land; a miscarriage of justice was attributed to the influence of money' since the certificate 'had not, like all previous inquiries of the kind, originated with the authorities of the gaol, but had been promoted and conducted entirely as a matter of professional business by Townley's legal adviser.' Justice had been thwarted by 'substantially transferring the power of life and death from the Crown to two justices and two medical men, put in motion by the prisoner's solicitor'.[30]

Grey was only administering the law; nevertheless, he appointed another commission to report on Townley's state of mind. This commission found him sane.

> The prisoner endeavoured to represent the catastrophe to us as due to the influence of sudden impulse, but the details which we elicited from him show that he used threats of murder for some time before he struck the first blow. We think that his clear memory of the events attending the crime, and also the attempts which he has made to misrepresent the state of his mind and memory at the time of these events, are evidence of his sanity.[31]

Grey solved the dilemma by commuting the sentence to penal servitude for life, and Townley returned to prison. At the same time, a bill was introduced to amend the 1840 Act.[32] Townley concluded the case by committing suicide.

Townley was found sane enough to be responsible by a jury (the judge concurring), was found insane though responsible in law by one commission, was certified insane by a process which corresponded to normal civil procedure, and was then found sane by a second medical commission.

This was disorderly boundary-drawing with a vengeance. Medical categories which were themselves unconsolidated cut across common-sense ideas of justice. Taylor cited Townley's case as exemplifying, in the public mind, the danger of the insanity plea.[33]

Even where commissions were officially appointed and able to develop their views in a neutral and private context, they still disagreed. This suggests that the popular medical idea of a court-appointed expert commission would not have been the definitive answer that its proponents hoped. It confirms that something other than legal procedure inhibited the expansion of the medical viewpoint. This lay within the confrontation between discourses.

A closer look at the language used to describe Townley supports this. Winslow based his opinion of Townley on three grounds: that he was suffering from a delusion of conspiracy against him, that he had perverted notions about his fiancée being his property, and that he was morally insane. The theory of insane delusion was rather weak because there was good reason to believe that the murdered woman's relatives had consistently opposed the marriage. Maudsley and Robertson, when they reviewed the case in order to dissociate the main body of alienists from Winslow's opinion, claimed that Winslow had been duped by Townley. 'It is to be regretted, therefore, that the unreliable evidence, so positively given, of a delusion which never existed, does seriously invalidate the rest of the medical evidence of Townley's insanity.'[34] This other medical evidence concerned possible insanity in remote relatives, habitual indulgence of his passion, and a history of anger and violence out of all proportion to the cause. Winslow was also reported as saying that Townley 'does not appear to have a sane opinion on a moral point . . . His moral sense was more vitiated than I ever found that of any other human being. His opinions were pretty much those of atheists, but he was beyond atheism. He seemed incapable of reasoning correctly on any moral subject.'[35] Winslow concluded that Townley was morally insane, thereby stating that medicine did not intend to call a complete absence of moral reasoning and conduct by its familiar name. This was consistent with his thesis that the behaviour of some of the great tyrants could be explained by insanity.

The implications of Winslow's argument were not lost. The *Saturday Review* commented: 'What the defence seems to come to is this: – That the greater rogue a man is, the more entirely is he free from responsibility. To do him only justice, Dr. Forbes Winslow went in his evidence one step further than the usual advocates of the plea of moral insanity, but it was a logical step.'[36] Winslow's 'logical step' took him from the claim that moral sentiments and conduct were subject to illness to the wider idea that depravity was illness. The *Saturday Review* rejected this approach as totally incompatible with ethics. Moral sentiment and conduct could not, by definition, be described in determinist language. Winslow's medical critics were equally committed to a pathology which reduced people to machines. But to retain public credibility they divorced this from the 'logical step' which Winslow took. They did this by implying that Winslow was a bad doctor because he drew conclusions which were *empirically* unsound. The error was located in one practitioner's observations, not in the structure of scientific medicine. Alienists were left nonetheless with an unresolved boundary problem where depravity and moral insanity overlapped.

Medicine's theoretical incoherence was dragged into public view by Baron Bramwell at William Dove's trial at York. As Dove had murdered his wife slowly with small doses of strychnine, the case was complicated by a debate, involving medical experts, over the symptoms and effect of the poison.[37] The prosecution evidence concerned the bad relations between husband and wife, Dove's procuring of the poison, and his reference to its effects and the course of his wife's 'illness'. Defence counsel tried to play this evidence down, but 'the substantial defence which gives the case its interest was, that the act was either not wilful or not malicious; and the evidence of this was, that Dove was insane, and was thus either prevented by mental disease from knowing that the act was wrong, or constrained by an irresistible impulse to do it'.[38]

The evidence in support of this plea concerned Dove's biography rather than the circumstances of the crime. He was reputed to be restless, difficult, irrationally violent, and sometimes physically dangerous. His conversation and conduct were often incoherent and extravagant; while in gaol he wrote a letter to the devil in his own blood.

> Dear Devil, – If you will get me clear at the assizes, and let me have the enjoyment of health, wealth, tobacco, beer, more food and better, and my wishes granted – life till I am sixty – come to me to-night and tell me.
>
> I remain your faithful servant,
> William Dove.[39]

This letter and his deference to a local wizard encouraged a suspicion that he was simulating insanity. But medical evidence stated that he had been morally insane from birth: he suffered from a 'perverted state of the moral feelings from infancy' and showed a 'general inability to comprehend or take his share in transacting the common affairs of life'.[40] Above all, moral discipline had had no effect. But, as Bucknill pointed out, this evidence applied just as much to 'a wilful, passionate, mischievous and cruel boy' as to moral insanity; there was no change in character to reveal the onset of disease.[41] Defence counsel argued that the life history itself was evidence of insanity prior to and independent of the crime. Medical witnesses admitted under cross-examination that there was every indication that Dove could distinguish right from wrong; they suggested, however, that this knowledge would not have informed his deed. They were therefore in the awkward position of arguing for the 'irresistible' repeated administration of small doses of strychnine.

Dr Williams, the chief defence witness, extricated himself by arguing that Dove suffered from homicidal mania.

[There is] an uncontrollable propensity to destroy, give pain, or take life. The propensity might continue as a permanent condition of the mind. It might select a special object and not injure any body or thing else. I think such a person would not know he was doing wrong. He might fear the consequences of punishment. He would probably know that he was breaking the law. He would not know at the time he did it he would be hanged for murder. I found that opinion on the occupation of the mind by the insane propensity. It is uncertain if he would know it before he did it.[42]

The prosecution defined 'a violent propensity to destroy' as depravity and therefore questioned whether Williams distinguished vice and insanity. Williams's reply wavered between congenital moral insanity and moral insanity following bad habits.

The prisoner's previous history would be required to determine whether it was vice or insanity . . . A man by nourishing an idea may become diseased in his mind, and then he cannot control it. This is moral insanity. It does apply to other cases: it might apply to rape; as if a man nourished the desire to possess a particular woman till the desire became uncontrollable, and then he committed the rape, that would be moral insanity. So of theft. If a man permits himself to contemplate the gratification of any passion or desire till it becomes uncontrollable, that is moral insanity.[43]

His language was badly chosen; one reporter suggested that Williams countenanced all vice if only it were carried on long enough. 'A doctrine more dangerous to society never was uttered in a court of justice. If the jury would support that theory, gone was the security of every hearth in the country. A man was only to be vicious, and to contemplate his crime for a given period, until it became uncontrollable, and then these gentlemen would say it was insanity.'[44] Williams later complained that he had not been allowed to explain what he meant. He *did* draw a line between vice and insanity – at the boundary of mind and body: the mind was inalienable, but when its instrument was disordered, then there was exculpatory insanity.

So long as the material structures of the brain are unaffected, so long the individual who yields to his inclinations and his passions must be considered accountable; but when the material organ of the mind has become affected in consequence of a life of vicious indulgences and depraved habits, then the measure of responsibility becomes proportionally diminished, and in the end he is found amongst the insane.[45]

Physicalism made it possible to separate morally accountable humans and insane machines. Williams could have no knowledge of Dove's diseased brain, but the ideal of physical objectivity gave him the confidence to stand up in court and argue for moral insanity.

The judge's direction to the jury was prejudicial to the alienists' evidence. Bramwell stated that deterrence rather than medical humanitarianism was needed in cases such as this. 'To a man of weak mind and strong animal propensities, the knowledge that the law would not punish him would be to take from him one of the first and most powerful reasons for not repeating his crime.' The jury agreed and found Dove guilty, though it added a recommendation of 'mercy on the ground of defective intellect', a recommendation which was ignored.[46]

Bramwell also expressed irritation at specialist medico-psychological evidence and firmly placed it outside the law.

His Lordship said he now came to one bit of evidence which he had reserved for the last, – evidence of a speculative and scientific character, – evidence which he approached with every respect for the medical profession; but he entirely concurred with the Learned Judge whose opinion had been quoted (Dr. Lushington), that it would be better, instead of listening to these speculative opinions, for the jury to decide upon the facts which were detailed before them. He certainly believed that the jury were as competent to form a correct opinion on matters of this kind as anybody else. In all matters of speculative opinion, they might always cull, from the large body of professors, a number of individuals who would swear up to what was required – not that they swore falsely, but because they held peculiar opinions. They knew this was so with men in all professions – architects and surveyors, as well as medical men.

Mr. BLISS [defence counsel]. – The prosecution might have called medical witnesses in reply.

BARON BRAMWELL. – And Mr. Bliss might have asked any question he pleased respecting the prisoner's alleged insanity from the medical witnesses called by the prosecution.

Mr. BLISS. – But they were not experts in madness, my Lord.

BARON BRAMWELL. – Experts in madness! Mad doctors! Gentlemen, I will read you the evidence of these medical witnesses – these 'experts in madness,' – And if you can make sane evidence out of what they say, do so; but I confess it's more than I can do . . . If the theory of these gentlemen were true of the prisoner, it would be equally true in the case of every criminal, and form a conclusive reason for liberating every person charged with crime. It would be affectation in him to pretend that he did not put a value of his own upon this scientific evidence. He frankly told them that he would rather take his own opinion upon the facts than the evidence of the three medical gentlemen that had been called before them – not that he undervalued these gentlemen, but he would rather exercise his own opinion than be led by the theories of gentlemen who held opinions which were extreme in their profession.[47]

Such remarks denied the relevance of mental pathology to the judicial process; a jury was expected to *know* depravity when it saw it. Further, Bramwell exploited the alienists' painful lack of professional standing.

It appeared to critics as if insanity specialists claimed knowledge which they did not have, manoeuvred for legal influence to which they had no right, and advanced moral judgements which commonsense knew to be wrong and socially damaging. The alienists responded that they were misrepresented on all three counts. As they believed that such misrepresentation proceeded from an ignorance of science, they devoted much effort both to stating the objective and progressive nature of science and to associating themselves with it.

This was much easier in theory than in practice, as the passion aroused in medical circles by the trial of Luigi Buranelli at the Old Bailey in 1855 illustrated. The case disturbed the alienists because Buranelli was hanged (and hanged badly!) after an unsuccessful insanity plea. Worse, the case produced conflicting courtroom evidence from medical specialists: defence witnesses described impulsive insanity, only to be contradicted by prosecution witnesses.

The action of the executive was indeed supported by the opinion of two physicians of reputation, so that it may possibly have been held that the evidence of the skilled witnesses on each side neutralized each other, and thus left the guilt of the accused to be decided upon principles of common sense, unaided by any rays of light shed from the lamp of science.

This trial has presented the painful and humiliating spectacle of mental pathologists differing entirely in their judgment, not only upon the particular question of sanity or insanity of the accused, but also upon the general questions of the nature of illusions and delusions, and the value of these and other phenomena as marks of cerebro-mental disease.[48]

The jury and the Home Secretary (when he considered commutation) were faced by alternative case histories: one of rejection in love and motives for revenge, another of delusion and distress. Buranelli was hanged because it was not clearly shown that at some point responsibility had ceased.

Buranelli was an Italian immigrant with an uneventful life until his wife's death. 'From that time, the prisoner laboured under melancholia and delusions; he became violent and ungovernable, and bent upon suicide.'[49] Evidence of insanity, right up to the time of the murder, was given by his landlady and others who described his wildness and

incoherence. More important, Buranelli had been under medical care for
an anal fistula; medical witnesses described how he magnified its effects
with delusions about urine flowing from the wound and soaking his bed.
He was a man 'who was not to be convinced by any appeal to his senses
or to his reason'.[50] These witnesses did not doubt that Buranelli was disordered of mind.

The crime occurred when Buranelli's mistress, whom he had made
pregnant, broke with him. His behaviour became intolerable and their
landlord insisted that he leave the house. Buranelli later returned with
pistols, shot dead the landlord, and rushed upstairs with the apparent
intention of shooting his mistress and then himself. After arrest, he continued to exhibit signs of melancholy, delusion and incoherence. It was
easy, however, to reconstruct a psychological state leading up to the crime
in a way which emphasised normal motives and consciousness of the
nature of the act. He had quarrelled with the man he killed and with the
woman he tried to kill. The jury therefore had grounds for linking crime
and responsibility.

The prosecution was further supported by two medical witnesses, Dr
Mayo and Dr Sutherland, both of whom had interviewed Buranelli on
the day before the trial. Neither found insanity and both sought to
minimise Buranelli's disorder by calling his delusions 'illusions', implying
that there was an objective basis for his perceptions (for example, that his
anal wound suppurated). The surgeon from the gaol where Buranelli
awaited trial held the same view.

Mayo was prepared to carry his general criticism of the insanity plea
into practice. He interpreted hypochondriacal illusions as evidence for
weakness of mind and also, for weakness of character, which was precisely why a deterrent law was needed. Mayo came before the court as a
leading expert on mental pathology. That he did so revealed the divisions
among the medical practitioners: Mayo's expert standing and his
opinions were attacked in *The Lancet*, a journal well known for its
antagonism to the Royal College of Physicians. 'Dr. Thomas Mayo came
forward to propound, not evidence, but metaphysical speculations; and
to apply to a living fellow-creature his famous doctrines of abstract mental
disease, of insane responsibility, and the propriety of making madmen the
subjects of criminal punishment.'[51] Mayo referred to his recent Croonian
Lectures as proof of medical prestige; yet alienists considered these
lectures proof that Mayo was both out of touch with the new scientific
approach and opposed to the new humanitarianism. *The Lancet* contrasted Mayo's and Sutherland's 'senseless anachronism' with 'the
current teaching of all those who have a right to the title of scientific and
practical psychologists'.[52] Conolly, the most famous doctor called by the
defence, was singled out for praise; his work symbolised modern
qualities of humanity, institutional care, and scientific knowledge. 'We

shall show that the testimony for the prosecution, in its theoretical or scientific aspect, was opposed to the physiology and pathology of the age; in so far as facts were concerned, utterly irrelevant; and that to apply it to the case before the jury was a violent and monstrous outrage upon decency and truth.'[53] Mayo, the jury, and the Home Secretary were therefore ignorant and vindictive in rejecting Conolly's evidence and the written statement of Buranelli's insanity signed by Conolly and four other specialists. Buranelli was a *cause célèbre* for the politics of science and humanitarianism.

> The execution of Buranelli will, we fear, be a foul stain and a 'damned spot' upon the humanity and intelligence of the nineteenth century, and will, we apprehend, do an incalculable amount of injury to the advancement of the science of medico-legal testimony in cases of alleged lunacy, and seriously retard the progress of British Medical Psychology . . .
>
> It has been our pride and pleasure to be engaged in such a work of LOVE and MERCY, and have ever estimed it a noble privilege to stand forward as advocates in so holy and righteous a cause.[54]

Buranelli's medical witnesses argued that his change of character was not self-caused and that his delusions and abnormal conduct were grounds for finding insanity. Such evidence on other occasions served the defence well; in this case prestigious physicians joined laymen in rejecting these grounds because they found a commonsense language of immorality adequate. Only someone predisposed to entertain the new mental physiology could accept that Buranelli's, Dove's, or Townley's murders were uncontrollable. As Prichard had earlier observed: 'The discrimination between effects of animal instinct, perverted by disease, and actions referable to the last degree of moral turpitude, cannot be aided by any general rules.'[55] Rather, this 'discrimination' depended on the discourse and on the power to apply it.

The mutually exclusive categories of depravity and insanity created a degree of incoherence within the law. This is strikingly illustrated by Charles Westron's verdict in 1856. Westron murdered his solicitor, Mr Waugh, in broad daylight on a respectable London street. It was a particularly offensive murder since Waugh had shown kindness and patience in relation to Westron's financial affairs. Westron was deformed from birth with spinal curvature; symptoms of insanity had also been present for some time, with a suggestion of hereditary disposition. Reconciling Westron's mental weakness with retributive justice perplexed the jury. It was 'bewildered by the test of guilt submitted to them: they appear to have considered the man insane, but that his insanity had not reached the legal standard of an absence of knowledge of right and wrong'.[56] The contradictory verdict, when it came, was greeted by laughter from the public gallery. 'We find the prisoner guilty of wilful murder; we do not think he ought to be acquitted on the ground of insanity, but we recommend him to mercy because in his case we find there were strong predispositions to insanity.'[57] *The Times* declared that 'nothing can be a greater mockery of all the solemnities of justice than the conclusion of this trial'.[58] The confusion was caused less by the jury than by the ordering imposed on social reality. Given existing ways of thinking, the jury was dealing with conduct of marginal intelligibility. While Westron showed symptoms of insanity, he also shot Waugh out of revenge for supposed injuries. Mr Justice Wightman acknowledged the difficulty by exercising his power to record rather than to pronounce the death sentence. 'The jury had come to the conclusion that although he might be insane on some points, yet that he knew right from wrong, and they recommended him to mercy. Under these circumstances, he should abstain from passing sentence, and merely order judgment of death to be recorded.'[59]

The marginality of Westron's crime was emphasised by other aspects of the case. He was committed to the Millbank prison, an example both of the law's mercy and of its function to deter 'idle habits and ill-regulated minds'.[60] The compromise followed from the inability to determine how far responsibility decreased through heredity and indulgence. Scientific theories emphasised the continuity of uncontrolled and uncontrollable habits; the law tried to separate them again. Once at Millbank, however, Westron's mental unsoundness became more apparent, and he was transferred on a Home Secretary's warrant to Bethlem, where he died of apoplexy.

The deep-seated antagonism between legal and medical positions surfaced again when Charles Fooks was tried for a vicious murder at Dorchester in 1863. He was found guilty and hanged in spite of an extensive history of mental weakness and delusions of persecution. Alienists particularly objected to the court's denial that his delusions were connected with an incapacity to control his conduct. As Maudsley and Robertson commented: 'Under this dictum it would be necessary to hang nine-tenths of the lunatics in England, in the event of their committing murder.'[61] The *Journal of Mental Science* stated:

> It is the old foolish story, that if a man has insane delusions, and yet if at the time of the act he knew the nature of the act and its consequences, he is guilty. The presiding judge only laid down, we admit, the law, and on the law the lunatic was convicted. It is against the dangerous ignorance of morbid mental conditions which the law thus evinces that we desire again to record our protest. A monomaniac with perverted emotions and homicidal tendencies cannot, says science, control his conduct, and cannot therefore be held responsible for his acts. The law says he can and shall be. The issue lies thus in a few words.[62]

For Fooks to be excused in law, it was necessary to demonstrate that his delusion left him unable to know the nature of his deed. Alienists stressed that diseases did not necessarily affect such knowledge, but they did necessarily affect the controlling faculties. The law searched for a scientifically unsound 'connection between, not the disease and the act, but the delusion and the act'.[63] It required jurors to assume the defendant's responsibility unless they could trace a *logical* connection – not a *disease* connection – between the delusion and an inability to tell right from wrong.

> And what is it which the law really demands ? That the sane and logical mind should dive into the dark wasteful depths of the lunatic's soul, and follow the incoherencies of his wild and wayward thoughts. And if the sound mind should fail in tracing out a connection where no path is, then the lunatic is to be sacrificed to the vengeance of the law which *not he, but his disease,* has outraged.[64]

This was an important point. The image of disease as an outside disruption of reason and control, with the lunatic a passive subject, summarised medical logic. The separation between person and disease was not a metaphorical but a literal representation of a world divided between rational egos and automatons. From the alienist viewpoint, the courts were arrogantly assuming that the real world could be made to conform to legal reason. This criticism took for granted a naturalist theory of knowledge. The law, by contrast, presupposed idealist categories which rendered reality comprehensible by reason. The limitations of naturalism were evident in alienism's incoherence about the mind-body relation. The limitations of idealism were shown in rigid classification of protean phenomena.

These philosophies were not remote from practice. The genuineness of Fooks's delusions was vouched for by an expert called in from London. Under cross-examination Dr Harrington Tuke described a link between the delusion and the uncontrollable impulse to murder. However, the question he was actually asked concerned a link between the delusion and knowledge of the crime.

> *The Judge.* – From what you have heard of this case and seen, can you, as a professional man, with due regard to the solemnity of your oath, say that, in your opinion, at the time he fired that gun, he did not know that what he was doing was wrong ?
> *Witness.* – I have the greatest difficulty in answering that question. He certainly knows it is wrong now. But, on my oath, whether he then knew it to be right or wrong or not, he was under an uncontrollable impulse.[65]

The judge used the idealist language of knowledge while the alienist used the mechanist language of causation. This linguistic division reappeared when the court debated the value of science and commonsense. The gaol surgeon rebutted expert evidence, claiming on the ground of common-sense that Fooks was sane when he committed the murder.

Q. Did you see anything that would indicate insanity ? A. Never.

Q. Have you ever discovered he suffered under any delusion ? A. No.

Cross-examined by Mr. Coleridge [defence counsel]. – I have not read Esquirol or Pritchard, but I have Taylor. My principal study of mania has not been obtained from books, but from common sense. Q. How far do you push common sense ? A. When you converse with a man I do not think much professional skill is required. In the course of a long conversation you might arrive at the truth. Q. Have you made a prolonged investigation into the state of his mind ? A. Yes; as far as my abilities would allow. Q. What made you enter upon that ? A. Public rumour. I had heard there was supposed to be something wrong about him. Q. How did you proceed? A. By watching narrowly and talking of his daily routine of life.[66]

Prosecution and defence counsel continued to wrangle over the merits of medical expertise (Esquirol and Prichard) and medical commonsense (Taylor's *Medical Jurisprudence* and informal observation). But the law's structure ensured that the latter prevailed. As Mr Sergeant Shee directed the jury: 'You are not to be deprived of the exercise of your common sense because a gentleman comes from London and tells you scientific sense.'[67]

Commonsense and scientific sense: the judge's summary was more apt than he probably realised. In assuming that legal procedure enabled commonsense to have a voice he revealed how socially constructed knowledge was reinforced. By stating that the court's decision need not reflect scientific sense, he denied the universalist claims for that sense, thereby assigning it a place as socially constructed knowledge. Mental physiologists and medical psychologists could not possibly accept such a view. With some justification, derived both from limited descriptive clinical successes and the social role which society had legislated for them, they looked forward to the triumph of science. It was not, however, a successful strategy to try and make the murder trial the vehicle for their triumph. The scientific discourse was at its least convincing in relation to individual depravity.

CHAPTER SEVEN

MEDICO-LEGAL VIEWS OF WOMEN

1 *Femaleness and Infanticide*

As with criminals generally, the majority of criminal lunatics were men. The most controversial – Oxford, M'Naghten, Buranelli, Townley – were men. Occasionally women were at the centre of attention, but there are reasons for dealing with them separately: first, because of their association with infanticide, second, because recent feminist historiography creates a new sensitivity to such issues. The degree to which it is valid to distinguish women is an important aspect of medico-legal debate.

Both major theoretical elements in nineteenth-century medical discourse, clinical nosology and physical aetiology, were significant in discussions of female insanity. Put very generally, conceptions of women's social position were integrated with naturalistic description of disease types and determinist explanatory schemes. It was relatively easy to objectify women as part of physical nature. Further, this facility was present within both medical discourse and lay thought systems, creating the possibility of some medico-legal consensus.

The argument is not that true or false scientific knowledge was misused to support the repression of women. Rather, woman and nature were terms with a degree of interchangeability in their meaning. It would be too mechanistic to think in terms of 'influences' (in one or both directions) between knowledge and practice. Nineteenth-century medical statements of woman's passive nature abounded; such statements also implied woman's intellectual, cultural and economic dependence on man. Natural passivity and cultural dependence were not separately definable. Cultural values entered into the accounts of woman's nature which were then taken to define cultural possibility.[1]

Feminist orientations involve the rethinking of a great deal of medical history. There are new studies of the establishment of male medical dominance over midwifery and gynaecology, medical antagonism to the increase in birth control during the nineteenth century, and opposition to medical education for women. In addition, there is new interest in women's diseases and in the medical element in family relationships as microcosms of society. It is relevant here to extract one general point from this extensive literature: the network of correspondences between woman, nature, passivity, emotion, and irresponsibility. These correspondences did not exist in themselves but in a socially contingent contrast to man, culture, activity, intellect, and responsibility.[2] Much nineteenth-century medical writing, however, discussed such polarities in terms of autonomous existence. In particular, medical men identified women as natural objects and therefore described them with all the objective standing associated with science. But because their account of femaleness was itself a cultural product, they merely restated the terms of woman's existing position. This was strikingly apparent in medico-legal debate.

Medical writing centred on reproduction, the social and biological function which was considered both the strength and weakness of femaleness. Women gave life, but at the cost of menstruation, emotional dependency, nervous weakness, and a world view restricted to the family. These strengths and weaknesses were ethical as well as biological: through the family, women transmitted moral feeling and improvement, but the larger plan was liable to be swept aside by narrow emotion. Medical practitioners shared this evaluative view of nature; they perceived an inseparable scientific and social duty to inform and guide their patients and the general public. In their view, they occupied a professional position at the heart (literally and metaphorically) of the social order. The description of female biology, character, diseases, and care made medicine a central resource in the political mediation between the individual and society.[3] This related to jurisprudence through the concept of responsibility; medical men were deeply engaged in exploring the mutual responsibilities of women and society. They were society's delegates in this task.

These responsibilities had specific medico-legal content in relation to infanticide and to puerperal insanity, which were often linked. Infanticide focused several medical concerns regarding motherhood and the family, while puerperal insanity (insanity following childbirth) was a model for the alienist view of a potentially dangerous insanity.

On the face of it, infanticide was the antithesis of nature: a mother's perverse rejection of her natural function would seem an outrage calling for the strongest possible retribution. Though an element of this was present, Victorians also felt that infanticidal women should be objects of mercy. Lay and medical discourse coincided to render women – especially in activities connected with reproduction – lacking in responsibility. The coincidence can be explained by the manner in which social assumptions entered into the medical discourse. But the willingness to excuse women is remarkable, especially as infanticide was thought to be widespread throughout the century; and further, it was a crime which drew horrified attention to itself. For a period on either side of 1860, a small number of activists created a stir not just about its prevalence but its growth. Nevertheless, their evidence failed to arouse a concerted social response to punish infanticidal women – for either retribution or deterrence. 'And indeed it is unhappily true that, from whatever cause it may have arisen, infanticide is not looked upon in the same light as other murders by the public generally ... There is no crime that meets with so much sympathy, often of the most ill-judged kind.'[4] Infanticide continued, bound up with the working-class experience of poverty, illegitimacy, abortion, wet-nursing, and child-minding ('baby-farms').[5] It was probably most common with illegitimate children, and in these cases there was a continuous gradation between killing and abandonment or neglect.

Infanticide came into separate legal existence only in 1922 (the Infanticide Act, amended 1938). Throughout the nineteenth century, the term referred to mothers killing their children of variable age, though usually still babies. This was technically murder, though in most discussions it was treated as a separate category. The harsh seventeenth-century law of concealment of bastard births, which placed onus of proof on the mother to show murder had not occurred, was changed in 1803. Infanticide was treated like any other murder once it was shown that the child had been born alive. But, if the court acquitted, it then had the power to treat this as a conviction for concealment. This applied only to bastard children, and there was no separate charge for concealment. In 1828 concealment became a separate charge and it became necessary to show in such cases whether the child died before or after birth. A move towards deterrence was apparent in 1861 when it was made a mis-demeanour for any person (not just the mother) to conceal a birth, whether the baby was born dead or alive.[6] At the same time the provision continued which allowed for the jury, on acquitting a woman of murder-ing her child, to find concealment of birth as if that had been the original indictment. Concealment carried a maximum sentence of two years imprisonment, and one year was cited as normal.[7]

The 1803 Act had been introduced in an attempt to obtain convictions of mothers; eighteenth-century juries were unwilling to find mothers guilty of concealment since this was punishable by death.[8] In the nine-teenth century it was still widely believed that the law was incapable of securing convictions for murdering children at birth. One writer assumed that 'little comment will then be called for on our part to show that these laws are virtually inoperative'.[9] Nevertheless, between 1849 and 1864 there were thirty-nine convictions for child murder by mothers, thirty-four of which were of illegitimate children and most a few days to a few weeks old.[10] Juries were prepared to convict some women, given clear evidence, though they were able to add a rider recommending mercy.

It is difficult to interpret the incidence of babies being destroyed at birth. First, many births and deaths happened either in isolation or in company which had a positive incentive not to record events. Second, where such murders were brought to the authority's attention, the lesser charge of concealment of birth was often brought or no notice taken at all. Third, accusations of killing the baby at birth were not always well founded; the conditions of confinement might well have caused the baby to be still-born or to die shortly after birth.[11] This was possible even when controverted by contemporary medical opinion; various illnesses and what is now called the 'sudden unexpected death syndrome' may have intervened. The line between murder and the baby not having lived independently must have been extremely fine, especially in conditions of gross poverty and undernourishment.

Jurists were conscious of this gradation, not out of interest in the circumstances of illegitimate births, but because of the different degrees of mental accountability which such circumstances implied. By the nineteenth century it was conceded that the benefit of doubt must go to the accused and that a conviction should follow only after clear evidence of an intention to murder. The Scottish legal authority Archibald Alison gave this account of unmarried mothers:

> Their distress of mind and body deprives them of all judgment, and they are delivered by themselves ... and sometimes destroying their offspring without being conscious of what they are doing. Accordingly it is a principle of law, that mere appearances of violence on the child's body are not *per se* sufficient, unless some circumstances of evidence exist to indicate that the violence was knowingly and intentionally committed; or they are of such a kind as themselves to indicate intentional murder.[12]

By the 1860s and 1870s parliament was arguing along similar lines that infanticide should not be a capital offence, even if the killing was deliberate.[13] Jurists admitted that the law concerning death at birth was unclear but, though legislation was tinkered with, there was no concerted effort to clarify it during the century. This suggests that vagueness had social advantages: it gave latitude for dealing with a crime which was formally murder, and needed deterrence as murder, but which everyone agreed should not actually be treated as murder. The law was indecisive in both practice and theory. It was difficult to prove that a crime had taken place (the defendant not being allowed to incriminate herself) and to define birth (before or after the separation of the cord; or before or after the first breath). Killing the child before 'birth', even if delivered, was not technically murder.[14] Baron Bramwell summarised the judicial view:

> Under the present contrivance, if I may venture so to call it, or practice of the law, the mother is never found guilty in what is undoubtedly a case of infanticide, the reason being, that if nobody is present who can be called as a witness (and nobody ever is present, except a person who will screen himself or herself upon the ground that the answer would criminate him or her) there is always a possibility that the fatal injury to the child may have taken place before the child was thoroughly separated from the mother's person, and in that case it is not the subject of the crime of murder. I will not

say whether it is a right condition of things that the jury should always be told as they always are, 'There is a possibility of this child not having been born alive, and, therefore, though you have medical evidence to show that it breathed, and although you have evidence to show that it was improbable that the mother could have inflicted such an injury as it died of during parturition, yet, inasmuch as there is a possibility of it,' – which the medical witnesses never will negative, – 'therefore you must acquit her of infanticide.'[15]

The cumulative effect was a legally exculpatory attitude towards infanticidal women. A blind eye was turned in the first place, a charge of concealment of birth was brought in the second, the criminal law gave women benefit of doubt about moment of birth in the third, and the Home Secretary ensured finally that women were not hanged. There was also an alternative strategy, to plead insanity during the criminal trial.

This filtering process left few women to face a capital sentence for murdering their children. The last hanging of a woman for killing her child occurred in 1849. Even this case (Rebecca Smith) was considered somewhat unusual at the time. That the sentence was carried out was owing to the coincidence of three factors: a strong suspicion that more than one child had been killed over a period of time; the use of poison, a method which implied intention; and local opinion favouring retribution. As Sir George Grey's evidence to the 1864 Royal Commission on Capital Punishment emphasised, Home Secretaries were aware that public opinion would not countenance hanging for infanticide. 'I do not think that it would be possible for any one, consistently with public opinion, which must have a great influence in these matters, to carry the sentence in these cases into effect; and that, I believe, is the opinion of almost every person who tries them.'[16]

The separation of infanticide from murder was suggested for three interrelated reasons: first, to remove vagueness and inconsistency from the law; second, to achieve some kind of conviction as a sanction against women killing their children; third, to appease sentiment about the special position of mothers. Nevertheless, some judges continued to argue for the utilitarian value of a severe law tempered with mercy.

> I rather think that a very great jurist has laid it down, that the greater the temptation the greater the necessity for punishment. If she [an unmarried mother] is under a passionate desire to conceal her shame, it is just as well that the law should step in with some strong deterrent against that which induces her to take away the life of the child which she is bound to take care of.[17]

Stephen, by contrast, attacked this policy of no change, though he too used arguments of utility and public opinion. He claimed that the theoretical harshness of existing law unjustly prevented the conviction of women who had indeed murdered their children. He also claimed that there were special circumstances which should be recognised in law: a woman's mind after confinement was abnormally weak; temporary insanity was common and well known at this time; it was a less serious crime because one could not estimate the loss as it affected the child; it caused no alarm because it was committed by a restricted group; and public sympathy was heightened in illegitimacy cases because of the father's lack of accountability.[18] His argument nicely balanced justice and mercy.

The jurists Alison and Stephen referred to weakness before and after confinement as common knowledge associated with common sentiment. Medical discourse emphasised the same weakness, often extending it to include all aspects of reproduction – in other words, the whole woman. Though a lawyer might describe stress of mind and a medical practitioner softness of nerves, there was a significant area of agreement. This was reflected in insanity verdicts for infanticidal women.

Medical men had long been required to give evidence in infanticidal cases to coroners', sessional and assize courts. Such cases played an important part in the emergence of a forensic medical specialism between the 1780s and 1830s. The courts themselves took the lead in demanding that medical evidence be used; there was therefore an established institutional framework into which medical evidence linking infanticide and lunacy could be placed. I have described the filtering which removed women from the possibility of being sentenced for murdering their children. The insanity defence fitted in with this, enabling a jury to 'acquit' even when faced by overwhelming evidence that a killing had occurred. This use of the special verdict was sometimes influenced by medical evidence; at other times the verdict expressed popular sentiment about woman's weakness in general or particular dreadful circumstances.

Emma Lewis was sent to Bethlem in 1854 after murdering her newly-born baby at Nottingham. The defence apparently produced no medical evidence; it merely recounted how the bastard child resulted from a cruel seduction. No evidence of insanity was recorded at Bethlem, only the note that 'her conduct has been uniformly excellent'.[19] She was released within five years.

Even when the court paid more attention to the law than it had in this case, the same long-term consequences often followed. Maria Clarke was tried at the Suffolk Spring Assizes in 1851 for murdering her illegitimate baby; she was found guilty and was sentenced to be hanged. She had clumsily buried her child alive after giving birth in extreme poverty; there was no money for a defence. Mr Justice Jervis left no room for the jury to find insanity because she was clearly conscious both of the nature of her act and of her guilt. Nevertheless, the trial shocked local philanthropists, who submitted testimony of her insanity to the Home Secretary. The sentence was commuted.

Bethlem case notes about infanticides suggest that poverty was a major element both in the crime and in the jury's willingness to find insanity.[20] Mrs Maria Borley, starving and grossly neglected by her husband, was acquitted after drowning her child. Mrs Maria Chitty killed her child from a desperate fear of poverty; her husband was in hospital and therefore without income. She was later pardoned. Eliza Dart tried to drown herself and her child, but they were saved and she faced a charge of attempted murder. Lord Justice Brett stated in her case that it was proper to make a commonsense response rather than a narrow legal ruling based on medical evidence for insanity: 'It was a mistake to suppose that, in order to satisfy a jury of insanity, scientific evidence must be adduced. If the evidence of facts were such as to indicate an unsound state of mind that was quite sufficient.'[21] Once again, a lay definition of 'insanity' prevailed, excluding medical expertise. This case demonstrates how in law, 'insanity' continued to mean psychological disturbance of a certain kind, rather than brain disease. Even the prosecution argued that destitution and miserable conditions had unsettled Mary Hamilton's reason, leading her to murder her child; again, no medical evidence was given.

These decisions showed a willingness to associate distressful circumstances and distress of reason. The meaning of 'illness' in this context was not formed by the workings of the body; rather, it derived from specifiable social conditions. Insanity specialists had no role in deciding these cases, only in administering the conclusion. 'Insanity' was a label used by juries to describe women who were passive by nature and circumstance, even in the face of their active violence.

Judges or jurymen were presumably aware, however, that 'insanity' was also a medical term and that civil legislation recognised this medical content. Lay meanings were therefore growing into medical meanings; social decision-making increasingly grew into medical practice. This merging was aided by a shared humanitarian language. But as the medical connotations of 'insanity' became stronger, this inevitably changed the perception of acts like infanticide. The medical language of individual internal disorder emptied the violent act of external social meaning. The insanity verdict classified child-killing as a problem to be solved by custodial therapy and managed by society's delegated specialists. This was humanitarian (in Victorian terms), but it also detracted from examining women's position in relation to power and wealth. It is important to take seriously the words of women who killed their bastard children. Even if most women producing children outside marriage did not do violence, the statements of those who did are not thereby meaningless. But once defined as insane, expressions of suffering lose their meaning.

This is illustrated by the case of Sarah Allen, indicted in 1856 for drowning her two children. She 'had the fancy that her children would suffer in this world if they lived, consequently she wished to send them to heaven'.[22] Evidence portrayed an exemplary life free from previous symptoms of insanity. Nevertheless, the court decided she had been incapable of distinguishing right from wrong and accordingly found her insane. Dr Winslow argued particularly that her stated reason why she had drowned her children was itself evidence of insanity.[23] Yet at one level it was rational enough, even if the act that followed it was abnormal. Winslow described her insanity by comparing her conduct with social norms that accepted suffering. Calling her insane emptied her act of meaning; she, and not society, had a problem. At Bethlem she was later described as 'furious'; but whether or not she suffered from functional disorder, the specific form her act took was symbolic. It was a symbolism which was disguised and lost.

The primary object of humanitarian sentiment towards such women was to prevent hanging; the result of investing in such values was only a secondary consideration. The consequences were left to experts whom society had equipped as custodians. The jury's concern to remove the possibility of hanging was evident in cases such as those of Martha Bradish, Esther Lack and Ann Martin. There was evidence for jealousy as a criminal motive in Bradish's case, and no symptoms of insanity were noted during her subsequent custody at Fisherton House. The opinion stated before the Royal Commission on Capital Punishment therefore seems reasonable: the jury was simply not willing to have her hanged. We must presume that a multitude of local factors affected decisions. But the category of 'insanity' came into its own when some mitigating circumstance was perceived in the defendant's position.

In spite of these feelings, some women pleading insanity were found guilty and even hanged, though this final retribution was less frequent nearer the end of the century. Mary Gallop, for example, was hanged for poisoning her father in 1844. It is noteworthy that the victim was adult, the murder involved poison, and the accused stood to benefit from the death. Similar evidence of criminal motive helped a jury find Mrs Jackson guilty in 1847 of an attempt to murder her son-in-law. In the cases of Elizabeth Harris and Constance Kent the victims were infants, but there was clear evidence of intent in the former and a – possibly false – confession in the latter which upset medical speculations about impulsive insanity.[24] Neither woman was hanged.

2 Mad Women

The medicalisation of infanticide was helped by a clear symptomology of mental disorder surrounding confinement. All parties agreed on the emotional perversity of pregnant women, on the shock of childbirth (especially *primae partum*), and on the physical weakness and poor spirits following confinement. This knowledge translated readily into medical terms. As medical men could assume that most people accepted the existence of puerperal insanity, it became an important model in polemics for the medical discourse.

In the first half of the century, 'puerperal mania' referred vaguely to any mental disorder from pregnancy to several years after confinement. By 1850 it was usually separated from insanity of pregnancy and restricted to the period immediately following confinement, though there was little agreement whether this meant a few weeks or anything up to a year. Puerperal insanity was common; moreover, it was accepted as such by alienists, general medical practitioners, and ordinary people. Bucknill and Tuke estimated that it accounted for one-eighth of the women in Bethlem Hospital.[25] Dr J. Batty Tuke estimated that between 1846 and 1864, 7·1 per cent of women admitted to the Royal Edinburgh Asylum were puerperal cases, though this included insanity of pregnancy and lactation.[26] Most of these cases were of short duration and recovery was spontaneous.

Puerperal insanity took many different forms – as different as the forms of insanity in general. Bucknill and Tuke borrowed a description from Dr John Reid:

> As the patient attacked by puerperal madness, becomes more decidedly insane, 'the talking is almost incessant, and generally on one particular subject, such as imaginary wrongs done to her by her dearest friends; a total negligence of, and often very strong aversion to, her child and husband are evinced; explosions of anger occur, with vociferations and violent gesticulations; and, although the patient may have been remarkable previously for her correct, modest demeanor, and attention to her religious duties, most awful oaths and imprecations are now uttered, and language used which astonishes her friends; the eye is wandering and unsteady, and the hearing most acute. The suicidal tendency is not uncommon, especially in the cases of melancholia.'[27]

Reid's account emphasised the consistent breaking of taboos surrounding female conduct. To understand this one must consider that the body was a metaphor for thinking about morality. Even alienists treated insanity as a condition in which the evil inherent in people broke out after the controlling action of a moral will was removed. Christian conceptions of sin were incorporated into scientific conceptions of illness. The presence of evil – 'there is a latent devil in the heart of the best of men' – made it all the more imperative for people to set their minds to work properly while they were in health.[28] Puerperal mania exemplified the manner in which disease released evil by eliminating mental control.

> Every medical man has observed the extraordinary amount of obscenity, in thought and language, which breaks forth from the most modest and well-nurtured woman under the influence of puerperal mania; and although it may be courteous and politic to

join in the wonder of those around, that such impurities could ever
enter such a mind, and while he repudiates Pope's slander, that 'every
woman is at heart a rake,' he will nevertheless acknowledge, that
religious and moral principles alone give strength to the female mind;
and that, when these are weakened or removed by disease, the sub-
terranean fires become active, and the crater gives forth smoke and
flame.[29]

Puerperal mania correlated with the physiological upheaval of giving
birth; it also expressed in symbolic form a deviance latent in every woman.
There was no incompatibility between the two in medical discourse. But
alienists sometimes felt disturbed and puzzled by what they uncovered.
'In three violent cases of puerperal mania I have noticed an extraordinary
amount of salacity a very few days after labour; masturbation was
excessive in all these patients, but whether this was the result of the
irritation consequent on the labour causing perverted sensation, or actual
salacity, I cannot say.'[30] Alienists also agreed that 'in no form of insanity
is the suicidal tendency so well-marked'.[31] Sometimes this violence
turned outwards to threaten the baby's life. Nevertheless, because its
duration was normally restricted, and because it was closely linked with
a period when women were in a special transitional state, this insane
conduct was not considered a serious threat.

Mrs Ryder's trial provides an example both of the symptoms and
relative social acceptability of puerperal mania. She appeared before the
Central Criminal Court in 1856 charged with murdering her recently-
born baby. Taylor described her case:

> There was an entire absence of motive in this as in most other cases
> of a similar kind. The mother was much attached to the child, and
> had been singing and playing with it on the morning of its death.
> She destroyed the child by placing it in a pan of water in her bed-
> room. The medical evidence proved that she had been delivered
> about a fortnight previously – that she had had an attack of fever,
> and that she had probably committed this act while in a state of
> delirium. She was acquitted on the ground of insanity: and Erle, J.,
> remarked that it was evidently a case in which the insanity was only
> temporary, and the prisoner might be restored to her friends on a
> representation being made in the proper quarter.[32]

Judge, jury and medical men concurred in placing Mrs Ryder within a
class defined by excusing circumstances. Whether these conditions fulfilled the Rules was another matter, though Taylor's reference to possible
delirium suggests a gesture in that direction. The judge's cooperation is
noteworthy; his statement about a future release perhaps hinted that he
would write a letter to the Home Office favourable to the defendant.

The plea of puerperal insanity was uncontroversial when delusion was
apparent, as in the case of Wilson (1864) who suffered from head pains

and despondency following her confinement. While awake one night she experienced a black shadowy figure urging her to drown her children in a cistern to save them from wickedness.

The victim of puerperal violence did not have to be a baby. Mrs Law (1862) killed and cut up both her newly-born baby and her husband. Her confinement had involved great loss of blood, suggesting to the court that she had become physically and mentally weak. In addition, she had previously exhibited morbid delusions. She was found insane.

Medical and lay discourses alike identified the period following childbirth as one of weakened control and unavoidable danger. This offered particular scope for the medicalisation of personal life. In Martha Prior's trial at Chelmsford in 1848, her surgeon testified that he had recommended the newly-born child to be kept from the mother since she was in 'a dangerous state'. The advice was not heeded. He explained the murder as 'an uncontrollable impulse acting upon a mind previously diseased'.[33] Lord Justice Denman considered this a rash opinion but assumed the jury would act upon it, which they did, even though the mother had obtained the murder weapon, a razor, under pretext of wanting to cut her nails.

The general willingness to adopt a medical description was helped by the lack of adequate motives or any attempts to avoid detection. Motivation and secrecy were important in lay definitions of crime, and their absence made juries turn to non-criminal categories. Criminal insanity filled the gap.

A similar pattern of events was present in other infanticides. Mary McNeil was tried before the Central Criminal Court in 1856 for murdering two of her illegitimate children while suckling a third. Defence counsel described hysterical, melancholic and hereditary symptoms and linked them to a character change following the last confinement. She was found insane. Whereas Mrs Ryder probably returned to a caring family, Mary McNeil became a long-term inmate of the criminal wing at Bethlem.

Bethlem and Broadmoor played a role in maintaining paupers who, had they not been in such straits, might have been more readily 'pardoned'. Mrs Mary Beveridge, who murdered her two children at separate times, was found not guilty on the ground of insanity. Evidence suggested that her insanity was not caused by puerperal complications but by the brutality of her husband. She was transferred from Winchester to Bethlem when the magistrates objected to supporting a person for whom the Home Office was responsible. At neither place was she described as exhibiting symptoms of insanity, but at Bethlem she was classed as 'incurable' with the onset of blindness. Institutional care therefore continued; in this context, 'sane' but 'incurable' did not have a narrow medical meaning.[34] Considering the pain of her married life, Bethlem's claim that she was glad to be provided for was probably accurate.

The Home Secretary's power to authorise releases was exercised more with puerperal maniacs than any other group. A major factor was presumably that women past child-bearing age could no longer commit the same murders. But cases such as Mrs Catherine Savell's show that an earlier release was possible. She was tried for murdering her three-month-old baby in 1854. Insanity was found after evidence that she had been depressed since her confinement and that her husband had been medically advised to place her temporarily in an asylum. She had a false pregnancy a year later in Bethlem, but the following year she was 'pardoned'.

Alienists recognised that insanities linked with infanticide had a socially meaningful distribution. Bucknill and Tuke attributed the low rates of puerperal mania among paupers in the lying-in hospitals to the better conditions there than outside.[35] J. Batty Tuke explained puerperal insanity in terms of 'moral causes . . . fright and sudden shocks being the most common'.[36] Medical aetiology was receptive to social and psychological factors, however physicalist the language of proximate causes. This was important for the medical discourse's ability to achieve some social standing through infanticidal cases. Mothers had a unique status in the criminal courts, reflecting medical and lay beliefs about weakness in confinement. The courts took into account woman's 'nature', precisely what alienists thought should happen in every lunacy case. Further, since infanticide was limited in its object and duration, fears about the spread of violence were overriden by other factors. Infanticidal women were particularly well-suited to be objects of mercy. If punishment had meaning in a social world which presupposed individual choice, its value would be enhanced by a reluctance to punish a class who by nature could not fully exercise choice. Women in general, and confined women in particular, were by definition passive.[37] Leniency and mercy gave this practical expression.

Even in this area, however, medical and lay opinion did not always coincide. A few highly controversial murder cases cast an interesting light on the limits of sympathy towards women. In these cases alienists found determinism a particularly attractive way of thinking about female deviance, but their critics preferred to think in terms of active depravity.

Celestina Somner, far from being an object of humanitarian sentiment, became notorious as the Brighton murderess. She was tried in 1856 for murdering her ten-year-old stepdaughter. The defence claimed that her responsibility was lessened by her husband's conduct, but this was no defence in law; the jury was unsympathetic and found her guilty. Subsequently, however, the Home Secretary used a certification of insanity to remove her to an asylum, even though she had been clearly aware of the wrongness and nature of her crime. His decision led to newspaper criticism and a question in the House of Commons. Critics argued that justice was thwarted by the Home Secretary treating Somner as an infanticide. Infanticides were legitimately excused, but Somner did not belong in that class and was not a fit object of mercy.[38] It was even claimed that her history after 'one of the most deliberate and cruel murders ever recorded' reduced the judicial system to a lottery.[39] This was stated about five years after she had really become insane, according to medical evidence, whatever her earlier condition might have been.

This case brought together disparate and not easily reconciled elements. Mrs Somner had been continuously ill-treated by her husband, but she killed deliberately. She was certified by experts, but laymen felt justice had been frustrated. The medical discourse prevailed, but it did not coincide with the commonsense view that there had been criminal intent. The case also illustrates the way alienists attained power – through administrative structures which were not directly overseen by public opinion.

It was no coincidence that, when alienists appeared to have been decisive in finding insanity in controversial cases, there was adverse comment from the medical establishment and newspapers. The public called Martha Brixey the Greenwich murderess. Alienists, however, declared that her verdict of not guilty was an important legal precedent for irresistible impulse.

Brixey was a domestic servant who murdered one of her employer's children in 1845. No doubt, her particular relationship with the child suggested a real danger to the newspaper-reading public. There was general surprise when she was found insane, since there was no evidence of disordered reason to bring her within the scope of the Rules. The defence argued that the accused had suffered from menstrual disturbance leading to an irresistible impulse to murder.

> The prisoner, a quiet inoffensive girl, a maidservant in a respectable family, was charged with the murder of an infant. She had laboured under disordered menstruation, and, a short time before the occurrence, had shown some violence of temper about trivial domestic matters. This was all the evidence of her alleged (intellectual) insanity, – if we except that which was furnished by the *act* of murder. She procured a knife from the kitchen on some slight pretence, and while the nurse was out of the room cut the throat of her master's infant child; she then went downstairs and told her master what she had done. She was perfectly *conscious* of the act she had committed; she treated it as a crime, and showed much anxiety to know whether she should be hanged or transported. There was not the slightest evidence that at the time of the act, or at any time previous, she had laboured under any delusion or intellectual abberration. The prisoner was acquitted on the ground of insanity probably arising from obstructed menstruation.[40]

This case exemplified the type of logic alienists were trying to establish. They claimed that a physical change associated with menstruation led to a breakdown in the nervous system. This caused the nervous system to operate automatically, without control, under the influence of an idea already present in the mind; the idea served as a stimulus for a complex reflex. Brixey had behaved like a machine, so her violence had meaning only in terms of her body. And since her violence was socially meaningless, retribution was inappropriate. It also followed that if proper institutional arrangements were made the public need have no further worries. To alienists, the violence was a matter for themselves and Brixey.

Two comments can be made about this. Though alienists considered the case a possible precedent for including uncontrollable impulse as an excusing condition, it did not become a precedent in law. It could be argued that, as in other cases, the verdict reflected the jurymen's own beliefs rather than esoteric medical knowledge. It is probable that the extreme nature of the crime, the absence of an ordinary motive, and the lack of any attempt to escape the consequences, amounted to an insane deed in commonsense discourse, at least in the jury's view. Put simply, the accused had not *behaved* like a criminal.

That the accused was a woman, and that she had been disturbed by menstrual disorder (commonly accepted as influencing emotions) increased the plausibility of the insanity label.[41] Disordered menstruation ('amenorrhoea') was also the reason for an acquittal in Shepherd's trial for stealing a fur boa. The magistrates accepted that her conduct was periodically erratic and discharged her. When Amelia Snoswell killed her baby niece, she was acquitted on medical evidence of disordered menstruation; extreme melancholy following a disappointment in love was an additional factor.

The second point that should be made about Brixey's trial concerns the content of her insanity. She was described at Bethlem as 'a young woman of most interesting appearance and amiable expression of countenance with great propriety of manner and a pattern of retiring, modest behaviour. There is no appearance of anything approaching insanity or delusion of any kind.'[42] She had been distressed by a servant's impropriety of dress during a period of mourning. She then cut off the child's head, explaining that in doing so she made an angel of it. 'There was no other cause assigned for the deed nor is it believed any other existed.'[43] Perhaps the cause assigned should be taken seriously; if she was obsessed by sin, her violence had a degree of subjective rationality. Alienists assumed that such a degree of obsession amounted to insanity, and the jury agreed. By explaining the insanity as the product of physical disorder, they emptied the violence of any meaning it might have had. Nevertheless, the critical reaction to the verdict suggests that the crime was perceived to have a social and not just a physical content. Apart from this single deed, Brixey was conspicuous for her virtue, as her case notes and her 'pardon' after thirteen years in Bethlem testified.

Alienists assumed that a hereditary disposition to insanity was often present. In the case of Mary McNeil medical evidence of hysterical despondency and symptoms of pending violence was supplemented by hints about insanity in near relatives. Such evidence was not always well received, particularly if it appeared an excuse for violence. Christiana Edmunds was found guilty of murder and then reprieved by the Home Secretary on certification of insanity. This provoked adverse comment. According to Maudsley, however, symptoms in members of the family told the whole story.

> Her father died raving mad in an asylum; her brother died epileptic and idiotic at Earlswood; her sister suffered from mental excitement, and once attempted to throw herself out of a window; her mother's father died paralysed and childish; a cousin on the same side was imbecile; she herself had been subject to somnambulism in childhood, had suffered from hysteria later in life, and had finally had an attack of hemiplegia.[44]

From the medical viewpoint, one could not expect a woman like Edmunds to control her conduct. Her inheritance assigned her firmly to the discourse of nature rather than culture.

Many special female elements and medico-legal problems came together at the trial of Mary Ann Brough. It was equally plausible to reconstruct her life in terms of depravity or of disease. The crime was child murder, with evidence of weakness following her last confinement. But her crime was also a vengeful act against her husband. Medical evidence played an important role in the defence, and though the jury found insanity, both lay and medical critics considered it an 'escape'. Her case is the most striking example of the constraints on meaning in Victorian discourses.

During the night of 11 June 1854, Mrs Brough systematically cut the throats of all her six children (aged eleven years to eighteen months) then living at home, near Esher. She attempted to cut her own throat but revived in the early morning and eventually attracted the attention of some neighbours. She insisted on giving a detailed statement to the police describing how she had been extremely tired and depressed; in particular she felt overcome by a 'black cloud' which had gone when she recovered consciousness.[45] The scale of the murders, coupled with royal associations, created a sensation; Mrs Brough had briefly been a wet-nurse to the Prince of Wales and her husband was in service at Claremont Palace (on loan to the exiled French monarchy). Charabanc parties of visitors toured the blood-soaked bedrooms of the cottage. The sensation was further tinged with marital scandal; the murders took place the same week Mr Brough had accused his wife of adultery. He had her followed to London, where she met up with a man from a neighbouring village. Mr

Brough then left home and began legal proceedings for a separation. His wife killed the children the night before he was due to return with a document requiring her signature. She had also written a letter for the eldest daughter, who was living away from home, leaving her possessions to her to prevent the husband benefiting in any way.

These events had all the elements of a Victorian morality play. Vice – adultery committed over many years – produced a crisis. Faced by the implications of her conduct, Mrs Brough acted with selfish vindictiveness, the inevitable result of her depraved habits. These individualistic terms went unquestioned; the historical sequence of indulgence was the key to understanding the events. Not even alienists, at or after the trial, supposed that the murders would have occurred without the history of adultery. But when Mrs Brough was tried at Guildford, her counsel set out to prove that the murders were the product of insanity.

The evidence for this was of two kinds. First, since her last confinement, Mrs Brough had suffered from partial paralysis with impaired speech. These symptoms had decreased, but her doctor stated that he had warned her to avoid over-excitement because of nervous weakness. She had also suffered from severe headaches and was physically exhausted from caring for her children who had measles. An expert, Dr Winslow, was brought in to give the second type of evidence. He described a general syndrome in which brain disease led to an inability to control actions; he then stated his belief that Mrs Brough belonged to this pathological class. His evidence was not rebutted by the prosecution, since their expert medical witness, Professor Taylor, agreed that Mrs Brough was insane; he was therefore not called. Mr Justice Erle summarised the evidence in a neutral and unemotive manner, but he did charge the jury that the law did not recognise irresistible impulse.

> The evidence for the prisoner . . . appeared to be founded upon the supposition that the crime had been committed under the influence of some uncontrollable impulse, and he said he would only observe that this was a most dangerous doctrine, for undoubtedly every crime was committed under some impulse, and the object of the law was to control impulses of that description and thus prevent crime.[46]

Nevertheless, the jury reached a verdict of not guilty on the ground of insanity and Mrs Brough was removed to Bethlem.

There were two alternative reconstructions of the antecedents of the crime: first, 'that she was discovered in the commission of an inexcusable act of gross immorality, that she was a vicious woman, had violated her marriage vow'; second, 'that some structural alterations must have occurred in the brain, as the result of her former cerebral attack'.[47] The greatest tension between these two accounts was not in deciding whether she was in control of her faculties while committing the murders, but in evaluating her responsibility for creating such circumstances. The judge instructed the jury to resolve this problem.

> If . . . they should be of opinion that, owing to the unfortunate relation in which she stood with her husband at the time, she was induced to meditate the commission of some act of violence, either towards herself or others, and that this created an excited condition, which, operating upon her brain in its diseased condition, drove her to a state of temporary insanity, during which she committed the act with which she was charged, he was bound to tell them that this would not excuse her from the consequences, and it would be their duty to find her guilty of the crime of wilful murder.[48]

Several commentators were surprised and upset that the jury did not condemn Mrs Brough for her past conduct: 'If she were insane, her mental derangement was the result of the immoral life she had led for years, and as her insanity was *self-created*, the gallows ought to have claimed her for its victim.'[49] Winslow answered by also pointing out that such a history could produce insanity: 'Insanity may be often traced to a criminal indulgence in depraved habits and vicious thoughts, to reckless and unprincipled conduct; to long indulged self-will; to a censurable neglect of the cultivation of habits of *self-control*; to an utter disregard of all mental discipline and training, and above all, to a repudiation of the principles of our holy and revered religion.'[50] Winslow did not pursue the deep-seated problem he raised; he did not reconcile disease as a physical event with disease as an event that could and should be avoided through choosing the good. Though his evangelical tone was stronger than that used by most alienists, his argument was unexceptional; all mental physiologists employed similar evaluations in theories of mental and bodily control. These evaluations were present in both medical and non-medical discourses, indicating their basis in a shared culture. The differences between the discourses emerged when deciding how society should label the climax of Mrs Brough's history. At this point the medical discourse had a logical disadvantage: it could not express itself intelligibly about the temporal boundary between choice and determinism. In the non-medical discourse the continuity was perfectly intelligible.

The choice of which discourse to use could never be an empirical one however minutely Mrs Brough's condition was described. It makes no sense to ask whether she was 'really' mad. This question ignores the historical conditions in which statements possess meaning. Winslow found a lack of responsibility because he considered it wrong to place a life in jeopardy when brain disease might be present. By contrast, an anonymous writer asked, 'Where would society be, if such a moral state were held sufficient to shield the agent from the sword of the law?'[51]

One can of course only surmise why the jury reached the decision that it did. But the widespread benevolence towards mothers who murdered their children should be taken into account. It was also likely that the enormity of the slaughter and the reversal of maternal feelings (Mrs Brough was shown to have been a loving mother) argued for insanity. The effect was so out of proportion to the cause, even a cause in which vice featured, that the language of pathology acquired utility. The scale of the murders was such that it was hard to imagine commonsense motives and intentions sufficient to make her responsible. Yet there was no evidence of abnormal mental function, except in her subjective account of the crime. The only real evidence for insanity was the deed itself; perhaps the jury decided that it was literally 'insane'. Given a history of neurological symptoms, there was additional scope for categorising her conduct as the product of disease. The surgeon William Lawrence later carried out an autopsy at Bethlem and found evidence sufficient for alienists to claim that their diagnosis was vindicated.[52]

As with Pierre Rivière, it would be foolish to offer a definitive account of this tragedy – one element of tragedy is its openness to reinterpretation. But the mother-child relationship was at the heart of it. Mrs Brough gave vent to her feelings about her husband through this relationship, the jury perceived events in its light, and alienists linked it with nervous weakness and uncontrollable movements. Femaleness was a major element in medico-legal decisions. Female criminal lunatics came nearest to enabling medical discourse to describe legally exculpatory conditions. This reflected a shared assumption that woman was closer to nature than man; medical discourse was therefore more appropriate to women's lives.

CHAPTER EIGHT

KNOWLEDGE AND RESPONSIBILITY

I   The Language of Mind and Body

The response to lunacy exemplified new patterns of social organisation in the early nineteenth century; medicine and management came together to reinforce both centralised power and its mirror image, universalist knowledge. Lunatics thus became natural objects. Yet there was no break with earlier traditions of authority; there persisted an uneasy and sometimes openly antagonistic relationship between direct and indirect ordering. Moreover, in spite of the enormous commitment to medical science in the twentieth century, this strategic irresolution continues to generate conflict and confusion. In this context, criminal lunatics had an understandable visibility: the insanity plea amounted to a repeated exploration of the meaning of responsibility. Their visibility was increased by associations of violent moral disorder, hanging and retribution. They were idols of fear. The alienist G.F.Blandford stated that 'folks think of [lunatics] as pariahs and outcasts, and stare at them as if each was a Macnaughten'.[1] Criminals and lunatics alike caused anxiety. Even clear cases of crime or madness created ambivalence about retribution and treatment. Penology claimed to introduce elements of treatment, and alienism perpetuated elements of punishment.

The historical task is to understand medical and legal discourse rather than to promote one or the other. Each discourse contained relationships which established the meaning conditions for particular statements. As Stephen observed: 'Men have an all but incurable propensity to try to prejudge all the great questions which interest them by stamping their prejudices upon their language.'[2] He intended a shrewd observation of human character; his point, however, can be reconstructed to render the 'prejudice' of language a collective property.

The insanity plea requires the public drawing of boundaries between discourses. This is not an empirical process: empirical statements are necessarily part of one of the discourses between which the choice must be made. Empirical statements describe the objects about which choice is made but the statements are never empty of evaluative meaning. Juridical and medical parties, however, each have an interest in claiming objective empirical statements as the unique basis for decisions. In legal discourse, the facts of insanity are mental states; it is proper for juries to assess them. In medical discourse, the facts are bodily states; it is proper for experts to pronounce on them. Conflict is avoided only when there is an agreed division of labour between discourses. This was not possible in the nineteenth century when the administration of miscreants was undergoing extensive, though very incomplete, reconstruction. Further, by arguing for insanity in murder trials, alienists proposed to destroy a potent form of traditional authority.

Verdicts were extremely variable. In the early 1840s courts showed some willingness to expand the insanity plea's range, but this was short-lived. Each verdict can be understood only in relation to individual circumstances. It was always possible (*vide* Martha Brixey) that the 'motivelessness' of a murder would lead the jury to describe it as insane; conversely, that criminal intent (*vide* Benjamin Haynes) would lead the jury to find a deluded man guilty. This is what one would expect if the insanity defence was a forum for arbitrating between discourses. Since the discourses were sometimes genuine alternatives (*vide* Mrs Brough and Luigi Buranelli), the boundary-drawing had to be examined anew on each occasion. Only with certain types of defendants – extremely deluded lunatics and infanticidal women – was there an overlapping of medical and legal descriptions. Criminal lunatics, therefore, were a collection of anomalies. The lawyer A.W.Renton was accurate (as well as sarcastic) when he described them as a 'motley crew'.[3] They shared only the administrative procedures which gave them a common label. These procedures were themselves controversial and liable to change.

Victorian administration tried to regulate people who offended not only the law but the available descriptive groupings. Mary Douglas argues that such anomalies are important for understanding belief systems.

> By focusing on how anomalous beings may be treated in different systems of classification, we make a frontal attack on the question of how thought, words and the real world are related ... Any universe is liable to harbour monsters which straddle across its major classes. But such creatures do not necessarily get any attention. If they are noticed, they can be judged very auspicious. Alternatively, they can inspire horror, aversion, disgust. When this is recorded, we have the strong guts reaction.[4]

There is some controversy about the correctness of approaching cate-gorisation by examining boundaries and of treating categories as bounded entities. In Douglas's work such categories as assumed and linked with social divisions.[5] This has a suggestive application to the correspondence crime-lawyers and lunacy-medical men, leaving criminal lunatics in the middle as a point of both cognitive and social strain. Two difficulties, how-ever, arise from this approach: first, there is a logical circularity in defining categories by their boundaries and then describing boundaries as belonging to categories; second, there is a problematic psychological assumption in the argument, namely, the emotional need for order. Thus, while it is tempting to treat criminal lunatics as 'monsters' – they plainly inspired horror – it is not clear that the analysis in terms of their position between discourses can be taken much further. If categories are instead treated as amorphous groupings around ideal types (the total evil act or the ravingly insane deed), the boundary between them becomes a secondary matter. The further from the ideal type, the more variable the description. Different group interests will be represented in these peripheral areas. Pragmatic and administrative investment, rather than cognitive boundary-drawing, will receive attention. This corresponds to the historical events.

The ideal types of 'depravity' and 'madness' contained elements found in everyone's experience. It is significant that courts acted on the assumption that 'everyone knows' such states. They were the logical point of reference for the grey areas of conduct which included everyday life and the dramatic extreme of criminal lunacy. Their 'ideal' form rarely corresponded with the 'real' mixture of types. Classification exploited the range of meanings generated by opposition between ideal types. Emphasis on different aspects suited different purposes. There is no necessary relationship between the horror aroused by 'motiveless' murders, conflict between judges and medical witnesses over exculpatory conditions, and conceptual indecision about describing a crime as an act or an impulse. The entire discourse analysis of medico-legal disputes must therefore be synthesised. It cogently describes many disparate historical sources, but its own logic must not be mistaken for the phenomenon requiring interpretation.

Categories are not necessarily simple; they may be inherently polarised or hierarchical. Thus 'crime-insanity' can be treated as a category of conduct which contains the possibility of many different instances. Arguments about whether conduct 'is' crime or 'is' insanity reify abstractions. The more useful categories recognise that existential reality is intrinsically multiple and our interest in it intrinsically judgemental. Legal and medical statements are incorporated into other polarised categories: freewill-determinism, responsible-non-responsible, mind-body, head-hand, higher-lower, man-woman, culture-nature. Victorians drew upon all these oppositions and treated each pole as a real element. Nevertheless, it was the set as a whole which had logical primacy and the hierarchy between the poles which gave each term its meaning.

What has been described as the switching between discourses may be rephrased as the placing of conduct within a hierarchy of 'real' possibilities between 'ideal' types. This is characteristic of everyday blame and sympathy; it is also characteristic of esoteric thought, where it becomes an aspect of the mind-body problem or the integration of levels in the nervous system.

The hierarchical category of mind-body became detailed, experimental, and intellectually challenging from neurophysiological research after 1800. Scientists like Pierre Flourens, Johannes Müller and Marshall Hall divided the brain and spinal cord between a lower automatic and a higher controlling region. British mental physiologists then proposed a hierarchy of reflex actions; the theory systematised a great deal of anecdotal, anatomical, experimental and clinical information. At first, the mind was considered the head of the body; later, primacy was given to cerebral processes, with the mind relegated to a parallel or merely epiphenomenal position. In both versions, the higher part (mind or brain) inhibited lower spinal reflexes. This formula had multiple meaning; hence it could accommodate the details of experimental neurophysiology *and* everyday experience. It could also create an objective standpoint for understanding lunacy.

The bodily hierarchy was a scale of being between the mechanical and the mental. The reflex concept was important precisely because of its utility in mediating between observable purposive movements and unobservable (but presumed) mechanical events. The hierarchy offered objective grounds for a graded response to failure of self-control. The criminal could have inhibited his baseness; the lunatic, by contrast, did not have brain capacity to regulate conduct. If 'the madman is reduced to a mere automatic or machine-like existence', he is rightly regulated from outside.[6] To give a reflex explanation for an offence was to invoke medical management, since self-control was impossible. If the alternative was hanging, as it was for James Atkinson and George Bryce, then to treat people like machines had the appearance of humanity. Alienists continued to maintain self-control as the ideal and they were able to reconcile this with scientific determinism through hierarchical concepts. This was possible since reflex theory allowed for the inhibitory capacity of the higher centres – the exercise of control. The theory's empirical foundation gave hope that crime and lunacy could be translated into a relationship between nervous levels. The law, however, preferred the traditional category of good-evil to give meaning to 'brutality': 'all this [impulsiveness] was merely indicative of the lowest moral depravation and degradation'.[7]

The body – in this case the nervous system – is an analogue for interactions between people.[8] Victorian social relations were conducted on the basis of humans controlling themselves. Responsibility was the individualised form of conformity with the social order. The presence of the mind or the cerebrum at the top of the bodily hierarchy made it intelligible to locate responsibility within the individual. Just as the cerebrum inhibited the lower brain, the mind regulated the body, and society imposed responsibility.

There was not a one-to-one relation between the bodily hierarchy and the social hierarchy. Though everyone was expected to exercise control, more finesse was expected from gentlemen and more brutishness from working men. The bodily hierarchy was a resource for articulating the complex meaning of *any* conduct.

Specialist neurophysiological papers graded into the writings of mental scientists. These more popular works also portrayed conduct as the interaction between mental volition and the lower reflexes, instincts, and habits. Henry Holland described the will and the body in a state of struggle; yet they do 'concur and harmonise in general results; giving order and stability to all the complex functions of life, and admitting of increase of power to those [actions] of the highest kind by their due and sufficient exercise'.[9] Lunatics broke free from brain control and social pressure. As Griesinger wrote:

> In man, the immediate transition of these sensations to movement is subject in a higher degree to the influence of the understanding, and through it duty and morality intervene to control and govern the sensuous desires. But there are cases where these lose their power. In the insane, in whom the influence of the understanding over the instincts is enfeebled, and moreover the sensuous impulses perhaps strengthened, we often see, for example, the appetite for food or the sexual instinct showing itself with the most open regardlessness.[10]

The contrast between normality and deviancy was relocated in nature; nature thereby legitimated the original evaluation.

Medical discourse was not so much in opposition to legal discourse but an alternative hierarchy of the same evaluations. Lack of control was the universal enemy, recognisable in the shared rhetoric of degeneracy, beastliness, barbarism, and impulsiveness surrounding both insanity as brain disease and depravity as moral evil. If the insanity plea could condense so many symbols into one social act, it was indeed a fit object of controversy.

Alienists alternated between mental and physical language in describing the causes and treatment of insanity and in portraying lunatics as responsible and not responsible. For instance, alienists argued that brain disease should be accepted as producing non-accountability, but in defending asylum incarceration they argued that institutions created conditions in which patients with brain disease might act responsibly. 'Much of our own improved treatment of the insane, in the present day, turns upon the power of self-control which they can be induced to exhibit.'[11] Faced by such apparent inconsistency one might conclude either that alienists were poor philosophers or that inconsistency had its own meaning. The former judgement is easy to make, but the latter is more historical.

There was general incoherence about the mind-body relation, and alienists were among the worst offenders. Though the alienist's 'very name and functions mark him as the student and exponent of physical laws', in practice he mixed mental and physical language.[12] The phrase 'lesion of the will' was one of the more contradictory in common use. It is therefore not surprising when Scull argues that physicalist language was a product of the search for professional status.

> A somatic interpretation of insanity would place it beyond dispute within medicine's recognized sphere of competence . . . the doctors . . . began by postulating a Cartesian dualism between mind and body. The mind, which was an immortal, immaterial substance, identical with the Christian doctrine of the soul, was forced in this world to operate through the medium of a material instrument, the brain . . . The brain, as a material organ, was liable to irritation and inflammation, and it was this which produced insanity.[13]

This type of explanation, however, does not take into account the dualism indigenous in the culture as a whole. It also ignores the way physical descriptions enriched the intellectual resources for responding to 'out of control' conduct. Alienists did not have to 'invent' terms to express their expertise. The terms were available generally: mind, culture and responsibility represented a collective interest, while body, nature and non-responsibility represented special interests. In exploiting the language of body, alienists obviously developed their own vocabulary, but its origins in a common culture are apparent.

The contrast between the mind with its collective content and the body with its individual content was considered a universal social phenomenon by Durkheim. 'The old formula *homo duplex* is therefore verified by the facts . . . On the one hand is our individuality – and, more particularly, our body in which it is based; on the other is everything in us that expresses something other than ourselves.'[14] According to Durkheim, this dualism necessarily has a 'painful character', since 'society has its own nature, and, consequently, its requirements are quite different from those of our nature as individuals'.[15] Discounting the universalism of such a claim, it does suggest how insanity disputes can be subsumed under the very general endemic difficulty of defining individual and social power.

This description of Victorian dualism also provides a historical approach to 'freewill'. For example, it was common (as Scull observes) to claim that medical physicalism did not undermine moral freedom because there was a spiritual principle which transcended the material sphere. Bucknill, a sincere Christian, reconciled his conventional definition of insanity as 'the deprivation of the power of the will' with a faith in inalienable moral truths.

> The sense of duty, the feeling of right and wrong, is an innate principle of the human mind implanted by the Almighty, and serving as a sure foundation for the responsibility of man for his actions . . . It seems needful to enquire to what extent this absolute and necessary part of human nature becomes capable of being perverted or

destroyed under the influence of cerebro-mental disease. It may be taken as an axiom, that *the innate and essential principles of mind are ever present where mind exists.*[16]

Bucknill believed the human soul remained inviolate. At the same time, he argued that medicine revealed physical disease as an excusing condition in mental life. Dr Williams, expounding on moral insanity at Dove's trial, declared that 'happily the mind – the immaterial principle – cannot be the subject of disease'.[17] The social meaning of such dualisms was explicit: 'The psycho-somatists find in the liability of the cerebral instrument to disease, a reasonable basis for the irresponsibility of the insane; and, in the freedom of the spiritual will, a just ground for the responsibility of the sane.'[18] To reconcile the freedom of the will and the determinism of disease was to make cogent both responsibility and excusing conditions. But, as Bucknill was candid enough to admit, 'the difficulty which perplexes [alienists] is the union of the two states'.[19] Legal circumstances required a boundary between higher and lower levels in the nervous system, between mind and matter, and between freedom and determinism; this was the weak point. The insanity defence was the most conspicuous circumstance in which society tried to construct a boundary which, logically, could not exist.

There was consistency of a sort in the alienists' 'paradoxical' claim to study physical disease and yet train the moral character. Doctor-patient relationships can be understood in terms of dualism. Physical disease is the ostensible object of a relationship which also involves many responsibilities, for example, the patient in seeking treatment, the doctor in judging what is health and ill-health, and society in establishing appropriate institutions. Bucknill expressed this another way: 'But neither [the alienist's] knowledge nor his belief can be restrained within the confines of physical law. Though his main duty may lie within such confines, his enquiries must extend beyond them, or his knowledge of mental disease will be a thing of shreds and patches.'[20] This is a commonplace, but it needs the resources which dualism provides if it is to be intelligible. 'Responsibility' is assigned by a dialogue between ideal types.

Inconsistency in mental and physical terms is not restricted to alienists. Everyday language about people continuously embodies statements implying and denying the existence of moral choice. For the most part this follows established expectations and therefore arouses little comment. But when there is no settled division between control coming from within or from without, controversy occurs. The insanity plea turned this problem into public drama.

2 *The Content of Controversy*

Medico-legal history has implications for recent debate about the insanity defence and other issues concerning science and law. There is a great deal of theoretical and practical confusion surrounding the concept of responsibility. Such confusion reflects divergent and frequently incoherent political aims, since responsibility varies with theories of social order. Like the Victorians, we assess responsibility in terms of mind and body: we switch between them in response to contingent factors. Our legal and medical frameworks pre-empt discussion in more inclusive terms.

These issues concern the general development of human science, with its claim that science establishes the standard for all other institutions. Generalisation of this sort is important; it counteracts pressure from decision-making institutions to restrict their range of reference. Such restriction leads to medical and legal discourses being treated as self-contained rational systems not requiring justification. One value of the insanity defence is its tendency to expose the limited coherence of each discourse.

The last century and a half has seen the growth of a medico-legal specialism particularly oriented towards practical decisions rather than systematic knowledge. Nevertheless, the insanity defence remains a challenge; indeed, a contribution on this topic is almost the hallmark of medico-legal specialists. The dispute can now be summarised in the following historical terms.

1   *Psychiatric Argument.* Medical men who began to specialise in lunacy in the nineteenth century were confronted by an established criminal administration. They declared that their own experience, scientific progress, and humanitarian feeling, required them to advocate the non-accountability of lunatics. Their views were resisted by powerful members of the judiciary, lawyers, journalists, and other physicians. Against such a background, alienists often portrayed themselves as fighting a moral and intellectual battle against the forces of prejudice. Their efforts achieved greatest success in the 1950s, when it appeared to some psychiatrists that comprehensive treatment of mental illness was around the corner, and when the judiciary and the public were most willing to grant the claims of medical authority. To achieve this, psychiatry exploited a historical portrait of scientific and social progress that died with critical thinkers before 1914.

However bigoted judges may be, it is still important to recognise weaknesses in the psychiatric argument. First, there is the *empirical* tenability of claims that there are specific criteria for distinguishing insanity. Victorian alienists convinced themselves but not others about their expertise; in particular, they did not have a unique ability to recognise exculpatory insanity because they too referred to states of mind and patterns of conduct. Second, there is the *logical* tenability of supposing that a certain sequence of causal events (illness), as opposed to another sequence (health), entails non-accountability. Alienists confused what they regarded as an empirical division between health and illness with a logical division between discourses. Third, there is the question of the *legal* validity of the view that courts should be concerned with medical descriptions rather than information to help fact-finders working under legal rules.

2 *Legalistic Argument*. Jurists argued that the courts had a social duty to restrict exculpatory conditions, and they expressed this with a mixture of retributive and utilitarian concepts of punishment. Accordingly, they considered it proper to subject 'neutral' scientific statements to the adversary process, to restrict evidence of insanity to characteristics which could be examined by such processes and assessed by the lay jury, and to leave the final decision to the jury. They found psychiatrists naive for failing to understand the distinctive function of judicial process. More reflective jurists upheld the courts' duty to maintain the concept of individual responsibility as fundamental to social order; this, they argued, was threatened by the medicalisation of human actions, with its short-sighted 'do-gooding' connotations.

The weakness of legalism is two-fold. First, the law allows insanity as an exculpatory condition, and yet it proves extremely difficult, if not impossible, to demarcate such conditions. This issue continues to attract attention.[21] Once again, there is an empirical and a logical question. Second, in practice, courts rely on statements from expert witnesses when neither judge nor jury is considered competent to understand the evidence. The use of expert evidence grew considerably in the nineteenth century, creating new procedures which encouraged alienists to think their expertise should be valued. There was some element of 'prejudice' when psychiatrists were scorned. In addition, of course, the law sometimes rode roughshod over individual suffering.

3 *Professional Rivalry*. One unspoken implication of legalism was that it preserved judicial power in decision-making and sentencing. Juries were responsible for finding facts, but the framework in which they did this was a product of legal control. When alienists began to argue the role of medical evidence, they had in mind the social status which its acceptance would confer. The vehemence with which alienists denounced the law is partly explained by their inferior status, the stigma attached to the administrators of lunacy as well as to lunatics themselves, and the complete lack of autonomy given to witnesses in court. Such vehemence has died away as psychiatry has become a profession, with courts using deferential language and accepting extra-judicial medical institutions. The insanity defence has often symbolised competition in the administration of deviance and between strategies of direct and indirect control.

4   *Contingent Historical Factors.* It is possible to argue that controversy resulted largely from a conjunction of unfortunate historical circumstances; these need only be explained for controversy to die. There are two proposals along these lines. First, that the insanity defence was used only for murder, since the consequence of an 'acquittal' for a lesser charge was worse than the possible sentence. Given the virtual restriction of hanging to murder from the 1830s, the success of the plea was widely perceived as an alternative to hanging, by critics and supporters alike. Hanging a lunatic was a brutality which alienists could not tolerate, and since there were a few cases where this appeared to have happened, condemnation of the law became a duty. Both lawyers and alienists hoped that once the capital sentence was abolished, controversy would disappear. This has not happened. The picture was more complex: the insanity defence was not limited to capital offences, a conviction for murder often did not result in hanging, and some alienists favoured hanging some criminals – even in cases when sanity had been questioned.

The second 'unfortunate' circumstance concerns the M'Naghten Rules. It is easy to accuse the Rules of determining the course of decisions and to suppose that, had the Rules been better, the decisions would have been less controversial. This mistakes the symptom of controversy for the controversy itself. One variation of this theme argues that there was precedent for a liberal interpretation of exculpatory conditions but that the Rules denied this precedent. The Rules are then explained as a reaction against the threat of violence following Chartist agitation and attacks on the Queen. This has the virtue of putting medico-legal debate into a social context, but it tends to obscure structural tensions within the insanity defence.

5   *Failure of Communication and Provision of Administrative Machinery.* The relationship between psychiatry and law has changed considerably since the late nineteenth century and especially over the last thirty years. It is a commonplace to describe how the medical profession has acquired influence and even dominance over our lives. In relation to criminal deviance, this has taken the form of procedures allowing doctors to make decisions outside the exposed conditions of the courtroom. This goes back to legislation which formalised the finding of insanity on arraignment and to the growth of a prison medical service attuned to inspecting for insanity. These developments provide alternative routes for classifying deviants as insane, routes administered by experts responsible only to other members of the same administration. Such extra-trial procedures presuppose agreement about the expertise of those administering them, and there is now much common ground among medical and legal professionals in this area. There are many technical problems – for instance, legal liability and hospitalisation orders – but there is considerable co-

operation in searching for solutions. This is possible, first, through the shared interest in professional standing, and second, through agreement about the utilitarian function of controlling deviance in a well-ordered, caring, and secular society. In the Victorian period, this professional administration barely existed; the deep-seated inconsistencies between utilitarian theories and traditional views of crime and justice were therefore much more apparent.

In spite of practical changes, medico-legal experts still argue. There is a central contradiction in the relationship between expert administrators and democratic politics. Inevitably, there are conflicts of interest between experts and other groups, and the gruesome nature of some criminal lunatic deeds means that experts are required on occasion to give an account of themselves. The experts also have to sustain a political commitment to individualist democratic values which their professional practice often contradicts. Further, it is difficult to sustain a fully utilitarian theory of law: problems range from the technical (that such a theory cannot make sense of the *mens rea* requirement) to the political (that it necessarily denies fundamental social conflict).

One further contribution to resolving controversy should be mentioned. The 1957 Homicide Act introduced the plea of diminished responsibility; this is much used in cases when there might earlier have been a divisive debate about exculpatory insanity. The utility of this plea is not in doubt, but it is a utility subject to the same strictures as the extra-trial administration of insanity. The plea functions as long as there *is* relative agreement about mixing care and punishment.

Medico-legal discussion has produced suggestions for muddling through rather than a coherent solution to the question of insanity. The issue must be regarded as an aspect of the general problem of responsibility and therefore one which is not specifically medical. Questions of insanity exactly mirror current views of responsibility.

> The basic outline of the defense is one which excludes from the ranks of criminals all persons who are mentally diseased and who cannot reasonably be used to serve the purposes of the criminal law. Unfortunately, we are at a point in history when it is not at all clear what those purposes are and, therefore, what the function of the insanity defense is or should be . . . the insanity defense has been rationalized in ways designed to satisfy all the prevalent theories.[22]

If this is so, then technical medico-legal answers – whether administrative or semantic – must remain palliatives.

Nineteenth-century law and medicine pursued different values: the law was identified with social values maintained through heavy-handed application of rules; by contrast, medicine was identified with humanitarian values, even expressing a degree of irresponsibility towards society at large. Historical interpretation must concern itself with the *argument* between these values, rather than with particular answers. The answers are only abstractions from a continuous process of assigning meaning to conduct.

To describe an intentional act assigns responsibility to the individual. It also reinforces a society in which values are located within an individual's mental attributes. The guilty verdict concerns an occasion on which these values should have received expression but did not. The law rectifies the individual failure to reinforce the social order. The insanity verdict, by contrast, assigns responsibility to society, through its delegated representatives, to intervene in lieu of the individual's mental attributes; it asserts values at the level of institutions. The insanity defence therefore symbolises the distribution of value and power between the individual and society. It becomes overburdened with content when there is a tension between a highly articulated individualism and a vast, little understood social structure. The insanity defence holds a special fascination because it appears (falsely) to be a limited technical issue which, if resolved, would release this tension. The point is that the technical issue keeps slipping away, since the real issue is to make decisions about how to distribute power.

Another way to approach this conclusion is through the concept of 'causal attribution'. The plea of insanity requires the jury to decide whether to attribute a crime to causal processes of a mental or a physical kind. Mental processes define what it is to be human; they constitute the lay or commonsense elements of causal attribution. The law, in as far as it seeks to represent the common person's construction of reality, embodies the same system of causal attribution, albeit refined by rules and definitions. It follows that to make a causal attribution in the physical sphere of illness is to assign a distance between the human sphere and what the accused is held to have done.[23] It depersonalises the event, finding reasons for its occurrence in the other-than-human. The medical expert then becomes accepted as the mediator between the human and the non-human realm. It is presumed that he will ensure as much connection as possible between the alien sphere and the residual humanity of the lunatic. From this point of view, medico-legal debate concerns definitions of what is human and how such definitions exist as institutional practice.

That the crime-insanity category is inherently evaluative is what gives crime or insanity descriptive meaning. This does not imply that Victorian or present practice could not be improved, only that debate is necessarily about what counts as improvement. Clarification is therefore concerned with the fact-value relationship and corresponding theories of knowledge and ethics. The issue is not technical but general. The Victorians, however, were not well equipped – by moralistic temperament, institutional pressure, or analytic concepts – to frame issues in these terms.

Medicine and law alike set out to make decisions on the basis of facts. As specific trials have shown, they had very different ideas of what qualified as a fact. This is the historical justification for referring to separate discourses. Nevertheless, such was the strength of institutional commitment to factual knowledge that each discourse assumed the other should be making factual statements commensurable with its own. If alienists considered the Rules 'utterly untrustworthy, because untrue to the obvious facts of Nature', psychiatrists are still criticised for 'their reluctance to clarify the state of the developing body of knowledge about human nature'.[24] Confusion about each institution's content and function then arose at two levels: first, in relation to the process by which facts acquired that status; second, in relation to the separate meanings which each discourse covertly embodied in its factual statements.

The courts exist as a forum for settling facts about which there may be legitimate disagreement. Courts have utility in so far as they succeed in doing this. Science, however, sustains a picture of facts being settled by patient research and non-adversary discussion. But recent studies of science show that scientific facts, like legal ones, are often in doubt; doubt is resolved through complex social negotiation. This does not mean that scientists invent facts, only that the criteria defining what is a valid statement develop in social contexts. 'It is not that agents operate by reference to goals and interests instead of to empirical adequacy; rather it is that their sense of empirical adequacy is intelligible only in terms of contingent goals and interests.'[25] Nevertheless, an increasing number of jurists since Stephen have been tempted into supposing that science uncovers knowledge applicable in all contexts.

Legal and medical claims to establish facts have been a major source of misunderstanding. This is because such valid claims slide into an invalid one, namely, that the facts established belong to the same order. In particular, universalist claims for scientific truth – so prominent with Victorian alienists – make it seem that legal facts must be either 'scientific' or false. This is quite wrong, since legal and scientific facts are of different orders: 'One can have clear, objective, and relevant ways of describing and explaining human conduct – descriptions and explanations subject to rational criticism, which nevertheless do not amount to scientific statements or even to approximations of scientific statements.'[26] During the period of scientific expansion in the nineteenth century, this point was often denied, with medico-legal conflict an inevitable result. To take this further would require consideration of the relationship between scientific and legal rationality, particularly European arguments that the law might become 'scientific'.[27]

There is a real difference between Victorian and present-day courts in the deference accorded to scientific knowledge (if not always to witnesses stating such knowledge). Further, over the last twenty years or so, politicians have increasingly used judicial procedures to 'resolve' so-called 'big technology' issues like the siting of nuclear installations. They exploit the status of courts to make planning decisions appear matters of fact rather than policy. The courts in turn exploit the status of science to establish facts of a supposedly universalist character.[28]

These new judicial practices have not produced consensus either. Controversy is as rife in the area of science and law as it ever was in relation to the insanity defence, and for some of the same reasons. Environmental litigation and planning decisions suggest new points of comparison for medico-legal debate. Even when judges formulate these issues as specific matters of fact, the use of scientific witnesses generates rather than resolves conflict. Proposals for a science court (reminiscent of the court-appointed panel of experts favoured by nineteenth-century alienists), freeing scientists to reach decisions unencumbered by irrelevant legal rules, seem ill-fated.[29] A judicial tendency to view disagreement as 'bad science' propagated by biased individuals must be rejected. Scientists possess complex institutions for generating consensual knowledge, but there are many areas where this is not achieved – not merely from lack of knowledge but also from differing criteria of factual adequacy. If scientists are expected to provide publicly usable facts when such facts have no agreed standing, they will necessarily increase controversy. This would seem to be the case for both psychiatric evidence and, for example, evidence about radiation risk.

Factual statements cannot be removed from the context which sustains them as factual and still retain all their meaning. Conversely, if they are isolated for a particular purpose – whether legal or medical – they will bring with them some meaning and evaluation from their context. Nineteenth-century alienists often made this clear when, in the same sentence, they criticised the law for a lack of science *and* humanity. Critics, defending the intrinsic value of judgemental law, have argued that medical facts cannot be decisive. 'We must first decide that specified states of mind qualify as grounds excusing behavior before we can admit expert testimony identifying those states . . . This is a moral and legal matter; it is a business of deciding how we want things to be, not a matter of discovering what in fact is the case.'[30] This needs to be taken further so that we recognise, not just the evaluative nature of law, but the futility of trying to free factual statements from the social purposes for which they were framed.

Debates about abortion or organ transplants illustrate this. There is little difficulty for most purposes in making factual statements about whether a person is alive or dead. At either side of the agreed knowledge, however, there is a great deal of controversy mixing factual claims and emotion. Gestation is a process; there can be no agreement about when the potentially human is actually human unless everyone accepts the same evaluative criteria for humanness. No amount of embryological or theological knowledge will resolve the matter, unless the possession of such knowledge enables one group to dominate politically. The same applies to decisions about time of death.

The courts are concerned with moral and political ends, whether overt or symbolic, which have their point independent of scientific knowledge. 'Our criminal law, founded as it is on the principle of individual responsibility, is not a mere means toward reducing antisocial activity; the institution is itself an essential end for the society.'[31] There is therefore no more reason to accept the decisions of experts than of any other group. Experts may better understand the consequences of certain decisions, but to consult a certain type of expert necessarily constitutes a choice as to which kinds of decisions are favoured. Jurists and psychiatrists alike create confusion and minimise the existence of political power by supposing that facts exist independently of the decision to accept them.

These issues are particularly difficult in ascriptions of responsibility. Victorian alienists assumed that observation established a determinist causal basis for lunacy and that this determinism logically created excusing conditions. Both parts of the assumption were unsound: the alienists' determinism logically preceded their factual statements about lunatics.[32] And *if* it was determinism which established non-accountability, then '*no* one (sane or mad) would be what we call responsible'.[33] Lawyers often declared that the acceptance of a discourse of scientific facts would eliminate responsibility. This view is still widely held, though philosophers differentiate between compulsion determined by physical circumstances and acting in a certain way because motives give a reason to do so. No amount of scientific determinism can impugn the view that deeds are excusable while acts are not.[34]

Responsibility is about which factual statements, formulated by which institutions, we agree to accept as describing human conduct. Since neither we nor the Victorians agree about this, 'we can do little more than draw the uneven line traced by the [insanity] defense as it serves first one objective, then another, and even a third, sometimes separately and sometimes together'.[35] Consensus is not possible in a compromise between different beliefs, interests and values. Compromise only has political value when it is created rather than imposed. In this sense historical interpretation engages with a living argument.

ABBREVIATIONS

Asylum JMS	*Asylum Journal of Mental Science*
Bethlem CBC	Bethlem criminal case note books
BFMCR	*British and Foreign Medico-chirurgical Review*
BFMR	*British and Foreign Medical Review*
BMJ	*British Medical Journal*
Broun	Reports of cases – Scotland; see 'List of sources for cases'
CCC	Central Criminal Court
Capital Punishment Commission	*Report of the Capital Punishment Commission,* 1866; see 'List of sources for cases'
Couper	Reports of cases – Scotland; see 'List of sources for cases'
Cox C.C.	Cox's reports of cases; see 'List of sources for cases'
EMJ	*Edinburgh Medical Journal*
EMSJ	*Edinburgh Medical and Surgical Journal*
E.R.	The English Reports; see 'List of sources for cases'
Howell's St.Tr.	Howell's & Howell's State Trials; see 'List of sources for cases'
Irvine	Reports of cases – Scotland; see 'List of sources for cases'
JMS	*Journal of Mental Science*
JPM	*Journal of Psychological Medicine and Mental Pathology*
MTG	*Medical Times and Gazette*
P.P.	Parliamentary Papers
St.Tr.N.S.	Reports of the State Trials, new series; see 'List of sources for cases'

CHAPTER ONE
Introduction
1 [H.Maudsley and C.L.
Robertson] *Insanity and Crime: A*
Medico-legal Commentary on the
Case of George Victor Townley
(London: Churchill 1864) 29.
2 ibid., 28.
3 e.g. J.Biggs, *The Guilty Mind:*
Psychiatry and the Law of Homicide
(Baltimore: Johns Hopkins Uni-
versity Press 1967); S.Glueck, *Law*
and Psychiatry: Cold War or
'Entente Cordiale'? (London:
Tavistock 1963); A.S.Goldstein,
The Insanity Defense (New Haven:
Yale University Press 1967); J.M.
Quen, 'Anglo-American criminal
insanity: an historical perspective',
Journal of the History of the Be-
havioral Sciences 10 (1974) 313-23;
idem, 'Isaac Ray: have we learned
his lessons?', *Bulletin of the Ameri-*
can Academy of Psychiatry and Law
2 (1974) 137-47; F.A.Whitlock,
Criminal Responsibility and Mental
Illness (London: Butterworths
1963). This hardly touches the
literature; cf. the selected list in
A.D.Brooks, *Law, Psychiatry and*
the Mental Health System (Boston:
Little, Brown 1974) 15-18.
4 J.F.Stephen, *A History of the*
Criminal Law of England, 3 vols.,
first publ. 1883 (facsimile reprint
New York: Burt Franklin, n.d.) 11.
152.
5 This is substantially true of
the collection of essays on M'Naghten: D.J.West and A.Walk (eds.)
Daniel McNaughten: His Trial and
the Aftermath (Ashford: Headley
Brothers for The British Journal of
Psychiatry 1977). Contrast the
historical account in J.M.Quen,
'An historical view of the M'Naghten Trial', *Bulletin of the History of*
Medicine 43 (1968) 43-51.

6 G.Williams, *Criminal Law.*
The General Part, 2nd edition
(London: Stevens 1961) 428-558;
The English and Empire Digest . . .
Replacement Volume 14. Criminal
Law and Procedure (London:
Butterworths 1956) sections 234-
314. For the United States: S.R.
Lewinstein, 'The historical develop-
ment of insanity as a defense in
criminal actions', *Journal of*
Forensic Science 14 (1969) 275-93,
469-500; A.M.Platt and B.L.
Diamond, 'The origins of the "right
and wrong" test of criminal re-
sponsibility and its subsequent
development in the United States:
an historical survey', *California*
Law Review 54 (1966) 1227-60; H.
Weihoven, *Mental Disorder as a*
Criminal Defense (Buffalo: Dennis
1954) 50-173.
Victorian authorities include:
W.O.Russell, *A Treatise on Crimes*
and Misdemeanors, 5th edition ed.
by S.Prentice, vol. 1 (London:
Stevens 1877); L.Shelford, *A*
Practical Treatise of the Law Con-
cerning Lunatics, Idiots, and Persons
of Unsound Mind, 2nd edition
(London: Sweet, Stevens, & Norton
1847) 585-601; A.Alison, *Principles*
of the Criminal Law of Scotland
(Edinburgh: Blackwood 1832)
644-61; F.Wharton and M.Stillé, *A*
Treatise on Medical Jurisprudence
(Philadelphia: Kay & Brother 1855)
an American text but including
English and European cases.
7 N.Walker, *Crime and Insanity*
in England, vol. I: The Historical
Perspective (Edinburgh: Edinburgh
University Press, 1968); N.Walker
and S.McCabe, *Crime and Insanity*
in England, vol. II: New Solutions
and New Problems (Edinburgh:
Edinburgh University Press 1973).
Cf. K.Jones, *Mental Health and*

Social Policy 1845-1959 (London: Routledge 1960) 178-203. The variety of procedures under this Act complicates the extrapolation of conclusions from history to the present. But controversy continues: *Report of the Committee on Mentally Abnormal Offenders* (London: HMSO 1975); The Law Commission, *Criminal Law: Report on the Mental Element in Crime* (London: HMSO 1978); P.Clyne, *Guilty but Insane: Anglo-American Attitudes to Insanity and Criminal Guilt* (London: Nelson 1973).

8   See Walker 1968 [7] 85-8, 264-7, 283. For the reliability of judicial statistics: J.J.Tobias, *Crime and Society in the Nineteenth Century* (Harmondsworth: Penguin 1972) 23-5.

9   W.A.Guy, 'On insanity and crime; and on the plea of insanity in criminal cases', *Journal of the Statistical Society* 32 (1869) 159-91, on 180-1.

10   I do not include references to the vast medical sociology literature; but see J.Woodward and D. Richards, 'Towards a social history of medicine', in idem (eds.) *Health Care and Popular Medicine in Nineteenth Century England: Essays in the Social History of Medicine* (London: Croom Helm 1977) 9-55. On lunacy legislation and government growth: D.J.Mellet, 'Society, the State and Mental Illness, 1790-1890. Social, Cultural and Administrative Aspects of the Institutional Care and Control of the Insane in Nineteenth-Century England', unpublished Ph.D. thesis, Cambridge 1978, 142-85.

11   M.Foucault, *Discipline and Punish: The Birth of the Prison* (London: Allen Lane 1977).

12   *Report of the Metropolitan Commissioners in Lunacy*, P.P. 1844, XXVI; A.T.Scull, *Museums of Madness: The Social Organization of Insanity in Nineteenth-Century England* (London: Allen Lane

1979); P.McCandless, 'Insanity and Society: A Study of the English Lunacy Reform Movement 1815-1870', unpublished Ph.D. thesis, Wisconsin 1974; Mellet 1978 [10] 133-85; W.L.Parry-Jones, *The Trade in Lunacy: A Study of Private Madhouses in England in the Eighteenth and Nineteenth Centuries* (London: Routledge 1972).

13   Jones 1960 [7] 7-40; the role and social composition of the Commissioners is analysed in Mellet 1978 [10] 266-346.

14   *Copy of the Special Report of the Commissioners in Lunacy to the Lord Chancellor on the Alleged Increase of Insanity*, P.P. 1897, XXXVIII; Scull 1979 [12] 221-53.

15   G.Rosen, 'Cameralism and the concept of medical police', *Bulletin of the History of Medicine* 27 (1953) 21-42; L.J.Jordanova, 'Policing public health in France 1780-1815', unpublished paper, University of Essex 1980; E.H. Ackerknecht, 'Early history of legal medicine', in C.R.Burns (ed.) *Legacies in Law and Medicine* (New York: Science History 1977) 249-71. Bibliographies in R.P.Brittain, *Bibliography of Medico-legal Works in English* (London: Sweet & Maxwell 1962); J.Nemec, *International Bibliography of Medico-legal Serials. 1736-1967* (Bethesda: National Library of Medicine 1969); idem, *International Bibliography of the History of Legal Medicine* (Bethesda: National Library of Medicine 1973); J.B. Speer, 'Essay review of T.R.Forbes *Crowner's Quest*', *Annals of Science* 37 (1980) 353-6.

The principal Victorian texts were: W.A.Guy, *Principles of Forensic Medicine* (London: Renshaw 1844); A.S.Taylor, *A Manual of Medical Jurisprudence* (London: Churchill 1844); idem, *The Principles and Practice of Medical Jurisprudence* (London: Churchill

1865); T.R.Beck and J.B.Beck, *Elements of Medical Jurisprudence*, 7th edition (London: Longman, Brown, Green, & Longmans 1842) an anglicised American text with useful bibliography.

16 Walker 1968 [7] 52-73. For a nineteenth-century opinion that pre-1800 verdicts were variable and could be reached without evidence of disordered reason: T.Mayo, *An Essay on the Relation of the Theory of Morals to Insanity* (London: Fellowes 1834) 44-9.

17 For the mid-century medical profession see M.J.Peterson, *The Medical Profession in Mid-Victorian London* (Berkeley: University of California Press 1978). For the professionalisation of alienists: Mellet 1978 [10]; Scull 1979 [12].

18 Q.Skinner, '"Social meaning" and the explanation of social action', in P.Laslett, W.G.Runciman and Q.Skinner (eds.) *Philosophy, Politics and Society. Fourth Series* (Oxford: Blackwell 1972) 136-57.

19 C.Taylor, 'Interpretation and the sciences of man', *Review of Metaphysics* 25 (1971) 3-51, on 27.

20 cf. B.Barnes, *Interests and the Growth of Knowledge* (London: Routledge 1977); B.Barnes and S. Shapin, *Natural Order: Historical Studies in Scientific Culture* (London: Sage 1979); D.Bloor, *Knowledge and Social Imagery* (London: Routledge 1976).

21 M.J.Cullen, *The Statistical Movement in Early Victorian Britain: The Foundations of Empirical Social Research* (Hassocks: Harvester 1975); cf. Woodward and Richards 1977 [10] 45-55, for further references.

22 The importance of science to this class after 1870 is examined in D.A.MacKenzie, 'Karl Pearson and the professional middle class', *Annals of Science* 36 (1978) 125-44; idem, *Statistics in Britain, 1865-1930: The Social Construction of Scientific Knowledge* (Edinburgh:

Edinburgh University Press 1981). The argument is generalised in relation to the British bio-medical sciences in L.S.Jacyna, 'Scientific Naturalism in Victorian Britain: An Essay in the Social History of Ideas', unpublished Ph.D. thesis, Edinburgh 1980.

23 Barnes and Shapin 1979 [20] 93. Cf. F.M.Turner, *Between Science and Religion. The Reaction to Scientific Naturalism in Late Victorian England* (New Haven: Yale University Press 1974) 8-30; Jacyna 1980 [22]; R.M.Young, 'The historiographic and ideological contexts of the nineteenth-century debate on man's place in nature', in M.Teich and R.M. Young (eds.) *Changing Perspectives in the History of Science* (London: Heinemann 1973) 344-438.

24 T.Laycock, 'On law and medicine in insanity. An introductory lecture', *EMJ* 7 (1862) 1132-46, on 1143.

25 H.Maudsley, *Responsibility in Mental Disease* (London: King 1874) 23-4.

26 The term has been popularised by translations of Foucault, who used the much more common French term 'discours'; I do not claim consistency with his usage. Cf. M.Foucault, *The Archaeology of Knowledge* (London: Tavistock 1972) 32-4, 178-95. For a valuable discussion of law and psychiatry as genuinely alternative accounts: H. Fingarette, *The Meaning of Criminal Insanity* (Berkeley: University of California Press 1972) 62-9.

27 H.Maudsley, 'Homicidal insanity', *JMS* 9 (1863) 327-43, on 331.

CHAPTER TWO
Medical Criticism and Penal Practice

1 M.Ignatieff, *A Just Measure of Pain: The Penitentiary in the Industrial Revolution, 1750-1850*

(London: Macmillan 1978) 193-204; A.H.Manchester, *A Modern Legal History of England and Wales 1750-1950* (London: Butterworths 1980); L.Radzinowicz, *A History of English Criminal Law and its Administration from 1750*, 4 vols. (London: Stevens 1948-68).

2 A common institutional position is emphasised in M.Foucault, *Discipline and Punish: The Birth of the Prison* (London: Allen Lane 1977); D.J.Rothman, *The Discovery of the Asylum: Social Order and Disorder in the New Republic* (Boston: Little, Brown 1971).

3 Ignatieff 1978 [1] 71-2, discusses the contradiction within the penitentiary movement between treating deviants as machines and as moral individuals capable of repentence.

4 A.Walk and D.L.Walker, 'Gloucester and the beginnings of the R.M.P.A.', *JMS* 107 (1961) 603-32; A.T.Scull, *Museums of Madness: The Social Organization of Insanity in Nineteenth-Century England* (London: Allen Lane 1979) 164-5.

5 See R.Hunter and I. Macalpine, 'Introduction' to J.Conolly, *An Inquiry Concerning the Indications of Insanity with Suggestions for the Better Protection and Care of the Insane*, first publ. 1830 (facsimile reprint London: Dawsons 1964); idem, 'Introduction', to J. Conolly, *Treatment of the Insane Without Mechanical Restraints*, first publ. 1856 (facsimile reprint Folkestone: Dawsons 1973); idem, *Three Hundred Years of Psychiatry 1535-1860* (London: Oxford University Press 1963) 805-9, 1030-8.

6 *Journal of Psychological Medicine and Mental Pathology*, 1848-60; *The Medical Critic and Psychological Journal*, 1861-3; reformed by his son Lyttleton S. Forbes Winslow under the original title, 1875-83. Cf. W.L.Parry-Jones, *The Trade in Lunacy: A Study of Private Madhouses in England in the Eighteenth and Nineteenth Centuries* (London: Routledge 1972) 95; Hunter and Macalpine 1963 [5] 964-5. It is very probable that the great majority of the unsigned articles in the *Journal* were written by Winslow himself.

7 *Asylum Journal*, vol. I, 1853-1855; *Asylum Journal of Mental Science*, vols. II-III, 1856-7. Many of the unsigned articles in early volumes were by J.C.Bucknill. Cf. G.F.Blandford, *General Index to the First Twenty-four Volumes of the Journal of Mental Science. With Historical Sketch by D.Hack Tuke* (London: Churchill 1879). Lists of Association members are at the back of several volumes. D.H.Tuke (ed.) *A Dictionary of Psychological Medicine*, 2 vols. (London: Churchill 1892) II, 1382-1408, contains a bibliography arranged by date and a list of psychological societies and journals.

8 Maudsley's money and planning led to the Maudsley Hospital (opened 1923), now part of the Bethlem Royal Hospital and the Maudsley Hospital (housing the Institute of Psychiatry) in London. Maudsley has no biographer; but see A.Lewis, 'Henry Maudsley: his work and influence', *JMS* 97 (1951) 259-77.

9 R.Smith, 'Physiological Psychology and the Philosophy of Nature in Mid-Nineteenth-Century Britain', unpublished Ph.D. thesis, Cambridge 1970, 69-100, 255-63.

10 T.Laycock, 'The scientific place and principles of medical psychology: an introductory address', *EMJ* 6 (1861) 1053-64; idem, 'On law and medicine in insanity. An introductory lecture', *EMJ* 7 (1862) 1132-46; idem, 'The teaching of psychological medicine and mental pathology at the University of Edinburgh', letter to the Editor, *BMJ* i (1871) 293; A. Morison, *Outlines of Lectures on*

the *Nature, Causes, and Treatment of Insanity*, 4th edition by T.C. Morison (London: Longman, Brown, Green, & Longmans 1848); [? F.Winslow], 'The instruction of medical pupils in mental diseases', *JPM* I (1848) 185-8. Cf. Hunter and Macalpine 1963 [5] 769-70, 1053; idem, Conolly 1964 [5] 22-5; G.M.Robertson, 'The teaching of psychiatry in Edinburgh: and Sir Alexander Morison', *EMJ*, new series 35 (1928) 192-205.

11 Lectures which were given assumed that the medical jurisprudence of insanity gave them added importance: Laycock 1861 [10]; J.M.Pagan, *The Medical Jurisprudence of Insanity* (London: Ball, Arnold 1840); lectures by R. Jamieson reported in 'Medical jurisprudence of insanity', *JPM* 4 (1851) 187-96.

12 D.Skae, 'On the legal relations of insanity: the civil incapacity and criminal responsibility of the insane', *EMJ* 12 (1867) 811-29, on 829. Cf. F.Fish, 'David Skae, M.D., F.R.C.S., founder of the Edinburgh school of psychiatry', *Medical History* 9 (1965) 36-53.

13 'The plea of insanity', *BFMCR* 55 (1875) 88-115, on 114.

14 See also publications by J. Burgess, C.M.Burnett, J.G.Davey, J.F.Duncan, R.Jamieson, T.M. Madden, T.C.Morison, S.W.North, M.B.Sampson, R.H.Semple, J.A. Symonds, T.S.Traill, J.W.H. Williams.

15 N. Walker, *Crime and Insanity in England, vol. I: The Historical Perspective* (Edinburgh: Edinburgh University Press 1968) 74-95.

16 J.F.Stephen, *A History of the Criminal Law of England*, 3 vols., first publ. 1883 (facsimile reprint New York: Burt Franklin, n.d.) 11. 151-9.

17 8 E.R. 722. Some difficulties were discussed by the Law Commissioners: *Second Report of Her Majesty's Commissioners for Revising and Consolidating the Criminal Law*, P.P. 1846, XXIV. 9-11, 50-1. The Rules are quoted and discussed in Walker 1968 [15] 97-102; and in G.Williams, *Criminal Law. The General Part*, 2nd edition (London: Stevens 1961) 477-509.

18 8 E.R. 720.

19 ibid., 722-3.

20 S.Glueck, *Law and Psychiatry: Cold War or 'Entente Cordiale'?* (London: Tavistock 1963) 45.

21 J.R.Reynolds, *On the Scientific Value of the Legal Tests of Insanity* (London: Churchill 1872) 9.

22 *Royal Commission on Capital Punishment 1949-1953: Report* (London: HMSO 1953) minute 227.

23 J.F.Stephen, 'On the policy of maintaining the limits at present imposed by law on the criminal responsibility of madmen', read 1855, in *Papers Read Before the Juridical Society: 1855-1858* (London: Stevens & Norton 1858) 67-94, on 67.

24 ibid., 71.

25 ibid., 73. Even lawyers, though, could not help sometimes treating the Rules as tests of insanity; this was pointed out in Dr Winslow's reply to Stephen: F. Winslow, 'The legal doctrine of responsibility in cases of insanity, connected with alleged criminal acts', read 1857, in *Papers Read 1858* [23] 595-635, on 599-601.

26 'Regina v. Fooks. Dorset Spring Assizes, 1863', *JMS* 9 (1863) 125-37, on 126.

27 cf. H.Maudsley, *Responsibility in Mental Disease* (London: King 1874) 164; J.R.Reynolds, *Criminal Lunatics: Are they responsible?* (London: Churchill 1856) 32; W.Wood, *Remarks on the Plea of Insanity, and on the Management of Criminal Lunatics* (London: Longman, Brown, Green, & Longmans 1851) 3-5, 19. This position was

criticised in Stephen 1883 [16] 11. 125.

28   J. Feinberg, 'What is so special about mental illness ?', in *Doing & Deserving: Essays in the Theory of Responsibility* (Princeton: Princeton University Press 1970) 272-92, on 272. A.G.N.Flew, *Crime or Disease?* (London: Macmillan 1973) argues for incapacity (the obverse of compulsion) as the test of responsibility. For biting criticism of doctors who confuse responsibility and illness: H.Oppenheimer, *The Criminal Responsibility of Lunatics: A Study in Comparative Law* (London: Sweet & Maxwell 1909) 9-16.

29   Walker 1968 [15] 188-92, 209-15.

30   Quoted in extracts from Ray's 5th edition (1871) in I.Ray, *A Treatise on the Medical Jurisprudence of Insanity*, first publ. 1838 (reprinted Cambridge, Mass.: Belknap Press of Harvard University 1962) 345. Doe, J. repeated the charge in State v. Jones. On State v. Pike (coming to trial in 1868 and to appeal in 1869) and State v. Jones (1871): Glueck 1963 [20] 79-83; S.R.Lewinstein, 'The historical development of insanity as a defense in criminal actions', *Journal of Forensic Science*, 14 (1969) 275-93, 469-500, on 480-2; J.M.Quen, 'Isaac Ray: have we learned his lessons ?', *Bulletin of the American Academy of Psychiatry and Law*, 2 (1974) 137-47; L.E.Reik, 'The Doe-Ray correspondence: a pioneer collaboration in the jurisprudence of mental disease', *Yale Law Journal* 63 (1953) 183-96. Ray's position among American alienists is discussed in C.E.Rosenberg, *The Trial of the Assassin Guiteau: Psychiatry and Law in the Gilded Age* (Chicago: University of Chicago Press 1968) 61-5.

31   See the approving citation of the New Hampshire cases in

Maudsley 1874 [27] 99-111. The New Hampshire example was taken up by a number of American states: Glueck 1963 [20] 49-58; Lewinstein 1969 [30].

32   Quoted by Glueck 1963 [20] 86, see also 83-91. Cf. Lewinstein 1969 [30] 482-90; A.S.Goldstein and M.Marcus, 'The McNaughton Rules in the United States', in D.J. West and A.Walk (eds.) *Daniel McNaughton: His Trial and the Aftermath* (Ashford: Headley Brothers for The British Journal of Psychiatry 1977) 153-69.

33   D.L.Bazelon, 'Psychiatrists and the adversary process', *Scientific American* 230 (1974) 18-23. Cf. A.D.Brooks, *Law, Psychiatry and the Mental Health System* (Boston: Little, Brown 1974) 193-7.

34   Important discussions include: A.S.Goldstein, *The Insanity Defense* (New Haven: Yale University Press 1967); H.Fingarette, *The Meaning of Criminal Insanity* (Berkeley: University of California Press 1972). See Brooks 1974 [32] 111-242, for a legal text; the A.L.I. Model Penal Code is quoted on page 165. Different states have varied considerably in practice.

35   *Royal Commission* 1953 [22] 73-158, and Appendix 8; Walker 1968 [15] 147-64; Williams 1961 [17] 541-8.

36   cf. *Report of the Committee on Mentally Abnormal Offenders* (London: HMSO 1975); The Law Commission, *Criminal Law: Report on the Mental Element in Crime* (London: HMSO 1978).

37   E.Bittner, 'The concept of mental abnormality in the administration of justice outside the courtroom', in A.V.S.de Rueck and R. Porter (eds.) *The Mentally Abnormal Offender* (London: Churchill 1968) 201-18; N.Walker and S. McCabe, *Crime and Insanity in England, vol. II: New Solutions and New Problems* (Edinburgh: Edin-

burgh University Press 1973).

38   Director of Public Prosecutions, evidence to *Royal Commission* 1953 [22] minute 233.

39   Walker 1968 [15] 78-81.

40   [J.Blackwell], 'Report on the treatment of lunatics', *Quarterly Review* 74 (1844) 416-47, on 416-17.

41   Pritchard's case. Cf. W.O. Russell, *A Treatise on Crimes and Misdemeanors*, 5th edition ed. S. Prentice, vol. 1 (London: Stevens 1877) 113 note (n); Walker 1968 [15] 219-25. The grand jury (which continued throughout the nineteenth century to sit at the beginning of the assizes to find whether there was a true bill against those indicted) had the power to throw out a charge if they considered there was no case to answer owing to the accused's mental condition; see Griggs's case. On another occasion (Hodges's case, 1838) the judge argued that insanity must be decided by a petty jury.

42   The issue of unfitness to plead during the course of the trial was discussed in Southey's case (1865). Southey began by objecting to being represented by counsel. For the wrangle over onus of proof in unfitness to plead: Davies's case (1853), Turton's case (1854), Peacock's case (1870). On onus of proof: Williams 1961 [17] 448-52, 516-21.

43   All those accused of felony were given a right to counsel by The Felonies Act (1836); Manchester 1980 [1] 168-9.

44   Walker 1968 [15] 226.

45   ibid., 226-8.

46   ibid., 228-9.

47   ibid., 207-10.

48   See 'Lunatic asylums', *Westminister Review* 43 (1845) 162-92, on 188-90; P.H.Alldberidge, 'Criminal insanity: from Bethlem to Broadmoor', *Proceedings of the Royal Society of Medicine* 67 (1974) 897-904; idem, 'Why was McNaughton sent to Bethlem ?', in

West and Walk 1977 [32] 100-12; Parry-Jones 1972 [6] 64-7; Walker and McCabe 1973 [37] 2-7.

49   *Report of the Metropolitan Commissioners in Lunacy*, P.P. 1844, XXVI. 195-9, and Appendix G, page 274. Of the 257, 205 were male and 52 female. For further statistics of criminal lunatics: *Pauper Lunatic and Idiots, and Criminal Lunatics. Returns of the Number of Pauper Lunatics and Idiots in Each County in England and Wales; – And of Criminal Lunatics, With their Places of Confinement*, P.P. 1837, XLIV; annual figures in the *Reports of the Commissioners in Lunacy; Report of the Commission Appointed ... to Inquire into the Subject of Criminal Lunacy*, P.P. 1882, XXXII, Appendix A.

50   J.C.Bucknill, *Unsoundness of Mind in Relation to Criminal Acts*, 2nd edition (London: Longman, Brown, Green, Longmans & Roberts 1857) 119; first published in 1854. Cf. [A.Wynter] 'Lunatic asylums', *Quarterly Review* 101 (1857) 353-93, on 361-2.

51   Alldberidge 1974 [48]; idem, *The Late Richard Dadd 1817-1886* (London: The Tate Gallery 1974) 26-33. The Bethlem archives include the Bethlem Sub-Committee Books, 1709-1948, and the Criminal Lunatic Books, 1810-85, which include full details of admissions, administration, dealings with the Home Secretary, etc. The nineteenth-century Bethlem records have not been examined in detail. Cf. Walker and McCabe 1973 [37] 285.

52   Parry-Jones 1972 [6] 66.

53   See Annual *Reports* of the Commissioners in Lunacy; extract from J.C.Bucknill, *On the Classification and Management of Criminal Lunatics* (1851) in idem 1857 [50] 141-8; W.C.Hood, *Suggestions for the Future Provision of Criminal Lunatics* (London: Churchill 1854); Wood 1851 [27]. For convict

lunatics, see also J.T.Arlidge, *On the State of Lunacy and the Legal Provision for the Insane* (London: Churchill 1859) 6.

54 D.H.Tuke, *Chapters in the History of the Insane in the British Isles* (London: Kegan Paul, Trench 1882) 265-84; *Commission of Criminal Lunacy* 1882 [49] 5-6; R. Partridge, *Broadmoor. A History of Criminal Lunacy and its Problems* (London: Chatto & Windus 1953); Walker and McCabe 1973 [37] 8-10.

55 The relevant legislation is reviewed in *Commission of Criminal Lunacy* 1882 [49]. From 1875 a lunatic wing at Woking convict prison was used to receive insane convicts (who were then transferred to Broadmoor towards the expiry of their sentence if still insane).

56 My percentages are approximations, calculated from figures collated by Barbara Bowron (for work for the Open University with a record deposited at Bethlem) from the records of criminal lunatic admissions between 1816 and 1864. 59 out of 650 men, and 28 out of 120 women (total of 87 out of 770) admitted were eventually 'discharged to friends'. The total admission figures include convicts becoming insane; 83 men and 17 women (total 100) are reported as being returned to prison in the same period, but figures are not given for admissions in this category. My percentages are therefore probably lower than the correct ones.

57 See case note comments on e.g. James Atkinson, Mary Ann Beveridge, Martha Bradish, Charles Forrester.

58 K.T.Erikson, 'Notes on the sociology of deviance', in H.S. Becker (ed.) *The Other Side: Perspectives on Deviance* (New York: Free Press 1967) 9-21, on 14. Cf. Foucault 1977 [2] 42-57.

59 J.C.Prichard, *A Treatise on Insanity and Other Disorders Affecting the Mind* (London: Sherwood, Gilbert, & Piper 1835) 398-9.

60 Maudsley 1874 [27] 129. Cf. T.H.Tuke, evidence in *Report of the Capital Punishment Commission*, P.P. 1866, XXI, minute 2442; A.H. Dymond, *The Law on its Trial; Or Personal Recollections of the Death Penalty and its Opponents* (London: Bennett 1865) 167; Oppenheimer 1909 [28] 233.

61 Radzinowicz 1948-68 [1] 1. 567, and IV. 303-26; Manchester 1980 [1] 244-9.

62 Ignatieff 1978 [1]. Cf. D.Hay, 'Property, authority and criminal law', in D.Hay et al., *Albion's Fatal Tree: Crime and Society in Eighteenth-Century England* (London: Allen Lane 1975) 17-63, on 40-9.

63 Walker 1968 [15] 194-218.

64 Russell 1877 [41] 807-8; Radzinowicz 1948-68 [1] IV. 341-2.

65 Convicts returning to sanity completed their sentence. In theory, this included hanging, but the execution of prisoners at one time found insane was not carried out; cf. Williams 1961 [17] 469; Walker 1968 [15] 205. I have not had time to pursue the records reviewing capital cases in which there was an unsuccessful insanity defence. The Home Office retains index files of Capital Cases 1846-1900, Index to the 'Old Criminal' Series, and especially a Chronological List of Capital Cases for the Period 1846-1900. These indexes are valuable guides to the records at the Public Record Office. I am grateful to Mr T.H.East (now retired) for guiding me through the Home Office indexes.

66 See the cases of Townley, Westron, Corrigan, George Clark, Dalmas and Somner.

67 Reynolds 1872 [21] 7-8. Cf. Skae 1867 [12] 820-9. Reynolds might have had a case like Broomfield (1865) in mind. Broomfield

was obviously insane – by medical opinion. Though he was found guilty, he was later certified.

68 Stephen, evidence in, *Special Report from the Select Committee on Homicide Law Amendment Bill*, P.P. 1874, IX. 7. Cf. Bucknill 1857 [50] 109. W.A.Guy, 'On insanity and crime; and on the plea of insanity in criminal cases', *Journal of the Statistical Society* 32 (1869) 159-91, on 161, calculated that for 1,452 in 10,000 murderers found insane or acquitted because of insanity, there were only 6 in 10,000 for other offences. For examples of minor offences in which the issue of insanity was raised: Bates' case (1850), and Shepherd's case (1845). Nevertheless, a majority among criminal lunatics had committed minor offences since this class included those found insane on arraignment or transferred before or after conviction. A causal theory linking petty crime and insanity became more prominent later: G.M.Bacon, 'The relation of crime and insanity', *Social Science Review*, new series 1 (1864) 431-47; C.Mercier, *Crime & Criminals: Being the Jurisprudence of Crime, Medical, Biological, and Psychological* (London: University of London Press 1918).

69 Bucknill 1857 [50] 113.

70 Radzinowicz 1948-68 [1] IV. 326-43; Dymond 1865 [60]; Manchester 1980 [1] 247-8; E.O.Tuttle, *The Crusade Against Capital Punishment in Great Britain* (London: Stevens 1961).

71 Wood 1851 [27] 4-5.

72 Pagan 1840 [11] 256.

73 A.S.Taylor, *The Principles and Practice of Medical Jurisprudence* (London: Churchill 1865) 1112. Taylor also accused some medical men of 'meddling' with the law: *A Manual of Medical Jurisprudence* (London: Churchill 1844) 450-1.

74 F.Winslow, *The Case of Luigi Buranelli Medico-legally Considered* [Supplement to vol. 8, *JPM*] (London: Churchill 1855) 63. Though Connolly (1964 [5] 453), Prichard 1835 [59] 399), and Wood (1851 [27] 264-7) were abolitionists, I think Winslow and Maudsley were not.

75 *Westminster Review* 1845 [48] 190.

76 Bucknill 1857 [50] 136. Cf. calls for an intermediate verdict in ibid., 113-18; idem, 'The pathology of insanity', *BFMCR* 15 (1855) 207-29, on 213; idem, 'Mayo, Winslow, & Parigot, on criminal lunacy', *BFMCR* 16 (1855) 370-88, on 379; Maudsley 1874 [25] 181; T.Mayo, *Medical Testimony and Evidence in Cases of Lunacy* (London: Parker 1854) 50-2, 86-90; Stephen 1883 [16] II. 175; Wood 1851 [27] 45-8; D.Yellowless, 'The trial of Alexander Milne for murder in Edinburgh', *JMS* 9 (1863) 119-25.

77 Walker 1968 [15] 186-93.

78 Oxford and Francis were tried for treason, though under the Act of 39 & 40 Geo. III, c.93, covering crimes against the sovereign, the trial procedure followed that of murder trials.

79 For the perception and reality of increasing crime rates: Ignatieff 1978 [1] 179-87; D.Philips, *Crime and Authority in Victorian England: The Black Country 1835-1860* (London: Croom Helm 1977); J.J. Tobias, *Crime and Society in the Nineteenth Century* (Harmondsworth: Penguin 1972). The crime rates were important to debates on prevention and policing: Radzinowicz 1948-68 [1] II and III; Manchester 1980 [1] 215-25. Cf. G. Pearson, *The Deviant Imagination: Psychiatry, Social Work and Social Change* (London: Macmillan 1975) 143-76.

80 Blackwell 1844 [40]; 'Moral insanity – Dr. Mayo's Croonian Lectures', *Fraser's Magazine* 51

(1855) 245-59; 'Homicidal mania and moral insanity', *Saturday Review* 15 (1863) 370-2. It was common for judges to say the defence must be 'jealously guarded': e.g. Lord Denman in John Smith's case, Erle, C.J. in Leigh's case, and Rolfe, B. in Alnutt's case.

81   Lord Campbell, *Hansard* 67 (1843) col.742.

82   Guy 1869 [68] 159.

83   W.C.Hood, *Criminal Lunatics. A Letter to the Chairman of the Commissioners in Lunacy* (London: Churchill 1860) 16.

84   Bethlem CBC/3, 203.

85   [? H.Maudsley], 'The suicide of George Victor Townley', *J M S* 11 (1865) 66-83, on 82. Cf. J.C. Browne, 'Notes on homicidal insanity', *J M S* 9 (1863) 197-210, on 197. It is likely that extreme arguments for the insanity plea embarrassed the medical Commissioners in Lunacy.

86   Guy 1869 [68] 180-1, 191. Walker's statistical study reaches a similar conclusion: Walker 1968 [15] 85-8, 264-7. Guy was Professor of Forensic Medicine, King's College, London, but he refused to appear as an expert witness; he was apparently upset by the adversary process for both personal and scientific reasons.

87   W.A.Guy, 'On the executions for murder that have taken place in England and Wales during the last seventy years', *Journal of the Statistical Society* 38 (1875) 463-86, on 468-75.

88   Evidence of Lords Cranworth, Wensleydale and Denman in *Capital Punishment Commission* 1866 [60] minutes 126, 360-1, 797.

89   Taylor 1865 [73] 1109. Cf. Conolly 1964 [5] 460-2.

90   Conolly 1964 [5] 462.

91   Winslow 1858 [25] 633-4. In other contexts, and in relation to other asylums, Winslow was of course an ardent defender of the non-punitive quality of incarceration.

92   J.G.Davey, 'Insanity and crime – communication by Dr. Dav[e]y', *J M S* 6 (1859) 31-8, on 31-2; T.Laycock, 'On the legal doctrines of the responsibility of the insane and its consequences', *J M S* 10 (1864) 350-66, on 351-2.

93   Reynolds 1856 [27] 33. Cf. Laycock 1862 [10].

94   J.G.Davey, 'A case of homicidal mania', *J M S* 7 (1860) 49-59; *Copy of the Fourteenth Report of the Commissioners In Lunacy to the Lord Chancellor*, P.P. 1860, XXXIV. 91-7.

95   E.H.Hare, 'Masturbatory insanity: the history of an idea', *J M S* 108 (1962) 1-25; H.T.Engelhardt, 'The disease of masturbation: values and the concept of disease', *Bulletin of the History of Medicine* 48 (1974) 234-48; A.N. Gilbert, 'Doctor, patient, and onanist diseases in the nineteenth century', *Journal of the History of Medicine* 30 (1975) 217-34; J.S. Haller and R.M.Haller, *The Physician and Sexuality in Victorian America* (Urbana: University of Illinois Press 1974) 195-211; R.P. Neuman, 'Masturbation, madness, and the modern concepts of childhood and adolescence', *Journal of Social History* 8 (1975) 1-27. For a criminal lunatic with progressive dementia attributed to masturbation see Touchet's case notes in Bethlem CBC/2, 86.

96   R.Cooter, 'The power of the body: the early nineteenth century', in B.Barnes and S.Shapin (eds.) *Natural Order: Historical Studies in Scientific Culture* (London: Sage 1979) 73-92. For a parallel analysis of the disease of chlorosis: K.M. Figlio, 'Chlorosis and chronic disease in nineteenth-century Britain: the social constitution of somatic illness in capitalist society', *Social History* 3 (1978) 167-97.

97   F.Winslow, 'The psychological vocation of the physician',

in *Lettsomian Lectures on Insanity* (London: Churchill 1854) 39; whole passage italicised in original.

98 Foucault 1977 [2] 170-92.

CHAPTER THREE
The Medical Viewpoint

1 H.Maudsley, *Body and Mind: An Inquiry into their Connection and Mutual Influence, Especially with Reference to Mental Disorders*, 2nd edition (London: Macmillan 1873) 113-14. Cf. idem, *Responsibility in Mental Disease* (London: King 1874) 1-15; J.C.Bucknill and D.H. Tuke, *A Manual of Psychological Medicine* (London: Churchill 1858) 64-85; D.H.Tuke, *Chapters in the History of the Insane in the British Isles* (London: Kegan Paul, Trench 1882); idem, *A Dictionary of Psychological Medicine*, 2 vols. (London: Churchill 1892) I. 26; E.Kraepelin, *One Hundred Years of Psychiatry* (London: Peter Owen 1962).

2 W.F.Bynum, 'Rationales for therapy in British psychiatry: 1780-1835', *Medical History* 18 (1974) 317-34; M.Fears, 'Therapeutic optimism and the treatment of the insane: some comments on the interpretation of psychiatric reform at the end of the eighteenth century', in R.Dingwall et al. (eds.) *Health Care and Health Knowledge* (London: Croom Helm 1977) 66-81; M.Foucault, *Madness and Civilization: A History of Insanity in the Age of Reason* (London: Tavistock 1967) 241-78; D.J. Rothman, *The Discovery of the Asylum: Social Order and Disorder in the New Republic* (Boston: Little, Brown 1971) 135-54; A.T.Scull, *Museums of Madness: The Social Organization of Insanity in Nineteenth-Century England* (London: Allen Lane 1979) 68-73, 119-124.

3 E.H.Ackerknecht, *Medicine at the Paris Hospital 1794-1848* (Baltimore: Johns Hopkins University Press 1967); M.Foucault, *The Birth of the Clinic: An Archaeo-*logy of Medical Perception (London: Tavistock 1973).

4 Ackerknecht 1967 [3] 170-1; R.Hunter and I.Macalpine, *Three Hundred Years of Psychiatry 1535-1860* (London: Oxford University Press 1963) 778-84, 1052-7; Bucknill and Tuke 1858 [1] 299-300, 325-9.

5 E.H.Hare, 'The origin and spread of dementia paralytica', *JMS* 105 (1959) 594-626, which includes a bibliography.

6 Further research is needed to understand the practical significance of the inclusion of GPI (along with epilepsy, moral insanity, monomania, etc.) in lists of lunatic types. Cf. *Report of the Metropolitan Commissioners in Lunacy*, P.P. 1844, XXVI. 102-3, 109-12; Bucknill and Tuke [1] 100.

7 J.Locke, *An Essay Concerning Human Understanding*, ed. by J.W.Yolton, revised edition, 2 vols. (London: Dent 1965) I. 127-8, (Book 2, chapter 11, para.13). Cf. P.Pinel, *A Treatise on Insanity*, first publ. 1806 (facsimile reprint New York: Hafner 1962) 13-14, 150-6; B.C.Brodie, *Psychological Inquiries: In a Series of Essays, Intended to Illustrate the Mutual Relations of the Physical Organisation and the Mental Faculties* (London: Longman, Brown, Green, & Longmans 1854) 89-90; Bucknill and Tuke 1858 [1] 87; J.C.Prichard, *A Treatise on Insanity and other Disorders Affecting the Mind* (London: Sherwood, Gilbert, & Piper 1835) 3-5; idem, *On the Different Forms of Insanity, in Relation to Jurisprudence* (London: Baillière 1842) 11-12; I.Ray, *A Treatise on the Medical Jurisprudence of Insanity*, first publ. 1838 (Cambridge, Mass.: Belknap Press of Harvard University 1962) 120-1.

8 Pinel 1962 [7] 20, 156. The English translation misleadingly rendered 'délire' as 'delirium'.

9 ibid., 20.

10 P.Pinel, *Traité médico-philosophique sur l'aliénation mentale*, 2nd edition (Paris: Brosson 1809) 158; my translation.

11 J.L.Casper, *A Handbook of the Practice of Forensic Medicine*, 4 vols. (London: New Sydenham Society 1861-5) IV. 201. Cf. ibid., 200-4, 290-337; criticism by J.P. Falret and B.A.Morel cited in R. Castel, *L'ordre psychiatrique: l'âge d'or de l'aliénisme* (Paris: Les éditions de minuit 1976) 179-80; T.Mayo, *Medical Testimony and Evidence in Cases of Lunacy* (London: Parker 1854) 53-90.

12 Ackerknecht 1967 [3] 149-60; G.Bass, *Die Gerichtsmedizin als Spezialfach in Paris von 1800 bis 1850* (Zürich: Juris-Verlag 1964) (Zürcher medizingeschichtliche Abhandlungen. Neue Reihe Nr. 22); Castel 1976 [11]; M.Foucault, *I, Pierre Rivière, Having Slaughtered my Mother, My Sister, and my Brother . . . A Case of Parricide in the 19th Century* (New York: Pantheon Books, Random House 1975) 263-9.

13 J.E.D.Esquirol, 'Manie', in *Dictionnaire des sciences médicales*, vol. XXX (Paris: Pankoucke 1818) 437-72 + 2 plates, on 452-4; this passage was removed from the altered section, 'De la manie' in Esquirol, *Des maladies mentales considérées sous les rapports médical, hygiénique et médico-légal*, 2 vols. (Paris: Baillière 1838) II. 219-318. Cf. articles on 'démence', 'fureur', 'folie', 'hallucinations', 'maisons d'aliénés', 'monomanie' (the section in *Des maladies mentales*, II. 1-130, is not equivalent), and 'suicide' in the *Dictionnaire*.

14 Note by Esquirol in J.C. Hoffbauer, *Médecine légale relative aux aliénés et aux sourds-muets, ou les lois appliquées aux désordres de l'intelligence* (Paris: Baillière 1827) 309-59; reprinted with alterations in Esquirol 1838 [13] II. 790-843; cf. 94-130.

15 Georget and C.C.H.Marc were involved in the most cited nineteenth-century medico-legal cases (especially of Henriette Cornier in 1825). Georget's papers are in *Archives générales de médecine* and the *Dictionnaire de médecine* (publ. from 1832); C.C.H.Marc, *De la folie, considérée dans ses rapports avec les questions médico-judiciaires*, 2 vols. (Paris: Baillière 1840) I. 239-45, and II. 24-154. Cf. Hoffbauer 1827 [14] 270-308; Prichard 1835 [7] 352-80; Castel 1976 [11] 174-90; Foucault 1975 [12] 274-85.

16 J.E.D.Esquirol, *Mental Maladies. A Treatise on Insanity*, first publ. 1845 (facsimile reprint New York: Hafner 1965) 364. Cf. Bucknill and Tuke 1858 [1] 193-202; H.Maudsley, 'Homicidal insanity', *JMS* 9 (1863) 327-43; J.M. Pagan, *The Medical Jurisprudence of Insanity* (London: Ball, Arnold 1840) 132-56, 209-56; F.Winslow, *The Plea of Insanity, in Criminal Cases* (London: Renshaw 1843) 193-202; P.Garnier and H.Colin, 'Homicidal monomania', in Tuke 1892 [1] I. 593-9; P.Dubuisson, 'De l'évolution des opinions en matière de responsabilité', *Archives de l'anthropologie criminelle et des sciences pénales*, no vol. (1887) 101-33. For a critical legal commentary on homicidal mania, based on the 1820s French cases: A.W. Renton, *Monomanie sans délire, an Examination of 'the Irresistible Criminal Impulse Theory'* (Edinburgh: T.& T.Clark 1886).

17 *Hansard* 67 (1843) cols.288-90.

18 This tension is evident, e.g. in: [H.Maudsley and C.L.Robertson] *Insanity and Crime: A Medicolegal Commentary on the Case of George Victor Townley* (London: Churchill 1864); F.Winslow, 'The legal doctrine of responsibility in cases of insanity, connected with alleged criminal acts', read 1857, in

Papers Read before the Juridical Society: 1855-1858 (London: Stevens & Norton 1858) 595-635. Maudsley and Robertson listed (p.18) 'monomania, or partial intellectual insanity', 'moral insanity', and 'impulsive or instinctive insanity' as the possible forms of partial insanity.

19 A.S.Taylor, *The Principles and Practice of Medical Jurisprudence* (London: Churchill 1865) 1101.

20 On Prichard: D.H.Tuke, *Prichard and Symonds in Especial Relation to Mental Science with Chapters on Moral Insanity* (London: Churchill 1891) 65-100; G.W. Stocking, 'Introduction' to J.C. Prichard, *Researches into the Physical History of Man* (reprinted Chicago: University of Chicago Press 1973) xxiv-xxxiii. J.O. Crump (30a College Road, Clifton, Bristol 8) is working on a biography and edition of Prichard's correspondence.

21 Prichard 1835 [7] 4; cf. 12-26, 34-71, and Prichard 1842 [7] 19.

22 Prichard first discussed the category in 'Insanity', in J.Forbes et al. (eds.) *The Cyclopaedia of Practical Medicine*, vol. 2 (London: Sherwood, Gilbert, & Piper, & Baldwin & Cradock 1833) 822-75, on 824, 826-31. Cf. T.Mayo, *An Essay on the Relation of the Theory of Morals to Insanity* (London: Fellowes 1834) 28-35. 'Moral insanity' gained some administrative approval in *Commissioners in Lunacy* 1844 [6] 108.

23 Prichard 1842 [7] 31.

24 ibid., 64. Cf. [J.Blackwell], 'Report on the treatment of lunatics', *Quarterly Review* 74 (1844) 416-47, on 446.

25 Prichard 1842 [7] 87. In Prichard 1835 [7], he uses the German term 'reine Tollheit' rather than 'instinctive madness'. Such deeds were most strongly described as medical facts in Ray 1962

[7], especially pp.127, 191-2. An English edition of Ray's first (1838) edition was published in 1839.

26 Prichard 1842 [7] 88.

27 Prichard 1835 [7] 380-404.

28 Prichard 1842 [7] 175. Cf. Dubuisson 1887 [16] 113-18.

29 W.B.Carpenter, *Principles of Mental Physiology*, first publ. 1874, 6th edition (London: Kegan Paul, Trench 1888) 658. Cf. Winslow 1858 [18] 597.

30 cf. A.S.Taylor, *A Manual of Medical Jurisprudence* (London: Churchill 1844) 627; Taylor 1865 [19] 1021-2, 1099; G.F.Blandford, *Insanity and its Treatment: Lectures on the Treatment, Medical and Legal, of Insane Patients* (Edinburgh: Oliver & Boyd 1871) 292-306, 314-23; Brodie 1854 [7] 99; Maudsley 1863 [16]; T.Mayo, *Medical Testimony and Evidence in Cases of Lunacy* (London: Parker 1854) 95-8, 113-15; F.Wharton and M.Stillé, *A Treatise on Medical Jurisprudence* (Philadelphia: Kay & Brother 1855) 145-7.

31 C.L.Robertson, 'A case of homicidal mania, without disorder of the intellect', *JMS* 6 (1860) 385-98, on 394.

32 Tuke 1891 [20] 17-18.

33 Ray 1962 [7] 192.

34 Victorian alienists did not question (as we might) the logic connecting physical determinism and non-responsibility.

35 D.Skae, 'On the legal relations of insanity: the civil incapacity and criminal responsibility of the insane', *EMJ* 12 (1867) 811-29, on 813.

36 F.Winslow, *Lettsomian Lectures on Insanity* (London: Churchill 1854) 144. Cf. Bucknill and Tuke 1858 [1] 186.

37 Scull 1979 [2] 158-62.

38 Winslow 1854 [36] 50. The extent to which insanity had been, and still was, treated as a 'spiritual malady' requires much more research.

39   ibid., 57-9. Cf. F.Winslow, *On the Incubation of Insanity* (London: Highley 1846) 3-4, 21; Maudsley 1873 [1] 122-3.

40   [Report], 'The antagonism of law and medicine in insanity, and its consequences. An introductory lecture. By Thomas Laycock', *JMS* 8 (1863) 593-7, on 597.

41   J.T.Merz, *A History of European Thought in the Nineteenth Century*, first publ. 1904-12, 4 vols. (reprinted New York: Dover 1967) 1; J.Ben-David, *The Scientist's Role in Society: A Comparative Study* (Engelwood Cliffs: Prentice-Hall 1971) 108-38; D.S.L.Cardwell, *The Organization of Science in England*, revised edition (London: Heinemann 1972).

42   See notes by J.S.Mill and A. Bain in J.Mill, *Analysis of the Phenomena of the Human Mind*, 2nd edition by J.S.Mill, first publ. 1869, 2 vols. (facsimile reprint New York: Kelley 1967); A.Bain, *Mental and Moral Science*, 3rd edition, 2 vols. (London: Longmans, Green 1872); R.M.Young, *Mind, Brain, and Adaptation in the Nineteenth Century: Cerebral Localization and its Biological Context from Gall to Ferrier* (Oxford: Clarendon Press 1970) 98-133.

43   J.G.Davey, 'On the relations between crime and insanity', *JMS* 5 (1858) 82-94, on 86; H.Maudsley, *The Physiology and Pathology of Mind*, 2nd edition (London: Macmillan 1868) 153.

44   L.S.Hearnshaw, *A Short History of British Psychology, 1840-1940* (London: Methuen 1964) 1-29; R.Smith, 'Physiological Psychology and the Philosophy of Nature in Mid-Nineteenth-Century Britain', unpublished Ph.D. thesis, Cambridge 1970; Young 1970 [42]; L.S.Jacyna, 'Scientific Naturalism in Victorian Britain: An Essay in the Social History of Ideas', unpublished Ph.D. thesis, Edinburgh 1980, 160-213.

45   Davey 1858 [43] 87.

46   T.Mayo, *Outlines of Medical Proof* (London: Longman, Brown, Green, & Longmans 1850) 49.

47   Bucknill and Tuke 1858 [1] 95.

48   ibid., 240-60. Asylum admission and case note books record causes. Social historians have started to use this material: D.J. Mellet, 'Society, the State and Mental Illness, 1790-1890. Social, Cultural and Administrative Aspects of the Institutional Care and Control of the Insane in Nineteenth-Century England', unpublished Ph.D. thesis, Cambridge 1978, 198-243, and Appendix; J.K.Walton, 'Lunacy in the industrial revolution: a study of asylum admissions in Lancashire, 1848-50', *Journal of Social History* 13 (1979) 1-22.

49   J.Conolly, *An Inquiry Concerning the Indications of Insanity with Suggestions for the Better Protection and Care of the Insane*, first publ. 1830 (facsimile reprint London: Dawsons 1964) 62.

50   Contrast the argument linking a change from psychological to physical explanation with social change: V.Skultans, *Madness and Morals: Ideas on Insanity in the Nineteenth Century* (London: Routledge 1975); idem, 'Moral order and mental derangement', in I. Lewis (ed.) *Symbols and Sentiments: Cross-cultural Studies in Symbolism* (London: Academic Press 1977) 117-28.

51   J.C.Bucknill, *Unsoundness of Mind in Relation to Criminal Acts*, first publ. 1854, 2nd edition (London: Longman, Brown, Green, Longmans & Roberts 1857) 13.

52   R.J.Cooter, 'Phrenology and British alienists, c.1825-1845', *Medical History* 20 (1976) 1-21, 135-51; idem, 'Phrenology: the provocation of progress', *History of Science* 14 (1976) 211-34; Young 1970 [42]; S.Shapin, 'Homo

phrenologicus: anthropological perspectives on an historical problem', in B.Barnes and S.Shapin (eds) *Natural Order: Historical Studies in Scientific Culture* (London: Sage 1979) 41-71.

53   Cooter, 'British alienists', 1976 [52] 11.

54   A.Combe, *Observations on Mental Derangement: Being an Application of the Principles of Phrenology to the Elucidation of the Causes, Symptoms, Nature, and Treatment of Insanity* (Edinburgh: John Anderson 1831); Conolly 1964 [49]; Ray 1962 [7].

55   Bucknill 1857 [51] p.iv. Cf. the summaries of existing knowledge in Prichard 1835 [7] 209-33; A.Addison, 'On the pathological anatomy of the brain in insanity', *JMS* 8 (1862) 37-61; Bucknill and Tuke 1858 [1] 390-433; Winslow 1854 [36] 50-61. For an example of an autopsy report: R.P.Brittain, 'Historic autopsies. I – The post-mortem examination of Daniel McNaughton', *Medicine, Science and the Law* 3 (1963) 100-4. The most comprehensive compilations of results appeared in the continental literature. Authorities included: C.Rokitansky, *A Manual of Pathology Anatomy*, 4 vols. (London: Sydenham Society 1849-54) III. 321-434; R.Virchow, *A Description and Explanation of the Method of Performing Post-mortem Examinations in the Dead-house of the Berlin Charité Hospital with Especial Reference to Medico-legal Practice* (London: Churchill 1876).

56   Bucknill 1857 [51] p.v. Cf. Maudsley 1868 [43] 453; Ray 1962 [7] 58-9; Cooter, 'British alienists', 1976 [52] 143-5.

57   Bucknill and Tuke 1858 [1] 387-90. The chapter on aetiology was written by Bucknill.

58   The former is evident in Prichard 1835 [7], the latter in Combe 1831 [54] 284-302.

59   Bucknill and Tuke 1858 [1]

358. Cf. ibid., 387-90; T.Laycock, 'On some of the latent causes of insanity', *JPM* 7 (1854) 159-84; Maudsley 1868 [43] 258-70; Maudsley 1873 [1] 102-5.

60   ibid., 104. Cf. W.B.Carpenter, *On the Use and Abuse of Alcoholic Liquors, in Health and Disease* (London: Gilpin, Churchill 1850); F.E.Anstie, *Stimulants and Narcotics, their Mutual Relations* (London: Macmillan 1864).

61   Bucknill and Tuke 1858 [1] 342; the whole passage is italicised in the original. Cf. Bain 1872 [42]; Blandford 1871 [30] 35-41; Carpenter 1888 [29]; T.Laycock, *Mind and Brain: Or the Correlations of Consciousness and Organisation*, 2 vols. (Edinburgh: Sutherland & Knox 1860); Maudsley 1863 [16] 343; H.Monro, *Remarks on Insanity: Its Nature and Treatment* (London: Churchill 1851); and almost any writing on physiological topics designed to influence conduct. See also, J.S.Haller and R.M.Haller, *The Physician and Sexuality in Victorian America* (Urbana: University of Illinois Press 1974) 9-15.

62   G.Canguilhem, 'Le concept de réflexe au XIXᵉ siècle', in K.E. Rothschuh (ed.) *Von Boerhaave bis Berger. Die Entwicklung der kontinentalen Physiologie im 18. und 19. Jahrhundert mit besonderer Berücksichtigung der Neurophysiologie* (Stuttgart: Fischer 1964) 157-67; E.Clarke and C.D.O'Malley, *The Human Brain and Spinal Cord: A Historical Study Illustrated by Writings from Antiquity to the Twentieth Century* (Berkeley: University of California Press 1968); C.Eckhard, 'Beiträge zur Geschichte der Experimentalphysiologie des Nervensystems. Geschichte der Entwicklung der Lehre von den Reflexerscheinungen', *Beiträge zur Anatomie und Physiologie* 9 (1881) 29-192; F.Fearing, *Reflex Action: A Study in the History of Physio-*

logical Psychology (reprinted New York: Hafner 1964).

63   M.Hall, *Memoirs on the Nervous System* (London: Sherwood, Gilbert, & Piper 1837); J. Müller, *Elements of Physiology*, 2 vols. (London: Taylor & Walton 1839-42) I. 706-22, 803-6.

64   cf. O.Temkin, *The Falling Sickness: A History of Epilepsy from the Greeks to the Beginnings of Modern Neurology*, 2nd edition (Baltimore: Johns Hopkins University Press 1971) 313-15, 328-46; Young 1970 [42] 197-248.

65   T.Laycock, *A Treatise on the Nervous Diseases of Women* (London: Longman, Orme, Brown, Green, & Longmans 1840) 106-14; idem, 'On the reflex functions of the brain', *BFMR* 19 (1845) 298-311. For his account of the development of brain reflex action theory: 'Examination of Dr. Carpenter's claim of priority as to the discovery of the law of unconscious cerebral action', in Laycock 1860 [61] II. 465-80; Laycock, 'Reflex, automatic, and unconscious cerebration: a history and a criticism', *JMS* 21 (1876) 477-98, and 22 (1876) 1-17. Cf. Smith 1970 [44].

66   T.Laycock et al., 'Correspondence between Geo. Combe Esq., Professor Reid, and Dr. Laycock on the reflex anatomy and physiology of the brain', *Lancet* ii (1845) 231-3, 255-8, 383-4, 308-10, 347-8, 364, on 364.

67   Conolly 1964 [49] 339.

68   O.M.Marx, 'Wilhelm Griesinger and the history of psychiatry: a reassessment', *Bulletin of the History of Medicine* 46 (1972) 519-44. For surveys of German medical psychology: E.H.Ackerknecht, *A Short History of Psychiatry*, 2nd edition (New York: Hafner 1968) 60-81; H.S.Decker, *Freud in Germany: Revolution and Reaction in Science, 1893-1907* (New York: International Universities Press 1977) (*Psychological Issues*, vol. XI,

no.1, Monograph 41) 25-72.

69   W.Griesinger, 'Ueber psychische Reflexactionen. Mit einem Blick auf das Wesen der psychischen Krankheiten', *Archiv für physiologische Heilkunde* 2 (1843) 76-113; idem, 'Neue Beiträge zur Physiologie und Pathologie des Gehirns', *Archiv für physiologische Heilkunde* 3 (1844) 69-98. The second edition (1865) of his textbook was translated as *Mental Pathology and Therapeutics*, first publ. 1867 (facsimile reprint New York: Hafner 1965); see especially pages 24, 74-8.

70   J.D.Morell, 'Modern English psychology', *BFMCR* 17 (1856) 347-64, on 351.

71   cf. Cardwell 1972 [41]; G.L. Geison, *Michael Foster and the Cambridge School of Physiology: The Scientific Enterprise in Late Victorian Society* (Princeton: Princeton University Press 1978) 13-47.

72   H.Holland, *Chapters on Mental Physiology* (London: Longman, Brown, Green, & Longmans 1852) 109.

73   e.g. Anstie 1864 [60] 80; Griesinger 1843 [69] 98-111; Laycock 1845 [65]; Monro 1851 [61]; J.A.Symonds, 'Sleep and dreams', first publ. 1851, in *Miscellanies* (London: Macmillan 1871) 145-208. The history of experimental studies of 'inhibition' in neurophysiology has not been studied, but see: Eckhard 1881 [62] 99-120; H.E.Hoff, 'The history of vagal inhibition', *Bulletin of the History of Medicine* 8 (1940) 461-96.

74   R.Darnton, *Mesmerism and the End of the Enlightenment in France* (Cambridge, Mass.: Harvard University Press 1968); H.F. Ellenberger, *The Discovery of the Unconscious: The History and Evolution of Dynamic Psychiatry* (London: Allen Lane 1970) 53-192.

75   J.Braid, *Neurypnology; or, the Rationale of Nervous Sleep,*

Considered in Relation with Animal Magnetism (London: Churchill 1843) 71.

76 A.Gauld, *The Founders of Psychical Research* (New York: Schocken 1968) 57-77; G.K. Nelson, *Spiritualism and Society* (London: Routledge 1969) 89-110.

77 Morell 1856 [70] 353-4. For similar explanations of mesmerism: J.H.Bennett, *The Mesmeric Mania of 1851; With a Physiological Explanation of the Phenomena. A Lecture* (Edinburgh: Sutherland & Knox 1851); W.B.Carpenter, 'Electrobiology and mesmerism', *Quarterly Review* 93 (1853) 501-57; Holland 1852 [72] 30; A.Wood, *What is Mesmerism? An Attempt to Explain its Phenomena on the Admitted Principles of Physiological and Psychical Science* (Edinburgh: Sutherland & Knox 1851).

78 [T.Laycock], 'Modern necromancy', *North British Review* 34 (1861) 110-41, on 114-20.

79 M.Faraday, 'Experimental investigations of table-turning', *The Athenaeum*, no.1340 (1853) 801-3.

80 J.E.Carpenter, 'Memorial sketch', in W.B.Carpenter, *Nature and Man: Essays Scientific and Philosophical* (London: Kegan Paul, Trench 1888) 1-152; R.Smith, 'The human significance of biology: Carpenter, Darwin, and the *vera causa*', in U.C.Knoepflamacher and G.B.Tennyson (eds.) *Nature and the Victorian Imagination* (Berkeley: University of California Press 1977) 216-30.

81 W.B.Carpenter, 'On the influence of suggestion in modifying and directing muscular movements, independently of volition', *Proceedings of the Royal Institution* 1 (1852) 147-53; idem, *Principles of Human Physiology*, 4th edition (London: Churchill 1853) 799, 826-33.

82 This moralistic psychology was developed systematically in Carpenter 1888 [29], but the ideas

were already present in Carpenter 1853 [81] 801-61. Cf. R.Dunn, *An Essay on Physiological Psychology* (London: Churchill 1858); idem, *Medical Psychology* (London: Churchill 1863); D.Noble, *Elements of Psychological Medicine* (London: Churchill 1853); idem, *The Human Mind in its Relations with the Brain and Nervous System* (London: Churchill 1858). Reference to the faculty of 'attention' – as a naturalistic description of a moralistic ideal of social control – was widespread: J.Abercrombie, *Inquiries Concerning the Intellectual Powers and the Investigation of Truth* (Edinburgh: Waugh & Innes 1830) 99-101, 129-56; idem, *The Philosophy of the Moral Feelings* (London: Murray 1833) 120-5; Brodie 1854 [7]; Conolly 1964 [49] 40-53; Holland 1852 [72].

83 Carpenter 1850 [60]; Carpenter 1888 [29] 636-60.

84 W.F.Bynum, 'Chronic alcoholism in the first half of the nineteenth century', *Bulletin of the History of Medicine* 42 (1968) 160-85; A.A.Pruitt, 'Approaches to alcoholism in mid-Victorian England', *Clio Medica* 9 (1974) 93-101.

85 F.H.Bradley, 'The vulgar notion of responsibility in connexion with the theories of freewill and necessity', in *Ethical Studies*, first publ. 1876, 2nd edition (Oxford: Clarendon Press 1927) 1-57, on 4.

86 Taylor 1865 [19] 1128.

87 B.Harrison, *Drink and the Victorians: The Temperance Question in England 1815-1872* (London: Faber & Faber 1971); for insanity and drunkenness, Mellet 1978 [48] 218-43.

88 Maudsley 1874 [1] 286.

89 cf. M.D.Alexander, 'The Administration of Madness and Attitudes toward the Insane in Nineteenth-Century Paris', unpublished Ph.D. thesis, Johns Hopkins 1976, 83-129; Acker-

knecht 1968 [68] 54-9.

90　Maudsley 1868 [43] 325.

91　T.Ribot, *Heredity: A Psychological Study of its Phenomena, Laws, Causes, and Consequences*, 2nd edition (London: King 1875) 226.

92　ibid., 222.

93　Maudsley 1868 [43] 351.

94　Maudsley and Robertson 1864 [18] 39.

95　Laycock 1860 [42]; Maudsley 1868 [43] 1-40.

96　Maudsley 1863 [16] 327.

97　ibid.

98　J.C.Browne, 'Notes on homicidal insanity', *JMS* 9 (1863) 197-210, on 204.

99　Maudsley 1868 [43] 316.

100　Maudsley 1874 [1] 151.

101　ibid., 150-1.

102　e.g. Ackerknecht 1968 [68] 54-9; C.E.Rosenberg, 'The bitter fruit: heredity, disease, and social thought in nineteenth-century America', *Perspectives in American History* 8 (1974) 189-235. Skultans 1977 [50] places undue emphasis on the change from environmentalist/psychological to hereditarian/physicalist accounts. Hereditarian theories were widespread in medicine before 1850.

103　Ribot 1875 [91] 119. Ribot estimated one third to one half of lunatics had heredity as the main cause of their affliction. Maudsley reckoned one quarter to one half, and the French alienist Moreau de Tours up to ninety percent.

104　Prichard 1835 [7] 157. Prichard was vague about distinguishing acquired and inherited dispositions.

105　Ribot 1875 [91] 121.

106　The inheritance of acquired characteristics was a major aspect of Herbert Spencer's evolutionary psychology, and Maudsley was indebted to this. On Spencer: Young 1970 [42] 172-90.

107　Maudsley 1874 [1] 41.

108　W.L.Lindsay, *Mind in the Lower Animals in Health and Disease*, 2 vols. (London: Kegan Paul 1879) I. 16. That Lindsay wrote on insanity in animals at all illustrates the power of the comparative approach.

109　H.Spencer, *First Principles* (London: Williams & Norgate 1862). Cf. J.D.Y.Peel, *Herbert Spencer: The Evolution of a Sociologist* (London: Heinemann 1971). B.A.Morel, *Traité des dégénérescences physiques, intellectuelles et morales de l'espèce humaine et des causes qui produisent ces variétés maladives*, first publ. 1857 (facsimile reprint New York: Arno 1976) 344-56, for the integration of mental alienation into his general scheme. Cf. Rosenberg 1974 [102]. Alexander 1976 [89], argues that Morel made the decisive contribution to French psychiatric pessimism. Cf. Dubuisson 1887 [16] 118-24; Maudsley 1868 [43] 330-4, 472-3; Maudsley 1873 [1] 45; Ribot 1875 [91] 90-4, 119-31, 267; Winslow 1854 [36] 155-7. L.J.Ray relates the rise of degeneration theories to British professional interests in 'Models of madness in Victorian asylum practice', forthcoming in *European Journal of Sociology* (1981).

110　Maudsley 1868 [43] 361. Cf. Maudsley 1873 [1] 66-7, 128-31; Maudsley 1874 [1] 29-30. On epileptics as degenerates: Temkin 1971 [64] 364-70.

111　Maudsley 1868 [43] 357.

112　Mayo 1834 [22] 43-4.

113　Maudsley 1874 [1] 22-35.

114　Dubuisson 1887 [16] 124-33; A.E.Fink, *Causes of Crime: Biological Theories in the United States 1800-1915* (Philadelphia: University of Pennsylvania Press 1938); A. MacDonald, *Abnormal Man, Being Essays on Education and Crime and Related Subjects, With Digests of Literature and a Bibliography* (Washington: Government Printing Office [Bureau of Education. Circular of Information no.4] 1883)

287-434, especially 411-15 for bibliography; H.Mannheim, *Pioneers in Criminology* (London: Stevens 1960); C.Mercier, *Crime & Criminals: Being the Juris-prudence of Crime, Medical, Bio-logical, and Psychological* (London: University of London Press 1918); A.H.Manchester, *A Modern Legal History of England and Wales 1750-1950* (London: Butterworths 1980) 235-9; R.A.Nye, 'Heredity or milieu: the foundations of modern European criminological theory', *Isis* 67 (1976) 335-55; Rosenberg 1974 [102]; W.C.Sullivan, *Crime and Insanity* (London: Edward Arnold 1924). The reconciliation of scientific and retributive modes of reaction to criminals in the con-cept of delinquency is discussed in M.Foucault, *Discipline and Punish: The Birth of the Prison* (London: Allen Lane 1977) 256.

115   Maudsley 1863 [16] 342.
116   T.Laycock, 'On the medico-legal relations of insanity, with reference to the Townley case', *JMS* 10 (1864) 293-4, on 294.
117   Evidence in *Report of the Capital Punishment Commission*, P.P. 1866, XXI, minutes 2777-84. The post-mortem reports for criminal lunatics are in the Bethlem archives.
118   J.F.Stephen, *A History of the Criminal Law of England*, first publ. 1883, 3 vols. (facsimile re-print New York: Burt Franklin, n.d.) II. 131; Stephen took Gries-inger 1965 [69] as his principal authority. On codification: *Special Report from the Select Committee on Homicide Law Amendment Bill*, P.P. 1874, IX; *Report of the Royal Commission Appointed to Consider the Law Relating to Indictable Offences*, P.P. 1878-9, XX; Man-chester 1980 [114] 44-8.
119   J.F.Stephen, *A Digest of the Criminal Law (Crimes and Punish-ments)* (London: Macmillan 1877) xxix-xxx. For a modern judge's

similar frustration: D.L.Bazelon, 'Justice stumbles over science', in A.S.Blumberg (ed.) *The Scales of Justice* (New York: Aldine 1970) 123-39; idem, 'Psychiatrists and the adversary process', *Scientific American* 230 (1974) 18-23.
120   Maudsley 1868 [43] 473. Cf. H.L.A.Hart, *Punishment and Res-ponsibility: Essays in the Philosophy of Law* (Oxford: Clarendon Press 1968) 254 note.
121   [F.Winslow], 'Recent trials in lunacy', *JPM* 7 (1854) 572-625, on 617.
122   [G.F.Blandford], '"Acquitted on the ground of insanity." (From a "mad doctor's" point of view.)', *Cornhill Magazine* 12 (1865) 426-40, on 435.
123   Bucknill and Tuke 1858 [1] 267. (Bucknill and Tuke wrote separate chapters of their book.)
124   H.Maudsley, *The Physiology of Mind* (London: Macmillan 1876); idem, *The Pathology of Mind* (London: Macmillan 1879).
125   Casper 1861-5 [11] IV. 94-181. This pragmatic approach was also followed by Griesinger 1965 [69] 1-11.
126   J.S.Mill, *A System of Logic Ratiocinative and Inductive*, 8th edition, first publ. 1872 (reprinted London: Longmans 1970) 556-7 (Book 6, chapter 4, sect.2).
127   cf. P.F.Cranefield, 'The organic physics of 1847 and the biophysics of today', *Journal of the History of Medicine* 12 (1957) 407-23; Jacyna 1980 [44] 146-7, notes the discrepancy between theoretical medical chemistry and practical knowledge (which was restricted to toxins).
128   A valuable review of pro-cedure and evidence in Wharton and Stillé 1855 [30] 70-114. Cf. Bucknill and Tuke 1858 [1] 267-340.
129   e.g. Bucknill 1857 [51] 79-81.
130   The German specialist J.C.A.

Heinroth, quoted by Wharton and Stillé 1855 [30] 80.

131 See frontispiece to Bucknill and Tuke 1858 [1]; plates in J. Conolly, 'The physiognomy of insanity', *MTG* 16 (1858) 2-4, 56-8, 134-6, 238-41, 314-16, 397-8, 498-500, 623-5, and 17 (1858) 81-3, 210-11, 367-9, 651-3, and 18 (1859) 183-6; plates in Esquirol 1965 [16] 11; plates in Morel 1976 [109]; plates in A.Morison, *The Physiognomy of Mental Diseases* (London: for the Author, 1840). Splendid photographs taken in Bethlem's criminal wing in the 1850s are in the archives.

132 Bucknill and Tuke 1858 [1] 288.

133 'Criminal irresponsibility of the insane', *Law Magazine*, 3rd series 1 (1872) 215-19, on 218.

134 Winslow 1846 [39] 9.

135 Bucknill and Tuke 1858 [1] 322.

136 ibid., 324. Cf. Maudsley and Robertson 1864 [18] 25; Ray 1962 [7] 110-12, 134-5; Winslow 1854 [36] 149.

137 Reported in 'The late assault on the Queen. Important medico-legal decision in cases of alleged lunacy', *Medical Times* 1 (1850) 64-5, on 65.

138 Prichard 1842 [7] 126. Cf. Ray 1962 [7] 169-70; Casper 1861-65 [11] IV. 103-30; Taylor 1865 [19] 1100-3.

139 The Lord Justice-Clerk in Macklin's case, reported in 3 Couper 260.

140 *Medical Times* 1850 [137] 65.

141 [? J.C.Bucknill], 'The annual reports of county asylums, etc. in England and Wales', *Asylum JMS* 2 (1856) 257-85, on 264, quoting a report from Dr Hitchman, the Superintendent Physician, Derbyshire County Asylum.

142 Maudsley 1874 [1] 188.

143 ibid.

144 Reported in 176 E.R. 114, note (a).

145 Maudsley 1874 [1] 194-5.

146 Bucknill 1857 [51] 78.

147 Maudsley 1874 [1] 215.

148 ibid., 133.

149 Robertson 1860 [31] 386. For other illustrative cases: Browne 1863 [98] 208-10; J.G.Davey, 'A case of homicidal mania', *JMS* 7 (1860) 49-59; J.F.Duncan, 'Brief notice of a case of moral insanity, unaccompanied by any obvious symptoms of intellectual aberration', *JPM* 6 (1853) 274-80; S. Haynes, 'Clinical cases illustrative of moral imbecility and insanity', *JMS* 10 (1865) 533-49; Maudsley 1863 [16] 332-43.

150 Robertson 1860 [31] 391.

151 ibid., 392.

152 C.L.Robertson, 'A case of homicidal mania, with auditory hallucinations', *JMS* 7 (1861) 120-7, on 122.

153 Maudsley 1868 [43] 348.

154 ibid., 473. Cf. J.R.Reynolds, *On the Scientific Value of the Legal Tests of Insanity* (London: Churchill 1872) 39; R.H.Semple, 'On criminal responsibility', *MTG* 12 (1856) 58-60; Taylor 1844 [30] 649; Taylor 1865 [19] 1108; W. Wood, *Remarks on the Plea of Insanity, and on the Management of Criminal Lunatics* (London: Longman, Brown, Green, & Longmans 1851) 18-19.

155 Wharton and Stillé 1855 [30] 35.

CHAPTER FOUR
Law and Responsibility

1 R.G.Hodgkinson, *The Origins of the National Health Service: The Medical Services of the New Poor Law, 1834-1871* (London: Wellcome Historical Medical Library 1967) 176-84, 575-91. For the development of poor law services: W.C.Lubenow, *The Politics of Government Growth: Early Victorian Attitudes toward State Intervention, 1833-1848* (Newton Abbott: David & Charles 1971);

D.Roberts, *Victorian Origins of the British Welfare State* (New Haven: Yale University Press 1960).

2 J.F.Archbold, *The New Statutes Relating to Lunacy* (London: Shaw 1854); D.P.Fry, *The Lunacy Acts* (London: Knight 1854); idem, *The Lunacy Acts*, 2nd edition reprint (London: Knight, Maxwell 1877); C.P.Phillips, *The Law Concerning Lunatics, Idiots, & Persons of Unsound Mind* (London: Butterworths 1858); G.Pitt-Lewis et al., *The Insane and the Law* (London: Churchill 1895); L. Shelford, *A Practical Treatise of the Law Concerning Lunatics, Idiots, and Persons of Unsound Mind*, 2nd edition (London: Sweet, Stevens & Norton 1847); A.S.Taylor, *The Principles and Practice of Medical Jurisprudence* (London: Churchill 1865) 1052-67.

3 A.H.Manchester, *A Modern Legal History of England and Wales 1750-1950* (London: Butterworths 1980) 52-8.

4 ibid., 79-82; C.H.S.Fifoot, *Judge and Jurist in the Reign of Victoria* (London: Stevens 1959). W.Holdsworth, *A History of English Law*, vol. xv (London: Methuen, Sweet & Maxwell 1965) 395-510, discusses the approach of individual judges.

5 'The lunacy laws', *Law Magazine*, 3rd series 4 (1875) 447-54, on 451. This position was expressed most clearly following a case of questioned insanity, Nottidge v. Ripley (1849), to the anger of alienists: Lord Brougham, 'On partial insanity', *JPM* 2 (1849) 323-9; P.McCandless, 'Insanity and Society: a Study of the English Lunacy Reform Movement 1815-1870', unpublished Ph.D. thesis, Wisconsin 1974, 223-9; W.L. Parry-Jones, *The Trade in Lunacy. A Study of Private Madhouses in England in the Eighteenth and Nineteenth Centuries* (London: Routledge 1972) 236.

6 K.Jones, 'The Windham case: the enquiry held in London in 1861 into the state of mind of William Frederick Windham, heir to the Felbrigg Estate', *British Journal of Psychiatry* 119 (1971) 425-33. For the number and location of lunatics found insane by inquisition: Parry-Jones 1972 [5] 69-70.

7 McCandless 1974 [5] 173-202; idem, 'Liberty and lunacy: the Victorians and wrongful confinement', *Journal of Social History* 11 (1978) 366-86; Parry-Jones 1972 [5] 236-8.

8 McCandless 1974 [5] 204-48.

9 cf. Pitt-Lewis et al. 1895 [2] 245-73; Taylor 1865 [2] 1068-93.

10 J.Conolly, *An Inquiry Concerning the Indications of Insanity with Suggestions for the Better Protection and Care of the Insane*, first publ. 1830 (facsimile reprint London: Dawsons 1964) 438, 451; H. Maudsley, *Responsibility in Mental Disease* (London: King 1874) 111-20; I.Ray, *A Treatise on the Medical Jurisprudence of Insanity*, first publ. 1838 (reprint Cambridge, Mass.: Belknap Press of Harvard University 1962) 34; F. Winslow, *The Plea of Insanity, in Criminal Cases* (London: Renshaw 1843) 74-5. Thus a writer (probably Winslow) believed that Dove (convicted of murder) would have been found insane in a civil case: 'William Dove', *JPM* 9 (1856) 584-93, on 586.

11 Holdsworth 1965 [4] 142-67, 248-75; Manchester 1980 [3] 23-5, 38-48, 166-8.

12 The Felonies Act. Cf. Holdsworth 1965 [4] 157; Manchester 1980 [3] 168-9.

13 Carol Boyle, associated with the Centre for Socio-legal Studies, Wolfson College, Oxford, has studied these modern social networks; her work includes some historical material. A.S.Taylor achieved an informal 'official' status

in relation to crown forensic evidence. General forensic practice established habits which conditioned expectations about 'psychiatric' evidence in the mid-century.

14   A.Alvarez et al., *The Progress of Continental Law in the Nineteenth Century*, first publ. 1918 (reprinted South Hackensack: Rothman Reprints 1969); C.L.von Bar et al., *A History of Continental Criminal Law* (London: Murray 1916).

15   See comments: C.J.Foster, *Elements of Jurisprudence* (London: Walton & Maberly 1853), 'Introduction'; W.Markby, *Elements of Law Considered with Reference to Principles of General Jurisprudence* (Oxford: Clarendon Press 1871) 'Preface'; T.E.Holland, *The Elements of Jurisprudence* (Oxford: Clarendon Press 1880) v-vi.

16   W.Blackstone, *Commentaries on the Laws of England*, 11th edition, 4 vols. (London: Cadell 1791); H.J.Stephen, *New Commentaries on the Laws of England. (Partly Founded on Blackstone)*, vol. IV (London: Butterworth 1845). Cf. A.Alison, *Principles of the Criminal Law of Scotland* (Edinburgh: Blackwood 1832).

17   Austin's lectures were delivered in the 1830s but not fully published till 1861: J.Austin, *Lectures on Jurisprudence*, 3 vols. (facsimile reprint New York: Burt Franklin 1970). The negative response is reflected in Foster 1853 [15]; and in J.F.Stephen's work, e.g., *Liberty, Equality, Fraternity*, first publ. 1873, 2nd edition (reprinted Cambridge, England: Cambridge University Press (1967) 150-62. But Stephen was influenced by utilitarianism (though more by his experience in India) in relation to codification.

18   Particularly by the establishment of the English historical school. Cf. L.Radzinowicz, *Sir James Fitzjames Stephen 1829-1894*

and his Contribution to the Development of Criminal Law (London: Quaritch 1957); Fifoot 1959 [4]; Holdsworth 1965 [4] 341-68.

19   F.B.Sayre, *'Mens rea'*, *Harvard Law Review* 45 (1932) 974-1026. The logical relationship between *mens rea* and exculpatory insanity is questioned in H. Fingarette and A.Fingarette Hasse, *Mental Disabilities and Criminal Responsibility* (Berkeley: University of California Press 1979) 66-70.

20   J.F.Stephen, *A General View of the Criminal Law of England* (London: Macmillan 1863) 75-85; idem, *A History of the Criminal Law of England*, first publ. 1883, 3 vols. (facsimile reprint New York: Burt Franklin, n.d.) II. 94-123; Holland 1880 [15] 72-5. G.Williams, *Criminal Law. The General Part*, 2nd edition (London: Stevens 1961) 13, however, describes an act as behaviour accompanied by consciousness, even if the act is uncontrollable and the party insane. Cf. ibid., 11-27, 30-84, 89-99; H.L.A.Hart, *Punishment and Responsibility: Essays in the Philosophy of Law* (Oxford: Clarendon Press 1968) 90-112.

21   Stephen 1883 [20] II. 95.

22   A.M.Platt and B.L.Diamond, 'The origins and development of the "wild beast" concept of mental illness and its relation to theories of criminal responsibility', *Journal of the History of the Behavioral Sciences* I (1965) 355-67; N.Walker, *Crime and Insanity in England, vol. I: The Historical Perspective* (Edinburgh: Edinburgh University Press 1968) 15-51.

23   W.O.Russell, *A Treatise on Crimes and Misdemeanors*, 5th edition by S.Prentice, vol. I (London: Stevens 1877) 108; this is a paraphrase of Blackstone 1791 [16] IV. 20-1.

24   Stephen 1883 [20] II. 100.

25   Austin 1970 [17] II. 81-2. Cf. Hart 1968 [20] 97-9.

26 W.B.Carpenter, *Principles of Mental Physiology*, first publ. 1874, 6th edition (London: Kegan Paul, Trench 1888), was a compendium of voluntarist psychology. Voluntarism was applied to the mind itself in, e.g.: J.Barlow, *On Man's Power over Himself to Prevent or Control Insanity* (London: Pickering 1843); G.Moore, *The Power of the Soul over the Body, Considered in Relation to Health and Morals* (London: Longman, Brown, Green, & Longmans 1845). Samuel Smiles linked this voluntarism with economic man.

27 Stephen 1863 [20] 77.

28 A.Gibson, 'Insanity. Law', in *Encyclopaedia Britannica*, 9th edition, vol. XIII (Edinburgh: Black 1880) 111-13, on 112. The logic of 'ignorance' of law and possible insanity is discussed in Fingarette and Hasse 1979 [19] 23-43.

29 Austin 1970 [17] II. 82; T. Brown, *Inquiry into the Relation of Cause and Effect*, 3rd edition (Edinburgh: Constable 1818). Brown's analysis was better known in the first half of the nineteenth century than Hume's, now classic, discussion. Cf. J.Mill, *Analysis of the Phenomena of the Human Mind*, 2nd edition by J.S.Mill, first publ. 1869, 2 vols. (facsimile reprint New York: Kelley 1967) II. 327-95; J.S. Mill, *A System of Logic Ratiocinative and Inductive*, 8th edition, first publ. 1872 (reprinted London: Longmans 1970) 232-9 (Book 3, chapter 5, sect.11), and 547-8 (Book 6, chapter 2, sect.2).

30 E.Durkheim, *The Division of Labour in Society* (New York: Free Press 1964) 70-110, on 80, 73. Cf. C.E.Rosenberg, *The Trial of the Assassin Guiteau: Psychiatry and Law in the Gilded Age* (Chicago: University of Chicago Press 1968), on public attitudes to the trial. For philosophical accounts of the retributive nature of punishment: J.

Feinberg, 'The expressive function of punishment', in *Doing & Deserving: Essays in the Theory of Responsibility* (Princeton: Princeton University Press 1970) 95-118; Hart 1968 [20] 165-9. It is not necessary here to distinguish 'retributive' and 'denunciatory' components; but see J.Glover, *Responsibility* (London: Routledge 1970) 145-6.

31 Stephen 1883 [20] II. 81.

32 e.g. Lord Brougham, in discussing M'Naghten's case, *Hansard* 67 (1843) col.729; Baron Bramwell, in *Report of the Capital Punishment Commission*, P.P. 1866, XXI, minutes 152-68.

33 Stephen 1883 [20] II. 80.

34 Hart 1968 [20] 35-50, 174-7.

35 Legal opposition to the concept of strict liability because it eliminates the *mens rea* requirement is discussed in relation to food adulteration legislation in the late nineteenth century in I.Paulus, *The Search for Pure Food: A Sociology of Legislation in Britain* (London: Martin Robertson 1974) 61-5. Cf. Manchester 1980 [3] 202-4.

36 Austin 1970 [17] II. 179-80, 184-6.

37 Bramwell, in *Capital Punishment Commission* 1866 [32] minute 152.

38 F.H.Bradley, 'The vulgar notion of responsibility in connexion with the theories of freewill and necessity', in *Ethical Studies*, first publ. 1876, 2nd edition (Oxford: Clarendon Press 1927) 1-57, on 26.

39 ibid., 27-8.

40 ibid., 31. Cf. H.B.Acton (ed.) *The Philosophy of Punishment: A Collection of Papers* (London: Macmillan 1969); H.L.A.Hart, 'Punishment and the elimination of responsibility', in Hart 1968 [20] 158-85; N.Walker and S.McCabe, *Crime and Insanity in England*, *vol. II: New Solutions and New*

Problems (Edinburgh: Edinburgh University Press 1973); B.Wootton, *Crime and the Criminal Law: Reflections of a Magistrate and Social Scientist* (London: Stevens 1963).

41 cf. Williams 1961 [20] 50. For evidence of states of mind: Hart 1968 [20] 32-4.

42 Stephen 1883 [20] II. III.

43 Hart 1968 [20] 33.

44 Quoted and discussed by Walker 1968 [22] 99-102.

45 On the complexities of onus of proof: Williams 1961 [20] 448-52, 516-21.

46 [J.Blackwell], 'Report on the treatment of lunatics', *Quarterly Review* 74 (1844) 416-47, on 438.

47 Expert evidence did not feature as a topic in legal textbooks, e.g. J.F.Archbold, *Archbold's Pleading and Evidence in Criminal Cases*, 12th edition (London: Sweet & Stevens & Norton 1853); it did appear from a practical viewpoint in medical forensic texts. C.Crawford (Linacre College, Oxford) is studying the development of British forensic medicine 1780-1830. Pressure for medical evidence originated especially with coroners' courts: T.R.Forbes, *Crowner's Quest* (Philadelphia: American Philosophical Society 1978) (*Transactions of the American Philosophical Society*, vol. 68, part 1). For references to the much more established European specialism: J.B.Speer, 'Essay review of T.R. Forbes *Crowner's Quest*', *Annals of Science* 37 (1980) 353-6.

48 J.R.Reynolds, *Criminal Lunatics: Are they Responsible? Being an Examination of "the Plea of Insanity," in a Letter to the Right Hon. the Lord High Chancellor* (London: Churchill 1856) 35-6. This upset alienists: [? J.C.Bucknill], 'Dr. J.Russell Reynolds on criminal lunatics', *Asylum J M S* 3 (1857) 134-9.

49 Crowder, J. in Richards' case (1858), reported in Pitt-Lewis et al. 1895 [2] 169. Cf. W.A.Guy, *Principles of Forensic Medicine* (London: Renshaw 1844) 1-14; Taylor 1865 [2] pp.xvii-lix.

50 Reported in 4 Cox C.C. 58; also quoted in Ray 1962 [10] 358-9. Cf. Russell 1877 [23] 113-39; Walker 1968 [22] 102, 120.

51 Alderson, B. in Crouch's case (1844); the text in question was 'Cooper's Surgery'. Alderson was not against medical evidence as such, since he stated he would also prevent foreign law texts being read. Willes, J. did allow a medical text (Taylor's *Medical Jurisprudence*) to be read in Hill's case (1856). Bramwell, B. allowed this (in Dove's case, 1856) only if it was the defending counsel's opinion: C.Williams, *Observations on the Criminal Responsibility of the Insane; Founded on the Trials of James Hill and of William Dove* (London: Churchill 1856) pp.vii, lxxxv.

52 J.C.Bucknill, *Unsoundness of Mind in Relation to Criminal Acts*, first publ. 1854, 2nd edition (London: Longman, Brown, Green, Longmans & Roberts 1857) xlii-xliv, 120-3; idem, 'Criminal lunatics, by Dr. W.C.Hood', *J M S* 6 (1860) 513-19, on 518; S.Knaggs, *Unsoundness of Mind Considered in Relation to the Question of Responsibility for Criminal Acts* (London: Churchill 1854) 81-8; T.Laycock, 'On law and medicine in insanity. An introductory lecture', *E M J* 7 (1862) 1132-46; idem, 'On the legal doctrines of the responsibility of the insane and its consequences', *J M S* 10 (1864) 350-66, on 357; H.Maudsley, *The Physiology and Pathology of Mind*, 2nd edition (London: Macmillan 1868) 473; [H.Maudsley & C.L.Robertson], *Insanity and Crime: A Medicolegal Commentary on the Case of George Victor Townley* (London:

Churchill 1864) 12-13; Pitt-Lewis et al. 1895 [2] 57-9; Ray 1962 [10] 48-54; J.R.Reynolds, *On the Scientific Value of the Legal Tests of Insanity* (London: Churchill 1872) 52; T.H.Tuke, in *Capital Punishment Commission 1866* [32], minutes 2466-7, 2495-6a; F. Winslow, *Lettsomian Lectures on Insanity* (London: Churchill 1854) 88.

53 Stephen 1863 [20] 209-10, on 210. Cf. J.F.Stephen, 'On the policy of maintaining the limits at present imposed by law on the criminal responsibility of madmen', read 1855, in *Papers Read Before the Juridical Society: 1855-1858* (London: Stevens & Norton 1858) 67-94.

54 Stephen 1858 [53]; *Special Report from the Select Committee on Homicide Law Amendment Bill*, P.P. 1874, IX. 9; *Report of the Royal Commission Appointed to Consider the Law Relating to Indictable Offences*, P.P. 1878-9, XX. 17-18, 67-68. Stephen's work was a prolegomenon to a criminal code: J.F.Stephen, *A Digest of the Criminal Law (Crimes and Punishments)* (London: Macmillan 1877) 15-16; Stephen 1883 [20] II. 171; 'The plea of insanity', *BFMCR* 55 (1875) 88-115. A later legalistic attempt to broaden the Rules argued that, 'Judges who have dealt with the subject since *MacNaughten's case* have never said that there *can* be no insanity without delusions, though they have pointed out the *extreme difficulty* of proving such insanity' (Pitt-Lewis et al. 1895 [2] 220).

55 *Indictable Offences* 1878-9 [54] 18. Cf. *Royal Commission on Capital Punishment 1949-1953: Report* (London: HMSO 1953) 401-2; H.Oppenheimer, *The Criminal Responsibility of Lunatics: A Study in Comparative Law* (London: Sweet & Maxwell 1909) iii-iv.

56 On codification: Alvarez et al. 1969 [14]; von Bar et al. 1916 [14]; *Capital Punishment Report 1953* [55], Appendix 9; Oppenheimer 1909 [55] 37-90, containing a world-wide tabulation of the law in relation to criminal insanity.

57 Translated in G.O.W.Mueller (ed.) *The French Penal Code* (London: Sweet & Maxwell 1960) 39.

58 Bucknill 1857 [52] 121; [G.F.Blandford], '"Acquitted on the ground of insanity." (From a "mad doctor's" point of view.)', *Cornhill Magazine* 12 (1865) 426-40, on 438-9; Taylor 1865 [2] liii-lix.

59 Oppenheimer 1909 [55] 98-126; M.Foucault (ed.) *I, Pierre Rivière, Having Slaughtered my Mother, My Sister, and my Brother . . . A Case of Parricide in the 19th Century* (New York: Pantheon Books, Random House 1975). R.Castel, *L'ordre psychiatrique: l'âge d'or de l'aliénisme* (Paris: Les éditions de minuit 1976) 174-90, links discussions of 'monomanie homicide' with the establishment of medical expertise. He argues the category was an administrative solution in a judicial system committed to a rationalist view of human nature and the law. Acts of extreme violence and 'motivelessness' called into question the 'reason' of the law.

60 Paragraph 51, translated in Oppenheimer 1909 [55] 46-8. On German jurisprudence: ibid., 159-69; F.Wharton and M.Stillé, *A Treatise on Medical Jurisprudence* (Philadelphia: Kay & Brother 1855); J.L.Casper, *A Handbook of the Practice of Forensic Medicine*, 4 vols. (London: New Sydenham Society 1861-5); H.L.A.Hart and A.M.Honoré, *Causation in the Law* (Oxford: Clarendon Press 1959) 381-441.

61 Maudsley 1874 [10] 28.

62 J.H.B.Browne, 'Responsibility and disease', *Law Magazine*,

3rd series 1 (1872) 492-508, on 501.

63 See especially T.S.Szasz, 'The insanity plea and the insanity verdict', in *Ideology and Insanity: Essays on the Psychiatric Dehumanization of Man* (London: Calder & Boyars 1973) 98-112; idem, *Law, Liberty, and Psychiatry: An Inquiry into the Social Uses of Mental Health Practices* (London: Routledge 1974) 89-146. Szasz' work is discussed against the background of the politicisation of psychiatry in G.Pearson, *The Deviant Imagination: Psychiatry, Social Work and Social Change* (London: Macmillan 1975) 15-48. Moral philosophers have valued his emphasis on responsibility: A.G.N. Flew, *Crime or Disease?* (London: Macmillan 1973) 61, 118; H. Morris, 'Persons and punishment', in *On Guilt and Innocence: Essays in Legal Philosophy and Moral Psychology* (Berkeley: University of California Press 1976) 64-73. For a psychiatrist's cogent response: A. Clare, *Psychiatry in Dissent: Controversial Issues in Thought and Practice* (London: Tavistock 1976) 325-60.

64 T.Mayo, *Elements of the Pathology of the Human Mind* (London: Murray 1838) 2. The consequences of translating human problems into medical terms are detailed in I.Illich, *Limits to Medicine. Medical Nemesis: the Expropriation of Health* (Harmondsworth: Penguin 1977).

65 J.Abercrombie, *The Philosophy of the Moral Feelings* (London: Murray 1833) 129.

66 Mill 1970 [29] 551 (Book 6, chapter 2, sect.3).

67 Bradley 1927 [38] 48. Cf. B.C.Brodie, *Psychological Inquiries: In a Series of Essays, Intended to Illustrate the Mutual Relations of the Physical Organisation and the Mental Faculties* (London: Longman, Brown, Green, & Longmans 1854) 93-104. For a general discussion of habit in relation to the prevention of insanity: Maudsley 1874 [10] 268-308.

68 Stephen 1883 [20] 11. 177.

69 [F.Winslow], 'Recent trials in lunacy', *JPM* 7 (1854) 572-625, on 624.

70 Wharton & Stillé 1855 [60] 97.

71 Bethlem CBC/3, 6.

72 J.C.Bucknill and D.H.Tuke, *A Manual of Psychological Medicine* (London: Churchill 1858) 323.

73 Bucknill 1857 [52] 115. Cf. ibid., 113-18, 136; T.Mayo, *Medical Testimony and Evidence in Cases of Lunacy* (London: Parker 1854) 50-2, 86-90; Maudsley 1874 [10] 181; Stephen 1883 [20] 11. 175; W.Wood, *Remarks on the Plea of Insanity, and on the Management of Criminal Lunatics* (London: Longman, Brown, Green, & Longmans 1851) 45-8; D.Yellowless, 'The trial of Alexander Milne for murder in Edinburgh', *JMS* 9 (1863) 119-25. For diminished responsibility: Walker 1968 [22] 138-64.

74 D.Skae, 'On the legal relations of insanity: the civil incapacity and criminal responsibility of lunatics', *EMJ* 12 (1867) 811-29, on 825.

75 J.Abercrombie, *Inquiries Concerning the Intellectual Powers and the Investigation of Truth* (Edinburgh: Waugh & Innes 1830) 325.

76 [? J.C.Bucknill], 'Criminal jurisprudence of insanity', *Asylum JMS* 2 (1856) 391-2, on 391.

77 Blackstone 1791 [16] IV. 25-6; Stephen 1845 [16] 79.

78 For legal authority on crime and drunkenness: Russell 1877 [23] 114-16; *The English and Empire Digest . . . Replacement Volume 14. Criminal Law and Procedure* (London: Butterworths 1956) 69-74. See also: Ray 1962 [10] 309-24; Taylor 1865 [2] 1127-32; Wharton and Stillé 1855 [60] 47-60; Walker 1968 [22] 177-82.

79 Reported in 173 E.R. 132.

80 Reported in 175 E.R. 571. In a similar case two years later (Doody) intent was found however. Cf. Ann Coultass' acquittal for the drunken killing of her idiot child in 1856.
81 Taylor 1865 [2] 1131.
82 See report in 14 Cox C.C. 564.
83 cf. Oppenheimer 1909 [55] 32-4.
84 T.Mayo, *Clinical Facts and Reflections; Also, Remarks on the Impunity of Murder in Some Cases of Presumed Insanity* (London: Longman, Brown, Green, & Longmans 1847) 175-6.
85 The letters are interleaved in Bethlem CBC/4. See G.Johnston, *The Life of Captain Johnston, Late Captain of the 'Ship Tory,' With his Statement of the Circumstances of his Last Voyage* (Liverpool: privately printed [1850]).
86 Bethlem CBC/2, 100.
87 *The Times*, 8 February 1856, p.8.
88 Bucknill 1856 [76] 391. Bucknill (?) also pointed out how *The Times* falsely implied Westron had been found insane in order to support its attack on medical men.
89 A.H.Dymond, *The Law on its Trial; Or Personal Recollections of the Death Penalty and its Opponents* (London: Bennett 1865) 195-206. Sadly for this story, transportation was suspended in 1853.
90 Reported in 5 Irvine 479.
91 cf. Walker 1968 [22] 144-6.
92 N.Chevers, *A Manual of Medical Jurisprudence for India*, 3rd edition (Calcutta: Thacker, Spink 1870) 777-99. As Chevers pointed out (781-5) the Indian administration was also faced by a potential medico-legal problem with Indians running 'amok'.
93 W.C.Sullivan, *Crime and Insanity* (London: Edward Arnold 1924) 230.

CHAPTER FIVE
Medical Insanity and the Insanity Plea
1 V.Aubert and S.L.Messinger, 'The criminal and the sick', *Inquiry* 1 (1958) 137-60, on 143.
2 T.Laycock, 'On the legal doctrines of the responsibility of the insane and its consequences', *JMS* 10 (1864) 350-66, on 351.
3 'Criminal law of lunacy. Fatal assault at the Kent County Lunatic Asylum', *Medical Times* 3 (1851) 284-5, on 284. On another case of killing by an inmate, see Clapham (Wakefield Asylum).
4 Both reported in J.F.Stephen, 'On the policy of maintaining the limits at present imposed by law on the criminal responsibility of madmen', read 1855, in *Papers Read before the Juridical Society: 1855-1858* (London: Stevens & Norton 1858) 67-94, on 92 note. The anecdote about Martin also appeared in T.Mayo, *An Essay on the Relation of Morals to Insanity* (London: Fellowes 1834) 40; and was referred to by Lord Brougham (Martin's counsel) in *Hansard* 63 (1843) col.734.
5 J.C.Prichard, *A Treatise on Insanity and Other Disorders Affecting the Mind* (London: Sherwood, Gilbert, & Piper 1835) 318-27; J.E.D.Esquirol, *Mental Maladies. A Treatise on Insanity*, first publ. 1845 (facsimile reprint New York: Hafner 1965) 445-96; J.C.Bucknill and D.H.Tuke, *A Manual of Psychological Medicine* (London: Churchill 1858) 101-20. W.W.Ireland, *On Idiocy and Imbecility* (London: Churchill 1877), became a standard work.
6 On the special provisions for idiots: K.Jones, *Mental Health and Social Policy 1845-1959* (London: Routledge 1960) 43-72; L.S.Hearnshaw, *A Short History of British Psychology, 1840-1940* (London: Methuen 1964) 151-4; W.L.Parry-Jones, *The Trade in*

Lunacy: A Study of Private Madhouses in England in the Eighteenth and Nineteenth Centuries (London: Routledge 1972) 70-2.

7 Reported in 172 E.R. 925.

8 October 1854. Campbell was returned to England and sent to Bethlem: Bethlem CBC/3, 77, and CBC/4, 121.

9 Erskine's defence, reported in 27 Howell's St. Tr. 1323.

10 Reported in *The Times*, 4 March 1843, p.5.

11 cf. J.Abercrombie, *Inquiries Concerning the Intellectual Powers and the Investigation of Truth* (Edinburgh: Waugh & Innes 1830) 262-364; W.B.Carpenter, *Principles of Mental Physiology*, first publ. 1874, 6th edition (London: Kegan Paul, Trench 1888) 568-610; H. Holland, *Chapters on Mental Physiology* (London: Longman, Brown, Green, & Longmans 1852) 109-44.

12 Editorial, '[The case of Luigi Buranelli]', *Lancet* i (1855) 441, 518-19, 540-1, 564-6, 589-91, on 590.

13 ibid.

14 Reported in 4 Irvine 343.

15 See favourable comments in: D.Skae, 'On the legal relations of insanity: the civil incapacity and criminal responsibility of the insane', *EMJ* 12 (1867) 811-29, on 822; D.Yellowlees, 'The trial of Alexander Milne for murder in Edinburgh', *JMS* 9 (1863) 119-25.

16 Reported in ibid., 119.

17 ibid., 123.

18 J.C.Bucknill, 'Trial of Robert Handcock for the murder of his wife, Philippa Handcock, at the Devon Winter Assize, before Mr. Baron Parke, Dec. 10th, 1855. Plea of insanity', *Asylum JMS* 2 (1856) 245-53, on 248.

19 T.Mayo, *Medical Testimony and Evidence in Cases of Lunacy* (London: Parker 1854) 55.

20 Bucknill and Tuke 1858 [5] 193, quoting W.B.Carpenter,

Principles of Human Physiology, 4th edition (London: Churchill 1853) 840. The modern legal definition of automatism distinguishes it from 'insane impulse': G.Williams, *Criminal Law. The General Part*, 2nd edition (London: Stevens 1961) 477-8, 482-90, 507-13. I use 'automatism' in a loose medical sense.

21 [H.Maudsley and C.L. Robertson], *Insanity and Crime: A Medico-legal Commentary on the Case of George Victor Townley* (London: Churchill 1864) 35.

22 Abercrombie 1830 [11] 292-302; A.Brierre de Boismont, *On Hallucinations: A History and Explanation of Apparitions, Visions, Dreams, Ecstasy, Magnetism, and Somnambulism* (London: Renshaw 1859); A.Gauthier, *Histoire du somnambulisme chez tous les peuples*, 2 vols. (Paris: Malteste 1842); [A. Thomson], 'Somnambulism, magnetic or artificial', in *Encyclopaedia Britannica*, 8th edition, vol.XX (Edinburgh: Black 1860) 413-46; D.H.Tuke, *Sleep-walking and Hypnotism* (London: Churchill 1884); F.Wharton and M.Stillé, *A Treatise on Medical Jurisprudence* (Philadelphia: Kay & Brother 1855) 119-30.

23 Reported in 4 Couper 75.

24 Dr D.Yellowlees (Superintendent of Gartnavel Asylum), 'Homicide by a somnambulist', *JMS* 24 (1878) 451-8, on 457. Medicine did add authority in this case, since the prosecution doctors (Yellowlees and Alexander Robertson, Physician to the Poorhouse, Glasgow) and defence doctor (Thomas Clouston, Superintendent of the Morningside Asylum) agreed.

25 H.Maudsley, *The Physiology and Pathology of Mind*, 2nd edition (London: Macmillan 1868) 351-5; idem, *Responsibility in Mental Disease* (London: King 1874) 227-47; 'States of unconsciousness. Irresistible impulses – epilepsy –

Treadaway', *JPM*, new series 3 (1877) 185-208; O.Temkin, *The Falling Sickness: A History of Epilepsy from the Greeks to the Beginnings of Modern Neurology*, 2nd edition (Baltimore: Johns Hopkins University Press 1971) 268-70, 320-2.

26   J.C.Bucknill, *Unsoundness of Mind in Relation to Criminal Acts*, first publ. 1854, 2nd edition (London: Longman, Brown, Green, Longmans & Roberts 1857) xxxvii-xxxviii.

27   J.H.Jackson, *Selected Writings of John Hughlings Jackson*, 2 vols. (reprinted London: Staples 1958); S.H.Greenblatt, 'The major influences on the early life and work of John Hughlings Jackson', *Bulletin of the History of Medicine* 39 (1965) 346-76; R.M.Young, *Mind, Brain, and Adaptation in the Nineteenth Century: Cerebral Localization and its Biological Context from Gall to Ferrier* (Oxford: Clarendon Press 1970) 204-10.

28   J.H.Jackson, 'On temporary mental disorders after epileptic paroxysms', first publ. 1875, in Jackson 1958 [27] 1. 119-34, on 122.

29   Wharton and Stillé 1855 [22] 116-19.

30   J.C.Bucknill and D.H.Tuke, *A Manual of Psychological Medicine*, 2nd edition (London: Churchill 1862) 214-15.

31   J.C.Bucknill, 'Mayo, Winslow, & Parigot, on criminal lunacy', *BFMCR* 16 (1855) 370-88, on 384. Cf. Maudsley 1874 [25] 165-70. The different links between epilepsy and insanity, and the debt to French alienists, are discussed in G.E.Berrios, 'Epilepsy and insanity in 19th-century French psychiatry', unpublished paper, University of Cambridge 1978.

32   Maudsley 1874 [25] 168.

33   Reported in H.Cowan, 'Report of the trial of Thomas Donelly, acquitted on the ground of insanity', *EMJ* 8 (1863) 772-5, on 773.

34   cf. Jackson 1875 [28]. Though Jackson drew attention to the medico-legal aspects of post-epileptic automatism, he knew of no cases where serious crimes during this condition reached the courts. The cases he cited were applied hypothetically to possible crimes, except for the self-mutilation and suicidal frenzy attributed to epilepsy in Emily A. (ibid., 131-4).

35   M.G.Echeverria, 'Criminal responsibility of epileptics, as illustrated by the case of David Montgomery', *American Journal of Insanity* 19 (1873) 341-425; idem, 'Violence and unconscious state of epileptics, in their relations to medical jurisprudence', *American Journal of Insanity* 19 (1873) 508-56; idem, 'On epileptic insanity', *American Journal of Insanity* 20 (1873) 1-51. Cf. Temkin 1971 [25] 361. Montgomery's case also aroused comment because Dr William Hammond gave evidence for *both* prosecution and defence. Hammond wrote one of several American medico-legal texts published at this time; cf. R.P.Brittain, *Bibliography of Medico-legal Works in English* (London: Sweet & Maxwell 1962).

36   A.S.Taylor, *The Principles and Practice of Medical Jurisprudence* (London: Churchill 1865) 1131.

37   Esquirol 1965 [5] 320.

38   Quoted in W.C.Townsend, *Modern State Trials*, 2 vols. (London: Longman, Brown, Green, & Longmans 1850) 1. 365-6.

39   I.Ray, *A Treatise on the Medical Jurisprudence of Insanity*, first publ. 1838 (reprinted Cambridge, Mass.: Belknap Press of Harvard University 1962) 32.

40   ibid., 13.

41   Quoted in Townsend 1850 [38] 1. 356.

42 Evidence of Mr M'Clure, surgeon, quoted in ibid., 1. 398.

43 F.Winslow, *Lettsomian Lectures on Insanity* (London: Churchill 1854) 109. Winslow defended his controversial appearance at M'Naghten's trial and quoted from interviews with M'Naghten in Bethlem to argue he was certainly insane: 'Medical evidence in cases of insanity', *JPM* 4 (1851) 574-82.

44 Taylor 1865 [36] 1113.

45 Reported in 3 Cox C.C. 276. Parke, B. referred to Rolfe, B. in Stokes's case (1848).

46 Reported in J.G.Davey, 'Insanity and crime – communication by Dr. Dav[e]y', *JMS* 6 (1859) 31-8, on 34.

47 Reported in ibid.

48 Bramwell, B. in *Special Report from the Select Committee on Homicide Law Amendment Bill*, P.P. 1874, IX. 27.

49 Dove's trial (1856), reported in C.Williams, *Observations on the Criminal Responsibility of the Insane; Founded on the Trials of James Hill and of William Dove* (London: Churchill 1856) cix. Cf. discussion comments to Winslow's paper read to the Juridical Society in 1857, reported in [F.Winslow], 'The Juridical Society, and the criminal responsibility of the insane', *JPM* 11 (1858) 166-72, on 168; trial of the arsonist Roberts (1860) referred to in Taylor 1865 [36] 1124-5; evidence in *Report of the Capital Punishment Commission*, P.P. 1866, XXI, minutes 152-5; Bramwell, B., 'Insanity and crime', *Nineteenth Century* 18 (1885) 893-9.

50 Ray 1962 [39] 39.

51 Davey 1859 [46] 35. This suggestion was also raised in other contexts (when it was also not developed): J.C.Browne, 'Notes on homicidal insanity', *JMS* 9 (1863) 197-210; J.R.Reynolds, *On the Scientific Value of the Legal Tests of Insanity* (London: Churchill 1872). A similar resolution was passed and presented to the Royal Commission on Capital Punishment by its proposer, Dr Thomas Harrington Tuke: *JMS* 10 (1864) 462-5; *Capital Punishment Commission* [49] minute 2394. Cf. deputation to the Lord Advocate (Scotland), reported in Editorial, 'Lunacy and crime', *BMJ* ii (1868) 498.

52 cf. comments by Dr Fayner in Davey 1859 [46] 36.

53 Presenting the Lunacy Regulation Bill to the House of Lords: *Hansard* 165 (1862) col.782. On Windham's inquiry: G.Pitt-Lewis et al., *The Insane and the Law* (London: Churchill 1895) 75, 83-7, 258; K.Jones, 'The Windham case: the enquiry held in London in 1861 into the state of mind of William Frederick Windham, heir to the Felbrigg estate', *British Journal of Psychiatry* 119 (1971) 425-33; P. McCandless, 'Insanity and Society: A Study of the English Lunacy Reform Movement 1815-1870', unpublished Ph.D. thesis, Wisconsin 1974, 198-9.

54 *Hansard* 165 (1862) col.783.

55 T.Laycock, 'On law and medicine in insanity. An introductory lecture', *EMJ* 7 (1862) 1132-46, on 1132. Laycock believed that Windham suffered from arrested development or idiocy, not from unsound mind. Cf. Maudsley 1868 [25] 473-4; Skae 1867 [15] 813-17.

56 As quoted by Stephen, from Dove's case (1856), in *Select Committee Homicide Law* [48] 9. Cf. Bramwell, B., in *Capital Punishment Commission* [49] minute 154.

57 Bucknill 1857 [26] 17.

58 Replying to a question from Mr Neate, *Capital Punishment Commission* [49] minute 168.

59 Maudsley 1868 [25] 355-6.

60 Bucknill 1857 [26] 87.

61 Taylor 1865 [36] 1120. Cf. Erle, C.J. in Leigh's case (1866).

62 Reported in [? F.Winslow], 'Medical jurisprudence – the plea of insanity', *JPM* 2 (1849) 331-8, on 337.

63 ibid., 338.

64 Stephen 1858 [4] 81; italics added.

65 The lawyer H.Oppenheimer, *The Criminal Responsibility of Lunatics: A Study in Comparative Law* (London: Sweet & Maxwell 1909) 27, cited the cases of Gill (1883) and Jordan (1872) as allowing the insanity verdict to cover irresistible impulse, but no information is given. Brixey (1845), Brough (1854), and Ovenston (1848) were sometimes seen as having permitted this defence. For possible American precedents for irresistible impulse: S.R.Lewinstein, 'The historical development of insanity as a defense in criminal actions', *Journal of Forensic Science* 14 (1969) 275-93, 469-500, on 470-5.

66 Evidence of her doctor Mr Bell, reported in 'Chelmsford – Friday, March 10. Charge of murder. – Acquittal on the ground of puerperal insanity', *JPM* 1 (1848) 478-83, on 479.

67 Reported in ibid., 479-80.

68 J.G.Davey, 'A case of homicidal mania', *JMS* 7 (1860) 49-59, on 54; quoting from *Copy of the Fourteenth Report of the Commissioners in Lunacy*, 1860.

69 Reported in W.Wood, *Remarks on the Plea of Insanity, and on the Management of Criminal Lunatics* (London: Longman, Brown, Green, & Longmans 1851) 37.

70 ibid.

71 ibid., 40.

72 Reported in 4 Cox C.C. 155.

73 Bethlem CBC/2, 164, reporting the comments of the surgeon of Oxford County Gaol where Layton was held after his arrest.

74 Reported from *The Sheffield and Rotherham Independent* in Williams 1856 [49] vi.

75 ibid., xi.

76 ibid., xv.

77 ibid., xiii.

78 J.F.Stephen, *A History of the Criminal Law of England*, first publ. 1883, 3 vols. (facsimile reprint New York: Burt Franklin, n.d.) II. 168-75; Taylor 1865 [36] 1096-7.

79 Referred to in ibid., 1097, and in 176 E.R. 111-15.

80 'The trial of a lunatic for murder', *JMS* 11 (1865) 446-9, on 446.

81 A.S.Taylor, *A Manual of Medical Jurisprudence* (London: Churchill 1844) 649-50; italics added.

82 Taylor 1865 [36] 1121. Cf. Bucknill 1857 [26] 93-4; Maudsley 1874 [25] 101-2.

83 [? F.Winslow], 'The plea of insanity in criminal cases', *JPM* 5 (1852) 103-23, on 106.

84 W.Markby, *Elements of Law Considered with Reference to Principles of General Jurisprudence* (Oxford: Clarendon Press 1871) 129-30.

85 Winslow 1852 [83] 104.

86 Bucknill and Tuke 1858 [5] 193.

87 ibid., 192.

88 Prichard 1835 [5] 17.

89 Modern 'psychopathy' is a personality disorder characterised by persistent anti-social conduct. Moral insanity described disorder of certain mental faculties. This distinction has been emphasised to me by Herman Berrios. Cf. N. Walker and S.McCabe, *Crime and Insanity in England, vol. II: New Solutions and New Problems* (Edinburgh: Edinburgh University Press 1973) 205-22; Williams 1961 [20] 534-5. The term 'psychopathia' was used in other senses in nineteenth-century European medical psychology.

90 Abercrombie 1830 [11] 348-9.

91 Townsend 1850 [38] I. 148.

92 Hood in *Capital Punishment*

Commission [49] minute 2886; Mayo 1854 [19] iv.

93 Winslow 1854 [43] 114-20.

94 Maudsley 1868 [25] 358.

95 ibid., 356. Alienists also objected to moral insanity on these grounds; see the discussion of the American J.P.Gray, in S.P.Fullinwider, 'Insanity as the loss of self: the moral insanity controversy revisited', *Bulletin of the History of Medicine* 49 (1976) 87-101.

96 Bucknill and Tuke 1858 [5] 159.

97 'Moral insanity. – Dr. Mayo's Croonian Lectures', *Fraser's Magazine* 51 (1855) 245-59, on 246. The 'men of note' were Dr Thomas Mayo and Sir Benjamin Collins Brodie of the Royal College of Physicians. The phrase 'homicidal orgasm' was not fashionable, but was a sarcasm. For a similar view: C.P.Phillips, *The Law Concerning Lunatics, Idiots, & Persons of Unsound Mind* (London: Butterworths 1858) 56 note.

98 J. Conolly, *An Inquiry Concerning the Indications of Insanity with Suggestions for the Better Protection and Care of the Insane*, first publ. 1830 (facsimile reprint London: Dawsons 1964) 454.

99 Reported in Bucknill 1857 [26] 82. Burton was tried twice for a legal technicality which is not made clear.

100 T.Mayo, *Clinical Facts and Reflections: Also, Remarks on the Impunity of Murder in some Cases of Presumed Insanity* (London: Longman, Brown, Green, & Longmans 1847) 217.

101 Mayo 1834 [4] 42.

102 T.Mayo, *Outlines of Medical Proof* (London: Longman, Brown, Green, & Longmans 1850) 52.

103 T.Mayo, *Elements of the Pathology of the Human Mind* (London: Murray 1838) 153-4; cf. 8-16, 61-4, 122-32.

104 Mayo 1847 [100] 174-5.

105 Mayo 1854 [19] 25. This

statement was attacked in: *Lancet* 1855 [12] especially p.591; Bucknill 1855 [31].

106 Mayo 1854 [19] 47.

107 Mayo 1847 [100] 204.

108 B.C.Brodie, *Psychological Inquiries: In a Series of Essays, Intended to Illustrate the Mutual Relations of the Physical Organisation and the Mental Faculties* (London: Longman, Brown, Green, & Longmans 1854) 102.

109 Laycock 1862 [55] 1141.

110 ibid., 1142.

111 ibid., 1141.

112 D.H.Tuke, 'The plea of insanity in relation to the penalty of death; or, the report of the Capital Punishment Commission psychologically considered', *Social Science Review*, new series 5 (1866) 289-309.

113 Evidence in *Capital Punishment Commission* [49] minute 3261.

114 Stephen 1883 [78] II. 91.

115 This view was cited as authority for producing evidence of hereditary insanity: Wharton and Stillé 1855 [22] 94. Such evidence could be rejected in Scotland on the basis of Gibson's case (1844).

116 Mayo 1847 [100] 175.

117 ibid., 169.

118 'Criminal irresponsibility of the insane', *Law Magazine*, 3rd series 1 (1872) 215-19, on 215.

119 Williams 1856 [49] 6. Cf. J.C.Prichard, *On the Different Forms of Insanity, in Relation to Jurisprudence* (London: Baillière 1842) 126.

120 Taylor 1865 [36] 1105-6.

121 Park, J. reported from Greensmith's trial (1837) in 'Dr. Blake on monomania', *Medico-chirugical Review* 28 (1838) 84-90, on 86.

122 See comments on the relation between atrocity and diagnosis: Bucknill and Tuke 1858 [5] 158-60; Maudsley 1868 [25] 354-5; Maudsley and Robertson 1864 [21] 15, 24-5; Prichard 1835 [5] 64, 86;

C.L.Robertson, 'A case of homicidal mania, without disorder of the intellect', *JMS* 6 (1860) 385-98, on 397; Winslow 1854 [43] 120.

123　Reported in 175 E.R. 515-16. Cf. Bramwell, B., reported in Haynes's case: 'Psychological quarterly retrospect', *JPM* 12 (1859) xxix-lxvi, on li.

124　Bucknill 1857 [26] 68-9. The young man in question was a chancery lunatic originally attended by Dr Alexander Sutherland. Cf. Taylor 1865 [36] 1106; Stephen 1858 [4] 82; Bramwell, in *Capital Punishment Commission* [49] minute 156.

CHAPTER SIX
Depravity and Madness in Controversial Trials

1　M.Foucault (ed.), *I. Pierre Rivière, Having Slaughtered my Mother, my Sister, and my Brother . . . A Case of Parricide in the 19th Century* (New York: Pantheon Books, Random House 1975) 249.

2　J.M.Quen, 'An historical view of the M'Naghten trial', *Bulletin of the History of Medicine* 42 (1968) 43-51.

3　The medical evidence is given in W.C.Townsend, *Modern State Trials*, 2 vols. (London: Longman, Brown, Green, & Longmans 1850) I. 135-43.

4　Quoted in 173 E.R. 950.

5　J.M.Quen, 'Anglo-American criminal insanity: an historical perspective', *Journal of the History of the Behavioral Sciences* 10 (1974) 313-23, on 319, 322, interprets Denman's statement as an important precedent for the defence of irresistible impulse which was later ignored. Nobody, however, including Denman, seems to have seen it as a precedent at the time and the whole tone of the summing up perhaps detracted from the quoted passage.

6　Townsend 1850 [3] I. 108-9.

7　Quoted in N.Walker, *Crime and Insanity in England, vol. I: The Historical Perspective* (Edinburgh: Edinburgh University Press 1968) 188. A similar attitude that 'everybody knows' the moral guilt of certain prisoners was expressed in 'Moral insanity. – Dr. Mayo's Croonian lectures', *Fraser's Magazine* 51 (1855) 245-59.

8　Reported in 'The late assault on the Queen. Important medico-legal decision in cases of alleged lunacy', *Medical Times* 1 (1850) 64-6, on 66; whole passage italicised in original.

9　[H.Maudsley and C.L. Robertson], *Insanity and Crime: A Medico-legal Commentary on the Case of George Victor Townley* (London: Churchill 1864) 28; italics added.

10　ibid., 28-9.

11　ibid., 27.

12　H.Maudsley, *Body and Mind: An Inquiry into their Connection and Mutual Influence, Especially in Reference to Mental Disorders*, 2nd edition (London: Macmillan 1873) 72. Cf. H.Maudsley, *Responsibility in Mental Disease* (London: King 1874) 161-3.

13　ibid., 160.

14　Maudsley and Robertson 1864 [9] 26.

15　According to the *Dictionary of National Biography*, A.S.Taylor wrote medico-legal editorials for the *British Medical Journal*; he may well have written this criticism.

16　T.Laycock, 'On the legal doctrines of the responsibility of the insane and its consequences', *JMS* 10 (1864) 350-66, on 353; also quoted in '[Legal responsibility of the insane]', *BMJ* ii (1864) 227-8, on 228.

17　*BMJ* 1864 [16] 228.

18　ibid.

19　Reported in 4 Irvine 525-6.

20　Laycock 1864 [16] 358.

21　D.H.Tuke, 'The plea of insanity in relation to the penalty of death; or, the report of the Capital

Punishment Commission psychologically considered', *Social Science Review*, new series 5 (1866) 289-309, on 291.

22 Bethlem CBC/4, 92.

23 Quoted from *The Times* in ibid.

24 [? H.Maudsley], 'The suicide of George Victor Townley', *J M S* 11 (1865) 66-83, on 82. Cf. W.C. Hood, *Criminal Lunatics. A Letter to the Chairman of the Commissioners in Lunacy* (London: Churchill 1860) 16. I have not managed to trace the parliamentary reference.

25 'James Atkinson's prison letters', *J M S* 5 (1859) 430-4.

26 Maudsley 1865 [24] 81-2. Cf. J.C.Bucknill, 'Criminal lunatics, by Dr. W.C.Hood', *J M S* 6 (1860) 513-19.

27 Reported in Maudsley and Robertson 1864 [9] 7; also in 176 E.R. 384-8.

28 Reported in Maudsley and Robertson 1864 [9] 7.

29 ibid., 9. The first report from the Commissioners was dated 28 December 1863 and was signed by the barristers Mr Campbell, Mr Wilkes and Mr Forster.

30 ibid., 10-11.

31 Their report was reprinted in ibid., p.12 note. The second report was dated 28 January 1864 and was signed by Drs Hood, Bucknill, Meyer, and Helps. Townley's sanity was also endorsed by Dr Hitchman (Superintendent Physician, Derbyshire County Asylum) who had a long interview with Townley while he was awaiting trial: J. Hitchman, 'An interview with George Victor Townley and reflections thereon', *J M S* 10 (1864) 21-34.

32 The Insane Prisoners Amendment Act. It was possible, if sanity returned, for the prisoner to be sent to complete the sentence. Cf. D.P. Fry, *The Lunacy Acts*, 2nd edition reprint (London: Knight, Maxwell 1877) 612-16; Walker 1968 [7]

207-10. The administration of this Act still provoked a feeling that those found guilty could be got off: 'Criminal irresponsibility of the insane', *Law Magazine*, 3rd series 1 (1872) 215-19, on 218-19, referring to Edmunds' case. For the parliamentary discussion of Townley: *Hansard* 173 (1864) cols.169, 218-19, 243-79, 328, 567-84, 1185, 1243-8.

33 A.S.Taylor, *The Principles and Practice of Medical Jurisprudence* (London: Churchill 1865) 1115-20.

34 Maudsley and Robertson 1864 [9] 23.

35 Reported in 176 E.R. 386.

36 'The insanity of criminals', *Saturday Review* 16 (1863) 776-7.

37 There were parallels between Dove's case and the famous strychnine poisoning case of William Palmer in the same year. Expert witnesses (notably A.S.Taylor) were involved at great length in establishing the legal standing of medical facts in Palmer's trial; here at least it seemed as if scientific expertise acquired status. Palmer was also a classic example of moral depravity; his history was not unlike Dove's, yet 'no one ever suggested that there was even a disposition towards madness in him; yet he was as cruel, as treacherous, as greedy of money and pleasure, as brutally hard-hearted and sensual a wretch as it is possible even to imagine'; J.F.Stephen, *A History of the Criminal Law of England*, first publ. 1883, 3 vols. (facsimile reprint New York: Burt Franklin, n.d.) III. 425. Palmer's case also established the national position of the Central Criminal Court; his trial was moved by a new statute from Stafford to London because it was feared a local jury would not be impartial.

38 J.F.Stephen, *A General View of the Criminal Law of England* (London: Macmillan 1863) 394.

39   Printed in J.C.Bucknill, 'Plea of insanity – the trial of William Dove', *Asylum JMS* 3 (1857) 125-34, on 130.

40   C.Williams, *Observations on the Criminal Responsibility of the Insane; Founded on the Trials of James Hill and of William Dove* (London: Churchill 1856) 13.

41   Bucknill 1857 [39] 132. Bucknill believed that Dove was not morally insane. Dove's case was characteristic of others in which defence counsel used biographical evidence, while prosecuting counsel emphasised the crime; cf. Foucault 1975 [1].

42   Reported in Stephen 1863 [38] 398.

43   ibid., 398-9.

44   The prosecution, reported by *The Leeds Mercury*, quoted in Williams 1856 [40] civ.

45   ibid., 24.

46   Judge and jury reported in ibid., cix, cxv.

47   Reported in ibid., cxiii-cxiv.

48   [J.C.Bucknill], 'The trial and conviction of Luigi Buranelli for murder. Plea of insanity', *Asylum Journal* I (1855) 209-13, on 209.

49   Editorial, '[The case of Luigi Buranelli]', *Lancet* i (1855) 441, 518-19, 540-1, 564-6, 589-91, on 540.

50   ibid.

51   ibid., 565.

52   ibid., 590. J.C.Bucknill, *Unsoundness of Mind in Relation to Criminal Acts*, first publ. 1854, 2nd edition (London: Longman, Brown, Green, Longmans & Roberts 1857) vii, also attacked Mayo for his 'metaphysical or spiritualist theory of insanity'.

53   *Lancet* 1855 [49] 566.

54   F.Winslow, *The Case of Luigi Buranelli Medico-legally Considered* [Supplement to vol. 8, *JPM*] (London: Churchill 1855) 3-4.

55   J.C.Prichard, *On the Different Forms of Insanity, in Relation to Jurisprudence* (London: Baillière 1842) 160.

56   Taylor 1865 [33] 1105.

57   Reported in *The Times*, 8 February 1856, p.8; and in Tuke 1866 [21] 301-2.

58   *The Times*, leader, 8 February 1856, p.9; quoted in [? J.C.Bucknill], 'Criminal jurisprudence of insanity', *Asylum JMS* 2 (1856) 391-2, on 391.

59   Reported in 'Psychological quarterly retrospect', *JPM* 9 (1856) xxv-xc, on lx.

60   'The late murder in Bedford-Row', *MTG* 12 (1856) 166-8. W. Wood, 'Lunatic criminals – their responsibility', [letter to the editor], *MTG* 12 (1856) 290, argued that Westron supported his view that the law should allow an intermediate verdict.

61   Maudsley and Robertson 1864 [9] 38.

62   'Regina v. Fooks. Dorset Spring Assizes, 1863', *JMS* 9 (1863) 125-37, on 126.

63   Maudsley and Robertson 1864 [9] 39.

64   ibid., 19; italics added.

65   *JMS* 1863 [62] 132.

66   ibid., 133.

67   ibid., 136.

CHAPTER SEVEN
Medico-Legal Views of Women

I   Criticism that some feminists draw on a 'misuse of science' argument is made in D.Haraway, 'Animal sociology and a natural economy of the body politic, Part I: a political physiology of dominance', *Signs* 4 (1978) 21-36. This argues from a radical position concerning knowledge in R.M.Young, 'Science *is* social relations', *Radical Science Journal* 5 (1977) 65-129.

2   The place of women in the nature-culture polarity is discussed in L.J.Jordanova, 'Natural facts: an historical perspective on science and sexuality', in C.P.MacCormack and M.Strahern (eds.) *Nature*,

Culture and Gender (Cambridge, England: Cambridge University Press, forthcoming 1981).

3   cf. J.L'Esperance, 'Doctors and women in nineteenth-century society: sexuality and role', in J. Woodward and D.Richards (eds.) *Health Care and Popular Medicine in Nineteenth Century England* (London: Croom Helm 1977) 105-27; K.Figlio, 'Chlorosis and chronic disease in nineteenth-century Britain: the social constitution of somatic illness in capitalist society', *Social History* 3 (1978) 167-97; J.S. Haller and R.M.Haller, *The Physician and Sexuality in Victorian America* (Urbana: University of Illinois Press 1974) 24-42, 46-87; E.Showalter, 'Victorian women and insanity', *Victorian Studies* 23 (1980) 157-81; C.Smith-Rosenberg and C.E.Rosenberg, 'The female animal: medical and biological views of woman and her role in nineteenth-century America', *Journal of American History* 60 (1973) 332-56; M.Verbrugge, 'Women and medicine in nineteenth-century America', *Signs* 1 (1976) 957-72.

4   W.B.Ryan, *Infanticide: Its Law, Prevalence, Prevention, and History* (London: Churchill 1862) 4. Cf. M.A.Baines, 'A few thoughts concerning infanticide', *Journal of Social Science* [2 vols. in 1] (1866) 535-40; G.Greaves, 'Observations on some of the causes of infanticide', *Transactions of the Manchester Statistical Society*, n.v. (1863) 1-24, on 4-8. This literature is discussed in G.K.Behlmer, 'Deadly motherhood: infanticide and medical opinion in mid-Victorian England', *Journal of the History of Medicine* 34 (1979) 403-27; K.Clarke, 'The status of the new-born child: infanticide, illegitimacy and the medical profession', unpublished paper, Birkbeck College, London 1980.

5   cf. R.Sauer, 'Infanticide and abortion in nineteenth-century Britain', *Population Studies* 32 (1978) 81-93.

6   Offences against the Person Acts in 1803, 1828 and 1861 (sect. 20). Cf. W.O.Russell, *A Treatise on Crimes and Misdemeanors*, 5th edition ed. by S.Prentice, vol. 1 (London: Stevens 1877) 801-7. Cases brought under these Acts were troubled by defining 'concealment'; there was no effort to interpret the law in a strict way. Cf. N.Walker, *Crime and Insanity in England, vol. I: The Historical Perspective* (Edinburgh: Edinburgh University Press) 126-32.

7   Sir George Grey, in *Report of the Capital Punishment Commission*, P.P. 1866, XXI, minute 1473.

8   R.W.Malcomson, 'Infanticide in the eighteenth century', in J.S. Cockburn (ed.) *Crime in England 1550-1800* (London: Methuen 1977) 187-209.

9   'Child-murder and its punishment', *Social Science Review*, new series 2 (1864) 452-9, on 453.

10   Grey, in *Capital Punishment Commission* [7], minute 1456.

11   Still-births were not recorded under the Registration Acts in the nineteenth century.

12   A.Alison, *Principles of the Criminal Law of Scotland* (Edinburgh: Blackwood 1832) 159.

13   J.F.Stephen, in *Capital Punishment Commission* [7], minute 1453. Cf. *Hansard* 234 (1877) cols. 1669-70; *Special Report from the Select Committee on Homicide Law Amendment Bill*, P.P. 1874, IX. 70, printing Stephen's draft code; *Report of the Royal Commission Appointed to Consider the Law Relating to Indictable Offences*, P.P. 1878-9, XX. 25, 102.

14   No clear definition of when a child was born was forthcoming: definitions were assessed anew at each trial. In law, before birth there is no person who can be killed within the description of

murder. The courts were liberal in interpreting death as occurring prior to the child being 'actually wholly produced alive' even when there was clear evidence of wounding. Cf. J.F.Archbold, *Archbold's Pleading and Evidence in Criminal Cases*, 12th edition (London: Sweet & Stevens & Norton 1853) 498-9; Russell 1877 [6] 646-7; J.F.Stephen, *A Digest of the Criminal Law (Crimes and Punishments)* (London: Macmillan 1877) 138; F.Wharton and M. Stillé, *A Treatise on Medical Jurisprudence* (Philadelphia: Kay & Brother 1855) 785-92. There was also a hiatus in the law between the felonies of procuring a miscarriage and of murdering a new-born baby. Destruction during birth was technically no crime: *Royal Commission Indictable Offences* [13] 108; Walker 1968 [6] 128.

15 Bramwell, in *Capital Punishment Commission* [7] minute 138.
16 ibid., minute 1470. Cf. A.H. Dymond, *The Law on its Trial; Or Personal Recollections of the Death Penalty and its Opponents* (London: Bennett 1865) 125-47.
17 Bramwell, in *Capital Punishment Commission* [7] minute 137. This view was supported by Grey, ibid., minutes 1453-86. The Commission proposed that infanticide, if committed within one week of giving birth, should be punishable by imprisonment and not death, but this was not taken up.
18 Stephen, ibid., minutes 2192-2204; *Committee on Homicide Law* [13] 19.
19 Bethlem CBC/3, 114.
20 According to admission figures (collated by Barbara Bowron, with a record deposited at Bethlem), between 1816 and 1864, out of 56 women admitted, acquitted of murder or manslaughter (out of a total of 120 criminally insane women admitted), 27 had killed their own child

within twelve months of birth, and a further 14 their own child of an older or unspecified age.
21 Reported in 14 Cox C.C. 144. Vaughan Williams, J. made the same point in Davies' case in 1853.
22 Bethlem CBC/3, 166.
23 [? F.Winslow], 'Important medico-legal trial – the plea of insanity', *JPM* 9 (1856) 126-42.
24 'Confession of Constance Kent', *JMS* 11 (1865) 427-31, citing comments from J.C.Bucknill. It is questioned whether Constance Kent's 'confession' was genuine or produced by religious manipulation: M.S.Hartman, *Victorian Murderesses: A True History of Thirteen Respectable French and English Women Accused of Unspeakable Crimes* (London: Robson Books 1977) 94-129. The case was also the subject of a BBC TV serial in 1980.
25 J.C.Bucknill and D.H.Tuke, *A Manual of Psychological Medicine* (London: Churchill 1858) 235-9.
26 J.B.Tuke, 'On the statistics of puerperal insanity as observed in the Royal Edinburgh Asylum, Morningside', *EMJ* 10 (1865) 1013-28.
27 Bucknill and Tuke 1858 [25] 235-9, on 238-9. The quotation is based on J.Reid, 'On the causes, symptoms, and treatment of puerperal insanity', *JPM* 1 (1848) 128-51, 284-94, on 134-5. Cf. J.E.D. Esquirol, *Mental Maladies. A Treatise on Insanity*, first publ. 1845 (facsimile reprint New York: Hafner 1965) 125-43; J.C.Prichard, 'Insanity', in J.Forbes et al. (eds.) *The Cyclopaedia of Practical Medicine*, vol. 11 (London: Sherwood, Gilbert, & Piper, & Baldwin & Cradock 1833) 822-75, on 867-72; idem, *A Treatise on Insanity and other Disorders Affecting the Mind* (Sherwood, Gilbert, & Piper 1835) 306-17; A.Tardieu, *Étude médico-légale sur l'infanticide* (Paris: Baillière 1868) 222-40; A.S.Taylor,

The Principles and Practice of Medical Jurisprudence (London: Churchill 1865) 1121-3. The extensive European literature on this topic attests to its significant role in the emergence of the forensic specialism.

28 Bucknill and Tuke 1858 [25] 273.

29 ibid.

30 Tuke 1865 [26] 1018.

31 ibid., 1015; Tuke placed most emphasis on the danger of suicide during pregnancy.

32 Taylor 1865 [27] 1122.

33 'Chelmsford – Friday, March 10. Charge of murder. – Acquittal on the ground of puerperal insanity', *JPM* 1 (1848) 478-83, on 479.

34 Mrs Beveridge was described as 'incurable' in Bethlem CBC/3, 160, and Incurable Case Book, 123.

35 Bucknill and Tuke 1858 [25] 236.

36 Tuke 1865 [26] 1020.

37 Jurisprudence established similarities between the legal incompetence of women and children. Women were 'passive' in the civil law of property: A.H.Manchester, *A Modern Legal History of England and Wales 1750-1950* (London: Butterworths 1980) 368-73. They were also 'passive' in criminal law, when a *'femme covert'* was not responsible while committing a crime accompanied by her husband. In addition, confined women might be considered – from an anthropological viewpoint – 'outside' society, if birth is considered a *rite de passage.*

38 *Hansard* 142 (1856) col.428.

39 W.Tallack, in *Capital Punishment Commission* [7] minute 1335.

40 Taylor 1865 [27] 1109-10.

41 On menstruation: V.Bullough and M.Voght, 'Women, menstruation, and nineteenth-century medicine', *Bulletin of the History of Medicine* 47 (1973) 66-82; Haller and Haller 1974 [3] 58-61; E.

Showalter and E. Showalter, 'Victorian women and menstruation', in M.Vicinus (ed.) *Suffer and Be Still: Women in the Victorian Age* (Bloomington: Indiana University Press 1973) 38-44. Bucknill suggested that disordered menstruation played a role in Constance Kent's supposed killing of her stepbrother: *JMS* 1865 [24]. Psychiatrists now argue that a 'premenstrual syndrome' should be recognised as an insanity defence; cf. A.D.Brooks, *Law, Psychiatry and the Mental Health System* (Boston: Little, Brown 1974) 240-2.

42 Bethlem CBC/2, 91.

43 ibid.

44 H.Maudsley, *Body and Mind: An Inquiry into their Connection and Mutual Influence, Especially in Reference to Mental Disorders,* 2nd edition (London: Macmillan 1873) 132.

45 Reported in *The Times,* 10 August 1854, p.12.

46 ibid.

47 [F.Winslow], 'Recent trials in lunacy', *JPM* 7 (1854) 572-625, on 623, 620.

48 Reported in *The Times,* 10 August 1854, p.12.

49 Winslow 1854 [47] 623; Winslow was parodying his critics.

50 ibid., 624.

51 'Moral insanity. – Dr. Mayo's Croonian lectures', *Fraser's Magazine* 51 (1855) 245-59, on 250.

52 Post-mortem Books, Bethlem archives; Hood in *Capital Punishment Commission* [7] minutes 2778-84.

CHAPTER EIGHT
Knowledge and Responsibility

1 [G.F.Blandford], '"Acquitted on the ground of insanity." (From a "mad doctor's" point of view.)', *Cornhill Magazine* 12 (1865) 426-40, on 440.

2 J.F.Stephen, *Liberty, Equality, Fraternity,* first publ.

1873, 2nd edition (reprinted Cambridge, England: Cambridge University Press 1967) 176.

3   A.W.Renton, *Monomanie sans délire, an Examination of 'the Irresistible Criminal Impulse Theory'* (Edinburgh: T.& T.Clark 1886) 52-3.

4   M.Douglas, 'Self-evidence', in *Implicit Meanings* (London: Routledge 1975) 276-318, on 282-3.

5   M.Douglas, *Natural Symbols: Explorations in Cosmology*, 2nd edition (London: Barrie & Jenkins 1973). These points are indebted to unpublished work by E.Nissan (London School of Economics).

6   J.G.Davey, '[On the relations between crime and insanity]', *JMS* 5 (1858) 82-94, on 90. J.C.Bucknill and D.H.Tuke, *A Manual of Psychological Medicine* (London: Churchill 1858) 105, where the reflex hierarchy is used to classify degrees of idiocy.

7   Wightman, J. in Burton's case (1863), reported in 176 E.R. 355 note (d).

8   On the exchange of meanings between the physical and social body: Douglas 1973 [5] 93-112. Other discussions of bodily hierarchies in relation to nineteenth-century knowledge include: B.Barnes and S.Shapin (eds.) *Natural Order: Historical Studies in Scientific Culture* (London: Sage 1979) 15-92; S.Shapin and B. Barnes, 'Head and hand: rhetorical resources in British pedagogical writing, 1770-1850', *Oxford Review of Education* 2 (1976) 231-54; J.V. Pickstone, 'Bureaucracy, liberalism and the body in post-revolutionary France. 1: Bichat's physiology and the Paris school of medicine', forthcoming in *History of Science*, 1981.

9   H.Holland, *Chapters on Mental Physiology* (London: Longman, Brown, Green, & Longmans 1852) 27.

10   W.Griesinger, *Mental Pathology and Therapeutics*, first publ. 1867 (facsimile reprint New York: Hafner 1965) 40.

11   T.Mayo, *Medical Testimony and Evidence in Cases of Lunacy* (London: Parker 1854) 47. Cf. idem, *An Essay on the Relation of the Theory of Morals to Insanity* (London: Fellowes 1834) 42; idem, *Clinical Facts and Reflections; also, Remarks on the Impunity of Murder in some Cases of Presumed Insanity* (London: Longman, Brown, Green, & Longmans 1847) 194; Davey 1858 [6]; H.Maudsley, *Responsibility in Mental Disease* (London: King 1874) 3-4; I.Ray, *A Treatise on the Medical Jurisprudence of Insanity*, first publ. 1838 (reprinted Cambridge, Mass.: Belknap Press of Harvard University 1962) 32; D.Skae, 'The legal relations of insanity', *EMJ* 6 (1861) 867-90, on 889; W.Wood, *Remarks on the Plea of Insanity, and on the Management of Criminal Lunatics* (London: Longman, Brown, Green, & Longmans 1851) 4-5.

12   J.C.Bucknill, *Unsoundness of Mind in Relation to Criminal Acts*, first publ. 1854, 2nd edition (London: Longman, Brown, Green, Longmans & Roberts 1857) 9.

13   A.T.Scull, *Museums of Madness: The Social Organization of Insanity in Nineteenth-century England* (London: Allen Lane 1979) 159-60. Scull's statement refers to the early nineteenth century, but the functionalist explanation of physicalism applies generally.

14   E.Durkheim, 'The dualism of human nature and its social conditions', in *Essays on Sociology and Philosophy*, ed. K.H.Wolff (reprinted New York: Harper Torchbook 1964) 325-40, on 328.

15   ibid., 338. A parallel dualism is found in Freud's account of the conditions of civilisation.

16   Bucknill 1857 [12] 28, 58-9. Cf. C.L.Robertson, 'A case of

homicidal mania, without disorder of the intellect', *JMS* 6 (1860) 385-98, on 393-4. For the inalienable will in popular form: J. Abercrombie, *The Philosophy of the Moral Feelings* (London: Murray 1833); J.Barlow, *On Man's Power over Himself to Prevent or Control Insanity* (London: Pickering 1843); G.Moore, *The Power of the Soul over the Body, Considered in Relation to Health and Morals* (London: Longman, Brown, Green, & Longmans 1845).

17 C.Williams, *Observations on the Criminal Responsibility of the Insane; Founded on the Trials of James Hill and of William Dove* (London: Churchill 1856) 24.

18 Bucknill 1857 [12] 15.

19 ibid.

20 ibid., 9-10.

21 cf. The Law Commission, *Criminal Law: Report on the Mental Element in Crime* (London: HMSO 1978); H.Fingarette and A. Fingarette Hasse, *Mental Disabilities and Criminal Responsibility* (Berkeley: University of California Press 1979).

22 A.S.Goldstein, *The Insanity Defense* (New Haven: Yale University Press 1967) 11.

23 cf. the discussion of causal attribution in relation to the development of American social science, in T.L.Haskell, *The Emergence of Professional Social Science: The American Social Science Association and the Nineteenth-Century Crisis of Authority* (Urbana: University of Illinois Press 1977) especially pp. 38-42.

24 J.R.Reynolds, *On the Scientific Value of the Legal Tests of Insanity* (London: Churchill 1872) 34; D.L. Bazelon, 'Justice stumbles over science', in A.S.Blumberg (ed.) *The Scales of Justice* (Chicago: Aldine 1970) 123-39, on 129. Cf. J.F. Stephen, *A Digest of the Criminal Law (Crimes and Punishments)* (London: Macmillan 1877) xxix-xxx.

25 B.Barnes, 'On the conventional character of knowledge and cognition', forthcoming in German in *Kölner Zeitschrift für Soziologie*, special issue, no.23, 1980.

26 H.Fingarette, *The Meaning of Criminal Insanity* (Berkeley: University of California Press 1972) 64.

27 e.g. V.Aubert, 'The structure of legal thinking', in F.Castberg (ed.) *Legal Essays* (Oslo: Universitatsforlaget 1963) 41-63. For comparison of scientific and legal explanations: H.L.A.Hart and H. Honoré, *Causation in the Law* (Oxford: Clarendon Press 1959).

28 Bibliography in M.L.Cohen, N.Ronen, and J. Stepan, *Law & Science: A Selected Bibliography*, ed. V.B.Shelanski and M.C.La Follette (Cambridge, Mass.: MIT Press 1980). Discussions with Brian Wynne (University of Lancaster) about his forthcoming study of nuclear decision-making and the 1977 Windscale Inquiry have suggested the continuity of nineteenth-century medico-legal problems and those of big technology. For the background to new approaches to institutional science, politics and technology: J.R.Ravetz, *Scientific Knowledge and its Social Problems* (reprinted Harmondsworth: Penguin 1973).

29 A.Mazur, 'Disputes between experts', *Minerva* 11 (1973) 243-62; idem, 'Science courts', *Minerva* 15 (1977) 1-14.

30 A.R.Louch, 'Scientific discovery and legal change', *The Monist* 49 (1965) 485-503, on 488.

31 Fingarette 1972 [26] 56.

32 This still causes difficulty, even for judges: e.g. the statement in Bazelon 1970 [24] 130, that 'scientists now generally agree that human behavior is caused rather than willed'.

33 F.H.Bradley, 'The vulgar notion of responsibility in connexion with the theories of freewill

and necessity', first publ. 1876, 2nd edition (Oxford: Clarendon Press 1927) 1-57, on 48 note, criticising Maudsley.

34   Fingarette 1972 [26] 71-81; A.G.N.Flew, *Crime or Disease?* (London: Macmillan 1973) 87-8, 100-8; J.Glover, *Responsibility* (London: Routledge 1970) 74-84; H.L.A.Hart, 'Legal responsibility and excuses', in *Punishment and Responsibility: Essays in the Philosophy of Law* (Oxford: Clarendon Press 1968) 28-53; Hart and Honoré 1959 [27] 30-41. For a medical attempt to tackle the conflict of medical determinism and legal (and commonsense) freewill: F.A.Whitlock, *Criminal Responsibility and Mental Illness* (London: Butterworths 1963) 54-71.

35   Goldstein 1967 [22] 225.

Date	Regnal year and chapter	Title and page reference
1800	40 Geo. III, c. 94	The Criminal Lunatics Act, pp.20, 71.
1803	43 Geo. III, c. 58	An Act for the further preventing of malicious Shooting, and attempting to discharge loaded Fire-arms, Stabbing, Cutting, Wounding, Poisoning, malicious using of means to procure the Miscarriage of Women . . ., pp.145, 212.
1808	48 Geo. III, c. 96	The County Asylums Act, pp.5, 22.
1816	56 Geo. III, c. 117	An Act to amend an Act . . . for the safe Custody of Insane Persons charged with Offences, p.21.
1828	9 Geo. IV, c. 31	An Act for consolidating and amending . . . Offences against the Person, pp.145, 212.
1836	6 & 7 Will. IV, c. 114	The Felonies Act, pp.70, 183, 197.
1840	3 & 4 Vict., c. 54	The Insane Prisoners Act, pp.21-2, 26, 92, 132.
1842	5 & 6 Vict., c. 51	The Treason Act, pp.28-9.
1845	8 & 9 Vict., c. 100	The Lunatics Care and Treatment Act, pp.3, 5, 68-9.
1845	8 & 9 Vict., c. 126	The Lunatic Asylums Act, pp.3, 5, 69.
1853	16 & 17 Vict., c. 70	The Lunacy Regulation Act, p.69.
1853	16 & 17 Vict., c. 97	The Lunatic Asylums Amendment Act, p.23.
1858	21 & 22 Vict., c. 90	The Medical Act, p.6.
1860	23 & 24 Vict., c. 75	The Criminal Lunatics Asylum Act, p.23.
1861	24 & 25 Vict., c. 100	The Offences against the Person Act, p.212.
1864	27 & 28 Vict., c. 29	The Insane Prisoners Amendment Act, pp.22, 132, 210.
1865	28 & 29 Vict., c. 126	The Prison Act, p.21.
1883	46 & 47 Vict., c. 38	The Trial of Lunatics Act, p.18.
1884	47 & 48 Vict., c. 64	The Criminal Lunatics Act, p.18.
1913	3 & 4 Geo. V, c. 28	The Mental Deficiency Act, p.116.
1922	12 & 13 Geo. V, c. 18	The Infanticide Act, p.145.
1957	5 & 6 Eliz. II, c. 11	The Homicide Act, pp.19, 171.
1959	7 & 8 Eliz. II, c. 72	The Mental Health Act, pp.2, 178.

[G.F.Blandford], '"Acquitted on the ground of insanity." (From a "mad doctor's" point of view.)', *Cornhill Magazine* 12 (1865) 426-40.

A.Broun, *Reports of Cases before the High Court and Circuit Courts of Justiciary in Scotland*, 2 vols. (Edinburgh: Clark 1844-6).

J.C.Bucknill, *Unsoundness of Mind in Relation to Criminal Acts*, first publ. 1854, 2nd edition (London: Longman, Brown, Green, Longmans & Roberts 1857).

C.T.Couper, *Reports of Cases before the High Court and Circuit Courts of Justiciary in Scotland*, 5 vols. (Edinburgh: Clark 1871-87).

E.W.Cox, *Reports of Cases in Criminal Law Argued and Determined in all the Courts in England and Ireland*, 30 vols. (London: J.Crockford and others 1846-1938).

A.H.Dymond, *The Law on its Trial; or, Personal Recollections of the Death Penalty and its Opponents* (London: Bennett 1865).

The English Reports, 176 vols. (Edinburgh: Green 1900-30).

The English Reports. Index of Cases, 2 vols. (Edinburgh: Green 1932).

T.B.Howell and T.J.Howell, *A Complete Collection of State Trials and Proceedings for High Treason and other Crimes and Misdemeanours*, vol. 27 (London: Longman, Hurst, Rees, Orme, & Brown 1820).

A.F.Irvine, *Reports of Cases before the High Court and Circuit Courts of Justiciary in Scotland*, 5 vols. (Edinburgh: Clark 1855-68).

H.Maudsley, *Responsibility in Mental Disease* (London: King 1874).

[H.Maudsley and C.L.Robertson], *Insanity and Crime: A Medico-legal Commentary on the Case of George Victor Townley* (London: Churchill 1864).

T.Mayo, *Clinical Facts and Reflections: also, Remarks on the Impunity of Murder in some Cases of Presumed Insanity* (London: Longman, Brown, Green, & Longmans 1847).

— *Medical Testimony and Evidence in Cases of Lunacy* (London: Parker 1854).

A.Morison, *Outlines of Lectures on the Nature, Causes, and Treatment of Insanity*, first publ. 1825, 4th edition by T.C.Morison (London: Longman, Brown, Green, & Longmans 1848).

Report of the Capital Punishment Commission, P.P. 1866, XXI.

Reports of the State Trials. New Series, ed. E.P.Wallis, vols. 4 and 8 (London: HMSO, 1892, 1898).

W.O.Russell, *A Treatise on Crimes and Misdemeanors*, 5th edition by S.Prentice, vol. 1 (London: Stevens 1877).

J.F.Stephen, *A History of the Criminal Law of England*, first publ. 1883, 3 vols. (facsimile reprint New York: Burt Franklin, n.d.).

A.S.Taylor, *The Principles and Practice of Medical Jurisprudence* (London: Churchill 1865).

D.H.Tuke, 'The plea of insanity in relation to the penalty of death; or, the report of the Capital Punishment Commission psychologically considered', *Social Science Review*, new series 5 (1866) 289-309.

N.Walker, *Crime and Insanity in England, vol. I: The Historical Perspective* (Edinburgh: Edinburgh University Press 1968).

W.Wood, *Remarks on the Plea of Insanity, and on the Management of Criminal Lunatics* (London: Longman, Brown, Green, & Longmans 1851).

Cases not indexed here (for example, M'Naghten's) will be found in the List of Cases; Acts of Parliament are in the List of Statutes. Not all place names are indexed; for places see also the List of Cases.